# Patriotism, Power and Print

For Edna Glover
and in memory of
Harry Glover

# Patriotism, Power and Print

## National Consciousness in
## Sixteenth-Century England

### GILLIAN BRENNAN

James Clarke
Cambridge

James Clarke & Co
P.O. Box 60
Cambridge
CB1 2NT

www.jamesclarke.co.uk
publishing@jamesclarke.co.uk

ISBN 0 227 67962 8

*British Library Cataloguing in Publication Data*
A catalogue record is available from the British Library

Printed in the United Kingdom
by Biddles

# ACKNOWLEDGEMENTS

I am grateful for the help and encouragement which I have received in the
preparation of this book from my colleague at St Helens College, Dr D.J.
Mellett. I also wish to thank Professor M.L. Bush and the staff of Manchester
University and St Helens College Libraries.

# CONTENTS

# ABBREVIATIONS USED IN NOTES

*Cal. S.P., Sp*  *Calendar of State Papers, Spanish*, 13 vols, 1862-1954 and 4 vols 1892-1899

D.N.B.  *Dictionary of National Biography*

*L. & P.*  J.S. Brewer and James Gairdner, eds, *Letters and Papers, Foreign and Domestic of the Reign of Henry VIII, 1509-1547*, 21 vols, 1862-1910, and R.H. Brodie, 1920

*S.P. Henry VIII*  *State Papers Published under the Authority of His Majesties Commission. King Henry VIII*, 11 vols, 1830-1852

T.R.P.  P.L. Hughes and J.F. Larkin, eds, *Tudor Royal Proclamations*, 3 vols, New Haven, 1964, 1969

*Ven. Cal.*  *Calendar of State Papers, Venetian*, 1864-1898

# I.

# INTRODUCTION

This study examines English patriotism in the sixteenth century to decide upon its nature, its modes of cultural expression and to consider its use in political and religious propaganda. In considering sixteenth-century English people's feelings for their country we are going back to a time before patriotism had been conceptualised. The first recorded use of the word 'patriot' in the sense of 'fellow-countryman' was in 1596. The patriot as 'one who disinterestedly exerts himself to promote the well-being of his country' was first used by Ben Jonson in the play *Volpone* in 1605, but the term occurs only rarely before the 1680s and it was the early eighteenth century before 'patriotism' came into use. The word 'nation' was used in the medieval universities to apply to a body of students who came from a certain district, country or group of countries,[1] and the same terminology was used for Church Councils. As voting was by nation rather than individuals, discussions as to what constituted a nation had power implications. At the Council of Constance in 1414 the French argued that the English could not be regarded as a separate nation from the Germans. English claims suggest an awareness of nationhood:

> Whether nation should be understood as people marked off from one
> another by blood relationships and habit of unity or by peculiarities
> of language, the most sure and positive sign and essence of a nation be
> understood as it should be, as a territory equal to that of the French nation.

But nation and state did not coincide. The English delegates argued they were a 'general nation' representing eight particular kingdoms: England, Scotland, Wales, The Isle of Man and 'four large and notable kingdoms in Ireland, near to England, Connaught, Munster, Galway and Meath'. Diversity of language was stressed: 'They comprehend five languages, English, Welsh, Irish, Gascon and Cornish.'[2] Throughout the sixteenth century 'nation' continued to be used to apply to any distinctive group as in Roger Ascham's reference to 'the nation of scholars'[3] and it was unusual for the word to denote country until the seventeenth century. 'Nationalism' was a much later phenomenon.

Although I intend to stay firmly grounded in the sixteenth century, I have inadvertently strayed into the controversy between modernist and revisionist writers concerning the timing of the birth of nationalism. The former, led by Eric Hobsbawm, John Breuilly, Ernest Gellner and Benedict Anderson interpret nationalism as a facet of modernism and place its origins firmly in the late eighteenth century.[4] They therefore play scant attention to the early modern period. There is currently a vogue for scouring medieval and early modern texts for signs of early nationalist tendencies. Adrian Hastings, for example, traced the origins of English nationalism back to Bede:

> The benefits of a defined territoriality, the politically unifying impact of ecclesiastical unity, the contribution of two geniuses, Bede and Alfred, the stabilising of an intellectual and linguistic world through a thriving vernacular literature, the growth of the economy and of an effective royal bureaucracy, all these are contributive to a firmly affirmative answer to 'Was England a nation-state in 1066?'[5]

He was critical of the modernist approach, writing that 'Understanding nations and nationalism will only be advanced when any inseparable bonding of them to the modernising of society is abandoned.'[6] Liah Greenfeld also criticises the modernist approach, but locates the birth of English nationalism firmly in the 1520s. She claims that a shift of attitude 'which was expressed in the application of the word nation to a people, and which in more than one way signified the beginning of the modern era, was already well under way by the 1530s.'[7] This conclusion is surprising in view of her definition of nationalism as a phenomenon which arises when sovereignty of the people provides the central object of loyalty and the basis for collective solidarity.[8] Few students of the early modern period would recognise her description of sixteenth-century England as a society which was 'fundamentally homogeneous', 'only superficially divided by the lines of status, class, locality . . .' and which was 'a nation perceived as a community of free and equal individuals.'[9] It will be my contention that the approaches of both Hastings and Greenfeld are problematic. I will suggest that their definitions of nationalism are different from those of the modernists, that they are too eager to attribute nationalist feelings to anyone who mentions the words 'England', 'English', 'country', or 'nation' and that they are insufficiently familiar with sixteenth-century historiography to interpret many of the texts they cite.

For present purposes, 'patriot' is defined as one who is loyal to and loves his country of origin. Patriotism does not have to be related to a nation state but can manifest itself in loyalty towards a town, city or province.[10] However, when one is dealing with patriotism towards a nation state, as England was becoming in the sixteenth century, there is inevitably some degree of national awareness involved and one should be careful not to confuse patriotism and nationalism. Barnaby Keeney, in an article on military service and the development of nationalism in the thirteenth and early fourteenth centuries, criticised H.M. Chadwick for interpreting nationalism as 'a virulent disease to which foreigners are subject and patriotism as a virtue peculiar to the British.'[11] I hope I will not be similarly accused for suggesting that the distinction should be clarified. In fact the emotions involved in, and the actions consequent on, patriotism and nationalism are different. The patriot tends to be less aggressive towards or resentful of foreign influences than the nationalist and is more likely to approve of patriotism in others. Perhaps more importantly, patriots love their country despite its failings and do not have the nationalists' belief in the superiority of their own nation. For the nationalist, personal ambition and religious and family loyalties are subordinated to the interests of the country; but patriots can love their homeland without it becoming an over-riding priority.

Graham Holderness attempts to relocate patriotism as a postmodern phenomenon. He argues that the nationalist needs a powerful state and, because Britain is no longer a 'great Imperial aggressor' its adherents are left with 'patriotism'. He explains the difference as follows:

> Patriotism as associated with 'poetry' with emotion, with the heart, with tears; 'nationalism with 'mindless aggression, with tub-thumping jingoistic assertiveness.'[12]

Some writers, either through carelessness or conviction, fail to make the distinction between patriotism and nationalism. E.D. Marcu brought together examples of what she called 'nationalism' in Europe in the sixteenth century. John Breuilly in his study of nationalism, which he recognised as of eighteenth century origin, assumed the difference must come because Marcu was dealing with cultural rather than political nationalism.[13] In fact she was dubious of meaning, beginning her work with the statement 'We should not ask too much of definitions, ideas might best be understood approximately,' and she preferred not to define nationalism. The consequent failure to differentiate between patriotism and nationalism undermined the value of her conclusions. She referred to the 'patriotic declarations' and 'patriotic sentiments' of her writers, yet used this as evidence for the existence of nationalism in the sixteenth century.[14] I will suggest that, in the cultural as well as in the political domain, sixteenth-century Englishmen were patriotic but were not nationalists. The patriotism of the educated elite had a variety of facets: they were proud of England's origins and history, her countryside and cities. Linguistic patriotism was increasing in the sixteenth century as pride in the vernacular replaced the idea that English was only for the uneducated and that the language itself was unsophisticated. However, the views of the elite were far removed from linguistic nationalism. They welcomed foreign influences on English, approved diversity of language within the political unit and celebrated national victories in a variety of languages.[15]

Definitions of nationalism emphasise the need for action to gain or to protect independence, whereas patriotism applies to existing boundaries so tends to be more passive. Elie Kedourie used three criteria in defining nationalism: that humanity is naturally divided into nations; that nations are known by certain characteristics which can be ascertained; and that the only legitimate type of government is self-government.[16] K.R. Minogue's definition of nationalism as 'an attempt to make the boundaries of the state and those of the nation coincide'[17] also implied a need for aggression. In *Nationalism and the State* Breuilly defined political nationalism as follows:

> There exist nations with an explicit and peculiar character. The interests and values of the nation take priority over other interests and values. The nation must be as independent as possible. This usually requires the attainment of political sovereignty.[18]

Anthony Smith mirrors Breuilly's three points and adds two of his own, suggesting the nationalist ideology included the beliefs that:

> 3. To be free, human beings must identify with a nation
> 5. World peace and justice can be built only on a society of autonomous nations.[19]

Hastings adopts a definition of nationalism to suit his own agenda:

> Nationalism does not necessarily or always imply that national values are placed above all other values, or that they alone are recognised as real, important and worth defending.

Among competing loyalties he mentions 'religion, family and class'.[20]

If one wants to engage with the modernists' position one should adhere to their definitions. I will argue, in chapter 3, that England's national identity was sufficiently developed in the sixteenth century for the first of Breuilly's criteria to apply but there were many patriots whose views did not fit the second and third. Priority was given to personal, religious and regional rather than national considerations; and foreign influences, or in some instances even foreign rule, could be accepted in the interests of the country. In the 1520s Henry was able to offer sovereignty to Charles V to protect the Tudor dynasty without arousing criticism. Although there was some hostility to Queen Mary's marriage to Charles's son, Philip II of Spain, in 1554, there were many who shared Stephen Gardiner's view that a Hapsburg marriage would bring peace to Europe, security to England and a boost to their careers. Gardiner's patriotism and that of other conservative clerics such as Cuthbert Tunstall, Bishop of Durham, was compatible with adherence to the international Catholic Church as was that of later opponents of the Elizabethan Religious Settlement such as Robert Parsons and Cardinal Allen.

As Elizabeth's reign drew to a close and interest in the succession again dominated the political scene, religion played a crucial role in determining polarities. Catholic exiles continued to advocate a Spanish heir as being in the best interests of the country and the faith. The authors of *The Conference about the next Succession to the Crown of England*[21] believed that the Commonwealth had the right to choose the most suitable monarch from the potential claimants. Of the nine discussed they favoured the Infanta of Spain, daughter of Philip II. The Protestants also looked to a foreign succession to secure their faith, that of James VI, King of the traditional national enemy, the Scots.

Patriotism is often seen as a precursor of nationalism. Leonard Doob explained the connection as follows:

> Patriotism is a predisposition of nationalism. Its most common definition, 'love of country' is obviously subjective and psychological. Nationalism arises psychologically when patriotism leads to demands and possibly also to action.[22]

The image is conjured of a harmless, docile patriotism awaiting transformation into something more hostile. John Edwards writes of 'pre-nineteenth century nations waiting as it were for the spark of consciousness which brought them alive'.[23] Gerald Newman refers to the 'low flame of patriotism, of irrational local attachments which were fanned into the consuming fire of nationalist demands and actions.'[24] These writers were concerned with nationalism and they were right to see patriotism as one of its components. The aim of the present study, however, is to deal with patriotism in its own right and not merely as nascent nationalism.

Studies of patriotism have been especially prone to subjective treatment. Many writers in the early to mid twentieth century saw patriotism as something to admire and emulate. Esme Wingfield-Stratford regarded patriotism as 'an emotion the purest of which our nature is capable, and its object which next to God is the utmost to which we can aspire'. In discussing Anthony Marten's response to the Armada he wrote:

> It is difficult even now to read this noble and stirring appeal without feeling something of the emotion which must have thrilled the nation in that glorious dawn, and ask ourselves, perchance, whether the England of George V be faced with perils less urgent than that of Elizabeth, and whether Marten's counsel does not equally apply to ourselves.[25]

Wingfield-Stratford rewrote his thesis on patriotism for publication in 1939, admitting earlier prejudices but explaining that he had not 'ceased to identify patriotism with the cult of the British Empire' in the earlier work but that he had now 'eschewed a patriotic or any other belief.' However, he had merely exchanged one ideology for another, as is indicated by his opening paragraph:

> I have in these pages, offered my infinitesimal contribution to the task of revealing Britain to herself, in the belief that an enlightened patriotism can only be built on a foundation of self-knowledge. That I cannot help feeling to be of supreme urgency at a time when free civilization, and all it stands for, is threatened with imminent destruction and when its sole guarantee of survival is the quality of greatness of its patriotism.[26]

With such an approach it is hardly surprising that Wingfield-Stratford painted a romanticised and distorted picture of the development of patriotism in England.

Writers in the 1940s were especially prone to see events in the 1580s as a mirror of their own predicament. The defeat of the Armada was taken as the embodiment of the spirit of Tudor patriotism. Garrett Mattingly began his account of the situation leading to the Spanish invasion plan with a reference to its contemporary relevance:

> The idea of writing this book about the defeat of the Spanish Armada first came to me, as it must have come to others in June 1940, when the eyes of the world were once again turned to England and their surrounding seas.

He was aware that it was the myth that was remembered and ended his work as follows:

> Meanwhile, as the episode of the Armada receded into the past, it influenced history in another way. Its story, magnified and distorted by a golden mist of time, became a heroic apologue of the defence of freedom against tyranny, and the eternal myth of the triumph of David over Goliath.[27]

Some historians were less interested in distinguishing legend and fact. In 1946, A.L. Rowse published a collection of essays, most of which were written during the war, to which he gave the title *The English Spirit*. These essays provide a clear example of propaganda superseding historical methodology. In an essay on Drake, July 1940 was compared to the time of the Armada; and in reference to Drake's ideas on defence, Rowse wrote that:

> It is inspiring to recall them, still more the man who held them and the memory of that great moment in our history when an altogether smaller people with vastly smaller resources than we have today faced undismayed the greatest power in Europe and America.[28]

In 1958, J.E. Neale published a collection of essays to commemorate the 400th anniversary of Elizabeth I's accession to the throne. He also compared Elizabethan times to his own:

> We recognise the Elizabethan period as an age strangely like our own and, understanding its problems see in the Queen a leader made for our own times: one endowed with wisdom, courage and tolerance, able to inspire a nation, save it from its perils and conjure immortal glory from its aspirations.

In referring to respect for the Queen he stated 'The like had never been seen before and has perhaps only been repeated since in the unique hold on Englishmen's affections won by Sir Winston Churchill during the late war.' This style of comparison can lead to a misunderstanding of sixteenth-century events, in general, and sixteenth-century patriotism, in particular. I will suggest, in chapter 2, that Neale's claim that 'the Virgin Queen identified herself with patriotism and the people to the exclusion of all earthly attachments'[29] is inaccurate.

A comment made by Hastings leads one to suspect that he also empathises with expressions of 'nationalism': 'Perhaps as I am myself very much an Englishman, they (i.e. sightings of 'nationalism' in sixteenth-century texts) may seem an expression less of historical enquiry than of English nationalism'. He seeks to justify rather than to deny the possibility of bias: 'Yet if there is such a thing as English nationalism it is surely right that an Englishman should explore it.'[30]

Neale would have been gratified by the amount of publicity the 400th anniversary of the Armada myth received in 1988. In general the many publications avoided presenting a view of the invasion plan which was too Anglocentric. Nor did they try to make national heroes out of the English seaman. However, although few still believe that Sir Francis Drake completed a game of bowls before going to beat the Spaniards single-handed, some myths do remain intact. For example, Elizabeth is still supposed to have made a patriotic and rousing speech to her forces at Tilbury:

> I am come among you as you see, at this time, not for my recreation and disport, but being resolved, in the midst and heat of battle, to live or die amongst you, and to lay down for my God and my kingdom and my people, my honour and my blood, even in the dust. I know I have

the heart and stomach of a king, and of a king of England too, and think foul scorn that Parma of Spain, or any Prince of Europe should dare to invade the borders of my realm.

Modern writers stress that the crisis was virtually over and the content was mere rhetoric, but most assume that the speech was made and was favourably received. Geoffrey Parker and Colin Martin, for example, quote the above version with the comment 'she delivered a short speech which has passed into legend.'[31] Felix Barker, however, writing in *History Today,* has reminded us that the speech was probably a seventeenth-century invention. The only eyewitness account is from James Aske whose poem, *Elizabetha Triumphans*, published in 1588, quotes a different speech which stresses devotion to the person of the Queen. According to Aske, she spoke of her subjects' 'loyal hearts to us their lawful Queen' and she promised to 'march with them like the Roman goddess Belladona'. Barker points out that neither Camden's *Annales* nor Nichols' *Progress of Queen Elizabeth*, quote the content of the speech. The version which is currently accepted first became known in 1691 when a letter, which had been written to the Duke of Buckingham by Leonel Sharp, was published. The letter was undated but must have been written before 1631, the date of Sharp's death. He was at Tilbury as Chaplain to the Earl of Essex and was asked to repeat the Queen's speech to the army the following day.[32] It is possible that the speech may have been Sharp's rather than Elizabeth's and it is interesting that it is the patriotic version that has become accepted. According to David Cressy, the legend of Elizabeth as a 'Protestant saviour and paragon of Princely virtues' was largely an invention of the seventeenth century. There had, of course, been flattering depictions during her lifetime mixing propaganda with literary conceit and genuine admiration. The legend grew slowly in James I's reign but became more potent in the 1620s and 1630s as the Stuarts fell short of the perceived success under Elizabeth and the war with Spain revived old memories. The anniversary of Elizabeth's accession date became an occasion for popular celebration. During each successive crisis monarchists and parliamentarians alike appealed to the memory of Elizabethan events. Cressy suggests that:

It is not without significance that the anti-Catholic processions in Charles II's reign culminated around the statue of Elizabeth at Temple Bar. Nor that Queen Anne adopted Elizabeth's motto, *semper eadam*, and attempted to attach the Elizabethan virtues to herself. Nor that the cult of Elizabeth should serve both Whig and Tory propagandists in the early eighteenth century.[33]

In considering sixteenth-century patriotism one must be aware, not only that much of the information is the product of the Tudors' effective propaganda machine, but also of the way in which successive generations have moulded personalities and events to suit their own circumstances. It is a testament to the success of Tudor propaganda that historians dealing with the sixteenth century have tended to regard loyalty to the monarch and loyalty to the state

as synonymous. Wingfield-Stratford wrote of sixteenth-century government
as follows:

> and when we speak of the people we speak of the nation as a whole,
> the essential John Bull, that undefinable unity of souls and purpose
> which is the condition of patriotism. It is the King's purpose to be the
> living symbol of that patriotism.

Although conceding that Henry VII could not be made into a 'patriot hero',
he stated 'there happened to be a great deal of John Bull embodied in the
billowing contours of Henry VIII'.[34] R.U. Lindabury's study of patriotism in
Elizabethan drama includes a chapter on the Queen which fails to recognise
the possibility of loyalty to the monarch and loyalty to the crown being in
conflict.[35] More recently, Gerald Newman made the following statement about
patriotism:

> In early times this sentiment usually focuses upon the King as the
> nation's chief in battle and the personification of political unity against
> the foreigner, and also upon the native land, the realm which he
> guarded – hence for example, Shakespeare's identification of king
> with nation.[36]

Greenfeld echoes Tudor propaganda in assuming that 'For nearly half a
century the person of the Queen was the chief object on which the national
sentiment focused.' She also assumes that the reign was 'remarkably tranquil'
and that 'the dominant motivation of the period – patriotism – 'was
'coterminous with the devotion to the reigning monarch and ensured zealous
concern for the preservation of her government.'[37]

Richard Helgerson is one of the few modern writers to recognise the
distinction between loyalty to the country and loyalty to the monarchy.[38] His
*Forms of Nationhood* is a generational study which looks at a variety of
texts produced by people who were born between 1551 and 1564, the most
important of whom are Shakespeare, Spenser, Coke, Camden, Drayton,
Hooker and Hakluyt. He criticises recent work, which has been categorised
as the 'new historicism', for putting too much emphasis on the ideological
power of the Court to the extent that Elizabeth and James become the 'authors'
of Elizabethan and Jacobean literature.[39] He is especially convincing in his
section on cartography and choreography. He traces the way that Christopher
Saxton, the producer of a collection of county maps, gradually developed a
higher profile than that of his patron, Thomas Seckford, who commissioned
the work, or Lord Burghley, who paid for it on behalf of the government.
This process is an example of the Renaissance discovery of self and the maps
form part of what Helgerson refers to as a 'Renaissance discovery of England'.
He thus links individualism and nationalism both of which operated in
opposition to royal absolutism:

> Not only does the emergence of the land parallel the emergence of
> the individual authorial self, the one enforces and perhaps depends
> on the other. Nationalism and individualism, to use dangerously
> convenient terms for these two tendencies, are as I have been arguing,

deeply implicated in one another. The mutual implication begins with
the sharing of a common term of difference. Each comes into being in
direct opposition to royal absolutism.[40]

In referring to the term 'nationalism' as 'dangerously convenient', however,
Helgerson hints at the key problem with his approach. He assumes that there
was an 'intense national self-consciousness' in Elizabethan England, and
argues that:

in most of that writing [i.e. about England] some other interest or
cultural formation – the nobility, the law, the land, the economy, the
common people, the church – rivals the monarchy as the fundamental
source of national identity.[41]

A major consideration of *Patriotism, Power and Print* is to examine the
way these alternative power bases provide a focus which works in opposition
to loyalty to the country as well as to the monarchy. One should not assume,
as Helgerson does throughout, that writings in or about the political and social
conditions in England at the time, or writings in or about the English language
were automatically engendered by a predominantly nationalist self-awareness.
Helgerson's difference of approach can, perhaps, be traced to the way that
his ideas on the development of the nation state in England are based on the
theories expounded by G.R. Elton in his *Tudor Revolution in Government*.
Elton's thesis, that a revolution occurred in the 1530s which transformed
England from a medieval feudal to a modern sovereign state, has been
challenged, especially by the work of Richard Starkey and John Guy.[42]
England was still undergoing the transition to a nation state during the
Renaissance and this was reflected in cultural as well as political formations.

There was a danger that national consciousness could develop into a force
which could threaten the monarchy, and there are indications that the Tudors
were aware of that possibility. Henry VIII and Elizabeth certainly sought to
increase their power by identifying themselves with the nation. But the attitude
of sixteenth-century monarchs to patriotism was ambivalent. They and their
councils realised that their use of the notion of loyalty to England could be
turned against them. Appeals to patriotism were made in response to fears of
internal disunity. When he broke with Rome to enable the Archbishop of
Canterbury to annul his marriage to Catherine of Aragon, Henry VIII claimed
to be acting in the interests of the country against the jurisdiction and financial
exactions of a foreign Prince. He called for unity against internal danger in
the form of the Pilgrimage of Grace and against external invasion threats.[43]
In the 1540s his return to a policy of dynastic expansion in France led to
failure; but there was no patriotic propaganda campaign to sell the war to the
English people at this stage as there was no threat to internal unity. It will be
argued, in chapter two, that during Mary's reign the use of patriotic
propaganda by opponents of the government was at its most effective.
Although willing to identify herself with the interests of the country as her
father had done there are indications that Elizabeth was aware of the dangers
of patriotic enemies. She was careful to emphasise the duty of obedience to

her person, especially in the early stages of her reign. In the 1580s, as had happened in the 1530s, danger from abroad, this time in the form of the Spanish Armada, highlighted internal disunity, and patriotic propaganda from the governing elite aimed to ensure the obedience of potential dissidents.

For Elizabeth, the 1590s were a retreat from, rather than a consolidation of the patriotism drawn upon during the previous decade. National expansion had provided an impetus for the patriotic element in Elizabethan propaganda. English activities overseas, whether involving trade, piracy or colonization attempts, provided writers with opportunities to express pride in their country. Richard Hakluyt, George Best and John Dee claimed that they wanted to publicise English exploits for the glory of the nation. Hakluyt explained that in travelling in France:

> I both heard in speech and read in books other nations miraculously extolled for their discoveries and notable enterprises by sea, but the English of all others for their sluggish security, and continual neglect of the like attempts, especially in so long and happy a time of peace, either ignominiously reported or exceedingly condemned.

He had undertaken *The principal navigations, voyages and discoveries of the English nation, made by sea or over land*, for 'stopping the mouthes of reproachers.' The purpose of the work was to encourage the 'honour of her majesty, the good reputation of our country, and the advancing of navigation, the very walles of this our island.'[44] George Best had a similar outlook in *A True Discourse of the late Voyages of Discoverie, under the conduct of Martin Frobisher,* published in 1578. He enumerated the riches to be gained overseas and hoped the English would not fall behind as they had in the reign of Henry VII. He listed Englishmen who had shown courage and enterprise abroad and praised them for the 'everlasting renoune, glorie and fame' they had brought to the English nation.'[45] John Dee's patriotic vision was especially imperialistic. His *General and Rare Memorials Pertayning to Perfect Arte of Navigation*, was partly made up of tables for the use of mariners, but it also had a theoretical section pleading for a strong navy, not just to defend England, but also to provide for her expansion. He justified this by referring to the lands reportedly held by King Arthur. Dee expressed the conventional devotion to his monarch as well as his country and he hoped the work would form a 'world-wide monument to the historical renown of Queen Elizabeth.'[46] But his efforts were not appreciated by the object of his dedication: he spent 1583 to 1589 on the continent and returned to disgrace and failure. Frances Yates has pointed out that his return 'coincided with a time after the defeat of the Armada which might have been seen as a triumph on the seas of the patriotic movement in which Dee had a share,' and that one reason for the way he was treated may have been that Elizabeth had abandoned any idea of the expansion associated with Dee's style of patriotism.[47]

Protestant polemicists also tried to give Elizabeth a role which she wanted to avoid – that of figure-head for Protestant Europe.[48] A Dutch engraving showed a similar representation of Elizabeth as leader of Europe. She was portrayed as Europa, her right arm made up of Italy and her left of England and Scotland, her feet planted in Poland. To her left was the defeated Armada, to the right a triple-headed Pope escaped in a boat rowed by clergy and escorted by a fleet of ships which were numbered to allude to papal allies. English depictions of the Armada defeat, however, emphasised Elizabeth's domination of England.[49] An engraving by Crispin de Passe shows Elizabeth standing between two columns on which are the Pelican and the Phoenix. She holds the orb and sceptre of rule and behind her is an island with forts, surrounded by shipping again depicting the defeat of the Armada. The two columns represent imperial power, not the power of world domination but of Elizabeth's authority in England.[50] The 'Ditchley portrait' is indicative of the image Elizabeth wished to project. It was a pictorial sequel to an entertainment provided by Sir Henry Lee in 1592. Standing with her feet in Oxfordshire Elizabeth towered over a map of England, symbolizing her domination over the realm.[51]

The image of Elizabeth's reign, which has survived into the twentieth century, is one of triangular identification of the crown, the Anglican Church and the nation. If we look at the strands which tied these aspects of the establishment power structure together we may detect that, although strained during Elizabeth's reign, they only began to fray with the accession of the Stuarts. The survival of the crown/religion link depended on the acceptability of the Anglican episcopacy, and this was not to survive the development of Arminianism in the reign of James I. The continuation of the crown/nation strand was based on patriotic propaganda which was ephemeral and which did not survive the changed outlook of the Stuarts towards diplomacy and the nature of their kingship.[52] The third side of the triangle – the link between Protestantism and the nation – was becoming stronger and it was this link which eventually caused the downfall of the monarchy in the reign of Charles I.

William Haller, in his *Foxe's Book of Martyrs and the Elect Nation*, popularised the idea that English Protestants believed their country to have a special role in God's providence. Critics of Haller have a point when they say that this conception of England cannot be found in the writings of John Bale and John Foxe, as Haller suggested, even though their account of the persecution of the faithful in England was interpreted by contemporaries as reflecting such a role.[53] Religious euphoria after the defeat of the Armada, spawned a more optimistic interpretation of the Apocalyptic prophesies and an enhanced perception of England's role as leader of the fight against Anti-Christ. Protestant support for the monarch was dependent upon them pursuing that role. John Foxe might have seen Elizabeth as the potential saviour of his faith – he dedicated his *Book of Martyrs* to her and the decoration in an initial letter shows her victorious over the Pope[54] – but the dedication contained an implied threat. He wanted people to learn about 'ecclesiastical history' and 'rules and precepts of doctrine' but he also warns of God's judgement in:

Overthrowing tyrants, in confounding pride, in altering states and kingdoms, in conserving religion against errors and dissensions, in

relieving the godly, in bridling the wicked, in loosing and tying up
again of Satan the disturber of commonweals.[55]

In the sixteenth century, religion was only rarely seen as an adequate
justification for the overthrow of a monarch.[56] A claim to be acting in the
interests of the commonwealth of England had greater propaganda value
than a claim to be serving God. Although patriotism was used only rarely to
justify opposition to specific policies or even the rights of individual rulers,
it was not used to question the validity of the institution of monarchy. This
was to change in the seventeenth century. In discussing the role of God in
the English Revolution, Christopher Hill distinguishes between the God of
the Parliamentarians, the God of the establishment and the God of the people.[57]
His conclusions make it clear that, by the early seventeenth century the
reluctance to use religion or patriotism directly to oppose the monarchy had
been overcome. The strength of the appeals to national interest combined
with Puritanism in the seventeenth century, in opposition to the crown, suggest
that Elizabeth was right to be apprehensive about the way patriotism was
used against her by opponents.

If one is interested in the role played by patriotic propaganda in bolstering
or challenging the power of a regime it is useful to consider the ideas of
Antonio Gramsci, many of which were formulated while he was in prison for
opposing the fascist regime in Italy after 1926. His early experience of
Sardinian nationalism, his need to provide an antidote to fascism and his
study of Italian history stimulated his interest in the role of the concept of
the nation in the establishment of class hegemony. He argued that to achieve
hegemony a ruling group must be seen to represent the interests of all sections
of the society it wished to control. He used the term 'national-popular' to
apply to a coincidence of popular and national interests, the formation of
which was to be achieved by the intellectuals whose contribution to 'moral
and intellectual reform' was essential. His conception of hegemony had
important consequences for the way he envisaged the role of the state:

> It is true that the state is seen as the organ of one particular group,
> destined to create favourable conditions for the latter's maximum
> expansion. But the development and expansion of the particular group
> are conceived of and presented, as being the motor force of a universal
> expansion, of a development of all 'national' energies.

He recognised the place of patriotism in the overall concept of hegemony as
follows:

> the particular form in which the hegemonic ethico-political element
> presents itself in the life of the state and the country is 'patriotism'
> and 'nationalism' which is popular religion, that is to say it is the link
> by means of which the unity of leaders and led is effected.[58]

Aspects of the 'national-popular' were often the basis for a fierce struggle
between classes fighting for hegemony; and Gramsci discussed the way such
terms as 'patriotism' and 'nationalism' underwent changes of meaning as
they were appropriated by different classes.

In his earlier works, Gramsci had been mainly concerned with the establishment of hegemony by the proletariat but in *Prison Notebooks* he used the concept to analyse practices by ruling groups in general. He discussed the way that rule by a 'concrete individual' could only work on existing national feeling:

> Its (i.e. the government based on the power of an individual) underlying assumption will be that a collective will, already in existence, has become nerveless and dispersed, has suffered a collapse which is dangerous and threatening but not definite and catastrophic, and that it is now necessary to reconcentrate and reinforce it – rather than that a new collective will which must be created from scratch. . . .[59]

Henry VIII endeavoured to work on existing patriotic feeling within Parliament, the Church and the country as a whole and to further his identification with the nation. When Elizabeth attempted to re-establish the link between ruler and country, which had broken down during Mary's reign, she became involved in a struggle to retain authority against different groups who were trying to use the national will for their own hegemonic pretensions – a struggle similar to that recognised by Gramsci as a stimulus to changes in the nature and meaning of patriotism.

A key aspect of Gramsci's interpretation of hegemony was that a relationship must be secured, not only in the economic and political domains but also with a basis of intellectual, cultural and moral unity. Anthony Smith sees an emphasis on cultural themes as a way to make the debates between modernists and revisionists fall into place. He writes:

> Ethnosymbolic approaches point to ways in which these earlier collective cultural identities may be related to modern nations while allowing for historical discontinuities between them. . . .[60]

Gramsci put special emphasis on linguistic unity, believing that the lack of a unifying vernacular was one of the reasons why there was no strong Italian state in the sixteenth century. In the *Prison Notebooks,* he dealt with the failure of the bourgeoisie at the time of the communes to unite nationally and blamed such factors as the attitudes of intellectuals and the Church, and what he called the 'language problem'.[61] In sixteenth-century England there was a dominant vernacular but Latin continued to be used by members of the intellectual elite. During the Middle Ages the Church fought to protect the status and power it derived from the use of Latin for religious purposes and the struggle continued into the sixteenth century as conservative clergy continued to portray Latin as the language of God and English as the language of the uneducated masses. Even when they conceded the inevitability of an English translation of the Bible, the conservatives were accused of keeping their version as obscure as possible. John Cheke was critical of Stephen Gardiner, Bishop of Winchester, who said that ninety-nine words were sacred and therefore should not be translated into English. Cheke suggests that Gardiner deliberately wanted to keep the Scriptures unintelligible to the lower orders.[62] The Roman Catholic translation of the New Testament, published at

Rheims in 1582, came under attach for similar reasons. William Fulke thought that the Roman Catholic Bible was:

> obscured without any necessary or just cause, with a multitude of strange and unusual terms, as to the ignorant are no less difficult to understand than the Latin of Greek itself.[63]

George Withers also believed that the obscurity was intentional: 'for they have hunted for words on purpose which the people do not understand.'[64]

During the Middle Ages the domains of the intellectual such as education, justice, charity, the production and dissemination of texts, and the administration of the state had been dominated by the clergy. By the sixteenth century their stranglehold had been weakened and lay intellectual were taking over. This did not lead to an immediate change in the perception of language. Just as ecclesiastical intellectuals had been criticised for hiding behind a linguistic barrier, lay experts were under fire for using language to protect their secrets. The humanist scholar, Thomas Elyot, wrote his *Castel of Health*, in 1534. In the second edition he justified his use of English, presumably in response to criticism from the medical establishment, referring to the 'envy and covatise of those who professed and practised phisyke.'[65] Andrew Borde, himself a doctor as well as a travel writer, was critical of his colleagues who 'write many obscure terms . . . the most being Greek words some few being Araby words' and explained that he chose to write in English 'that everyman might understand'.[66] Those members of the intellectual elite who saw language as an aspect of their power were fighting a losing battle as, by the middle of the sixteenth century, English was widely used for political, religious and cultural purposes. The role of printing was vital in breaking down barriers against publication in English. Printers could not have made their businesses viable without reaching customers who were literate but who did not have a classical education. In turn, print vernaculars could lay the basis for national consciousness by creating a unified field of exchange and communication below Latin and above the spoken dialects. But this does not mean that the intellectuals who were prepared to use English were conscious of language as a national force. In *Imagined Communities*, Benedict Anderson made the comment that 'nothing suggests that any deep-seated ideological, let alone proto-national impulse underlay this vernacularization when it occurred'.[67] Anderson was referring to Europe as a whole but I will argue in chapter three, which deals with the attitude of the intellectual elite to their mother tongue, and chapter four, which covers motives behind translation into English, that his generalization is appropriate to England. The impetus to use the English language came from the desire of intellectuals to inform, the desire of religious reformers to save souls, and the desire of the government to restrain the uneducated classes. The perception of language as a means of social control could, paradoxically, be a barrier to the establishment of wider hegemony. The continued use of classical languages by the clerical and lay elites is typical of one of the strategies identified by Gramsci as a barrier to 'expansive hegemony', which would always be limited if the language and culture of the intellectual elite was different from that of the community as a whole.

I will suggest, in chapter five, that the policies of the Tudor governments towards minority languages such as Welsh, Irish and Cornish were designed to increase their power rather than to indulge in linguistic imperialism on behalf of the English state.

Various myths associated with Tudor patriotism have affected the reading of Elizabethan literature. The myth of Tudor 'Englishness' has developed in the centuries since their deaths. The legend may have originated with the propaganda of the 1530s and been developed in the age of Shakespeare, but it has been elaborated by Protestants of the seventeenth and eighteenth centuries and by the so-called 'Whig Historians' of the nineteenth. This point is made by Norman Davies who writes of the 'deification of the English Monarchy as a focus for the founding of English Protestantism and of modern English patriotism'.[68] Many early twentieth-century critics made two inter-related assumptions – that a feeling of national euphoria greeted the defeat of the Spanish Armada which produced a unified country and contributed to a 'Golden Age' of literature; and that the literature itself was patriotic or even nationalistic in content. This interpretation owes more to the success of sixteenth-century propaganda than to an understanding of the complexities of Elizabethan politics and society. An example is provided by Professor Hales, writing in 1904:

> In no other century of English History was the national feeling more deeply roused and exalted than in the latter part of the sixteenth. In the earlier part of it there had been endless disquietude and uncertainty . . . a noble poetry could not flourish amidst such doubts and misgivings. Not until the accession of Elizabeth did a better state of things begin to be decided. The blessings of Elizabeth's reign were not immediately apparent: But slowly and with delight it (i.e. the country) at last recognised the happy transition that had taken place and then began the great Elizabethan period of literature.

Hales listed a 'high excitement of national feeling' alongside 'a suppression of religious quarrels' and 'a large increase of riches' as factors behind the 'golden age' of Elizabethan literature. When describing the climax of this mood of national achievement, Hales personified England:

> The valour of England was just then over-brimming; it could not conceive itself defeated or shamed. It could only imagine itself coming and seeing and conquering. It felt its strength in every limb. It could not dream of failure and ruin.[69]

Cumberland Clark shared Hales's views on the importance of national unity to Elizabethan drama. He wrote that 'in the stirring times of Elizabeth, exultant patriotism was an emotion which called for and received constant expression' and among the reasons given for this was a 'united national consciousness' which was 'represented in the monarch' and had 'replaced feudal loyalties'. He believed that 'one of the most prominent characteristics set forth in the plays, a characteristic which Shakespeare shared, is the patriotism of the

English.' For 'our' one should of course read 'English'. Clark was more open than most writers about his admiration of patriotism and his assumption that is was an English virtue:

> Other characteristics of the Elizabethan English are still true of our nation. Loyalty to the sovereign, different but no less sincere loyalty still persists. Respect for authority, for birth and rank, though not so deep-rooted perhaps, has been able to withstand all disruptive forces. Readiness to serve the country, even die for England, distinguishes the best elements of our population.[70]

Shakespeare has been reconstructed as a symbol of Englishness. Graham Holderness discussed the way in which the history plays and especially Henry V were used in 1944 to encourage a united response to the national crisis. G. Wilson Knight wrote a pamphlet entitled *The Olive and the Sword*. He believed that the voice of the nation was in its literature and that England's destiny was to be sought in her 'great heritage of letters' with Shakespeare having place of honour as custodian of the country's soul. He wrote:

> We need expect no Messiah, but we might, at this hour turn to Shakespeare, a national prophet if ever there was one, concerned deeply with the royal soul of England. That royalty has direct Christian and chivalric affinities. Shakespeare's life-work might be characterised as expanding, through a series of great plays, the one central legend of St George and the Dragon. Let us face and accept our destiny in the name both of Shakespeare and St George, the patron saint of literature and the nation.

In July 1941 he staged a production which involved an actor reading from Knight's commentaries and Knight himself reciting Shakespeare speeches. The production was billed as 'G. Wilson Knight's dramatisation of Shakespeare's call to Great Britain in Time of War.'[71] The idea of Shakespeare and St George as some kind of double act come to rescue England in her hour of need is so blatantly intended as propaganda that no one would take the comparisons between the contemporary and Elizabethan situations at face value. Paradoxically, a serious academic discourse purporting to be independent of the contemporary scene may have been more influential in establishing the myth of Shakespeare's England as a unified state. The dominant theme of E.M.W. Tillyard's *Shakespeare's History Plays*, first published in 1944, is that of order. He believed that the plays reflected the commonwealthmen's fixation with the idea of the body politic as part of a chain of being controlled by divine providence with the king as head.[72] He dismissed Machiavelli's view that 'disorder was the natural state of man' as alien to Elizabethans:

> Such a way of thinking was abhorrent to the Elizabethans . . . who preferred to think of order as the norm to which disorder, though lamentably common was yet the exception.

The comment in parentheses provides the clue to the ideological nature of Tillyard's discourse. It implied that he favoured the old society of hierarchy and deference rather than the end of poverty, unemployment and injustice which many of his contemporaries believed they were fighting for.[73]

The gushing empathy with their version of sixteenth-century patriotism shown by Clark, Hales and Wilson was not emulated by post-war critics. However, many assumed that Elizabethan society was both unified and loyal to its monarch, especially in the 1580s when the danger from Philip II of Spain was at its height. David Bevington refers to a 'united approach to the Armada threat by dramatists'[74] and A.L. Rowse, writing in 1972, made the statement:

> These were years in which a small, highly tensed society braced itself for a tough struggle for its future with a more powerful opponent and won through, its integration much heightened by the struggle. After the strain was over and the heroic days departed – people were conscious of them as such – things seemed to fall apart. As with society so with drama.[75]

Derek Traversi, in his introduction to *Renaissance Drama*, in 1980 took a similar line. He contrasted the closing years of Elizabeth's reign and the opening of that of James I with the 1580s:

> The unity between court and people, personified in the earlier years by the figure of Gloriana, the Virgin Queen, was giving way to a sense of separation which was not without its literary consequences. The war with Spain pursued in the past with immense patriotic fervour.[76]

Walter Cohen, writing in 1985, also referred to a 'unified national culture' in Elizabethan England emanating from political unity after the defeat of the Northern Rebellion (1569) and the Ridolfi plot (1570):

> Elizabeth's victories marked the end of the internal Catholic threat, the defeat of feudal particularism in the north and thus the unification of the nation.[77]

As late as 1992 Greenfeld still believed that:

> It is commonplace in contemporary literary history to note the remarkable, indeed striking in its omnipresence and intensity, nationalism in Elizabethan literature.[78]

By looking at a range of literature in chapters six and seven it will be possible to illustrate that the unity did not exist in literature any more than it did in politics and to challenge Greenfeld's surprising comment that 'Cultural creativity in this period (i.e. the first half of the sixteenth century) was almost invariably – and exclusively – motivated by patriotism'[79]

Sixteenth-century portrayals of foreigners are a key aspect of patriotism in literature. Theorists of nationalism emphasise the importance of an 'out-group' in the formation of collective consciousness.[80] The transition to nationalism involves a belief in the superiority of one's own countrymen and a desire to remain free, not only from foreign political control but also from alien cultural influences. Nationalism can also manifest itself in hostility to alien minorities within society. The patriot, however, can love his country to the extent of believing that foreign workers, cultural influences and even a foreign ruler can be beneficial to its welfare. I will be touching on attitudes to foreign states and rulers in chapter two and chapter eight consists of an analysis of

national stereotypes in literature, reactions to alien workers and travel abroad.
The portrayals of foreigners in literature were not as hostile as one would
expect had the cultural ethos been saturated with nationalism. Their role as
the outsider meant the national stereotype could be used for moral or comic
purposes, and in more realistic portrayals of foreigners' class, religion or
individual characteristics continued to be more important than ethnic origin.

It is perhaps in the economic sphere that the beginnings of the hostility to
foreigners, which is an inevitable component of nationalism, can be discerned. In
his study of the ideas of the 'commonwealthmen' in the first half of the sixteenth
century, W.R.D. Jones raised the possibility of their interest in economic welfare
leading theorists to a more nationally based economic policy:

> The traditional ideal envisaged the bridling of man's selfish acquisitive
> instincts in accordance with moral and religious criteria. . . . To what
> extent as this replaced, both in thought and actual policy, by desires
> to control and direct those instincts in the interest of national welfare,
> defined in terms of maximum wealth and economic efficiency.[81]

The transition to an awareness of England as unit whose interests should be
given priority was a gradual one. A treatise written by a London merchant,
Clement Armstrong, provides a typical example of the way concern for the
national interest could be combined with paying lip-service to the idea of a
unified Christendom. He called for protection for England against 'strange
merchantise and artificial fantasies devised to make Englishmen fools to get
riches out of the realm', yet he also suggested that a 'right ordinary Emperor'
might obviate the need for international competition.[82] Hatred of foreigners
surfaced during economic difficulties and was based on fears that alien
workers would take jobs or force up rents.[83] Towards the end of the sixteenth
century dislike of Spaniards, based on trade rivalry cut across religious and
political considerations and was beginning to provide a basis for a national
outlook.

The themes of *Patriotism, Power and Print* have a myriad of contemporary
resonances in early twenty first-century Britain. The Conservative Party's
use of the 'patriotism' card in the 1982 Falklands War was so successful that
politicians have since sought to portray themselves as defenders of the
nation's integrity. Margaret Thatcher's tone in her famous Bruges speech of
1988, when she spoke of 'our pride in being English' and 'our Island fortress',
has been emulated rather than demonised by subsequent governments. In
the recent 2001 election campaign, Tony Blair depicted his pro-European
Union stance as patriotic and it will be interesting to see both Euro-phile and
Euro-sceptic politicians trying to re-invent themselves as patriots when the
build up to the Euro referendum begins in earnest.

The devolution debate had pushed relations between England, Scotland and
Wales to the forefront of public awareness and cultural and political relations
with Ireland are as important as ever. The status of minority languages is still an
issue at the beginning of the twenty-first century. In 1999 politicians in the Irish,
Welsh and Scottish Assemblies used language to symbolise their move towards

greater autonomy. In the Scottish Parliament the veteran Nationalist, Winnie Ewing, was the first to take the oath and to make a brief declaration in Gaelic[84] and at its meeting, Gerry Adams addressed the Irish Assembly in Gaelic. Speakers in the Welsh Assembly are free to speak in either Welsh or English. The Cornish party, Mebyon Kernow, has been pressing for devolution for Cornwall for nearly half a century. The party chairman, Dick Cole is spearheading a campaign to have Cornish recognised by the government and to have it included in the charter of minority languages.[85]

The dismantling of the Soviet Union into its constituent ethnicities and the disintegration of the Eastern Bloc has also resulted in much soul searching on the subject of nationalism. The end of the cold war contributed to the demonising of Islam and has produced hostilities similar to the situation in the sixteenth century when Christendom was supposedly united against the Turks. By the end of the sixteenth century the Protestant Reformation had shattered the unity of Christendom, but the Turks were still the focus for common enmities. Shakespeare had Henry V make the following suggestion as part of his attempt to cement relations with France:

King Henry

> If ever thou be'st mine, Kate, as I have a saving faith within me tells thou shalt, I get thee with scrambling, and thou must therefore needs prove a good soldier-breeder: shall not thou and I, between St Denis and St George, compound a boy, half French half-English, that shall go to Constantinople and take the Turk by the beard? shall we not? what sayst thou my fair flower-de-luce?

Act 5 sc. 2 ll 196-208

Issues such as England's relations with the EU, the interactions of nations within the British Isles, the position of Islam in international affairs, the role of language in national consciousness look set to dominate the political agenda half a millennium later. It is gratifying to think that one is dealing with matters of such contemporary relevance. However, this is not without its teleological pitfalls. My aim is not to elucidate twenty-first century questions but to discuss those of the sixteenth century. Whatever their own agendas, I invite my readers to abandon them and attempt to see national consciousness through sixteenth-century eyes.

## Notes

1. Sir James A.H. Murray, ed., *A New English Dictionary on Historical Principles*, 1909.
2. L.R. Loomis, 'Nationality and the Council of Constance', *American History Review*, 44, 1938-9, pp 508-527, pp 524-5.
3. NED.
4. John Breuilly, *Nationalism and the State*, Manchester, 1982; Ernest Gellner, *Nations and Nationalism*, Oxford, 1983 and *Encounters with Nationalism*, Oxford, 1994; Benedict Anderson, *Imagined Communities: Reflections on the Origins and Spread of Nationalism*, 1991; Eric Hobsbawm, *Nations and Nationalism since 1780*, Cambridge, 1990.

5. Adrian Hastings, *The Construction of Nationhood: Ethnicity, Religion and Nationalism*, 1998, p. 43.

6. ibid p. 9.

7. Liah Greenfeld, *Nationalism: Five roads to Modernity*, Cambridge, Mass., 1992, p. 30.

8. ibid. p. 3.

9. ibid, pp 3, 30.

10. This definition of patriotism differs from that of James Kellas who interprets nationalism as loyalty to a country and patriotism as loyalty to the state. This means that Welsh nationalists would have patriotic feelings towards Great Britain. James G. Kellas, *The Politics of Nationalism and Ethnicity*, 1991, p. 3.

11. Barnaby C. Keeney, 'Military Service and the Development of Nationalism in England, 1271-1327', *Speculum*, xxii, 1947, p. 534. His opinion was based on H.M. Chadwick, *The Nationalities of Europe*, Cambridge, 1945.

12. Graham Holderness, ' "What ish my nation?" ': Shakespeare and National Identities', *Textual Practice*, 1991 pp 74-93 p. 75.

13. John Breuilly, *Nationalism and the State*, Manchester, 1982, p. 6.

14. E.D. Marcu, *Sixteenth-Century Nationalism*, New York, 1976, pp 3,73,83.

15. See chapter three.

16. E. Kedourie, *Nationalism*, 1961, p. 9.

17. K.R. Minogue, *Nationalism*, 1967, p. 12.

18. Breuilly, 1982, p. 3.

19. Anthony D. Smith, *The Nation in History: Historiographical Debates about Ethnicity and Nationalism,* 2000.

20. Hastings op. cit. pp 31-32.

21. *A Conference about the next succession to the crown of England . . . whereunto is also added a new and perfect geneology of the discents of the Kings and Princes of England.* See below, chapter two p. 27.

22. Leonard W. Doob, *Patriotism and Nationalism – their Psychological Foundations*, Yale, 1964, p. 6.

23. John Edwards, *Language, Society and Identity*, 1985, p. 13.

24. Gerald Newman, *The Rise of English Nationalism: A Cultural History 1740-1830*, 1987, p. 60.

25. Esme Wingfield-Stratford, *The History of English Patriotism*, 2 vols 1913, 1 pp,xviii, 211.

26. Esme Wingfield-Stratford, *The Foundations of British Patriotism*, 1940, pp xiii-ix.

27. Garrett Mattingly, *The Defeat of the Spanish Armada*, 1959, Preface, p. 377.

28. A.L. Rowse, *The English Spirit*, 1946, p. 44.

29. J.E. Neale, *Essays in Elizabethan History*, 1958, pp 13,17.

30. Hastings op. cit. p. 5.

31. Geoffrey Parker and Colin Martin, *The Spanish Armada*, 1988, p. 253.

32. Felix Barker, 'If the Armada had Landed', *History Today*, 38, 1988, pp 34-41.

33. David Cressy, *Bonfires and Bells: National Memory and the Protestant Calendar in Elizabethan and Stuart England,* 1989, pp 130, 140.

34. Wingfield Stratford, op. cit. 1940, pp 126,124, 141.

35. R.U. Lindabury, *A Study of Patriotism in Elizabethan Drama*, Oxford, 1931, chapter XIII.

36. Newman, op. cit., p. 53.

37. Greenfeld, op. cit. p. 65.

38. A similar point is made by Hastings 'in England, the nation both precedes, and can see itself contrasted with, royal power'. op. cit. p. 48.

39. Richard Helgerson, *Forms of Nationhood: The Writing of Elizabethan England*, Chicago, 1992, p9. Of the works which Helgerson has in mind, the most relevant here are: Jonathan Goldberg, *James I and the Politics of Literature*, Baltimore, 1983; Stephen Orgel, *Illusion and Power: Political Theatre in the English Renaissance*, Berkeley, 1975; Stephen Greenblatt, *Renaissance Self-Fashioning: From More to Shakespeare*, Chicago, 1980 and Leonard Tennenhouse, *Power on Display: The Politics of Shakespeare's Genres*, New York, 1986.

40. Helgerson, op. cit., p. 122.

41. ibid p. 10.

42. ibid. p. 4. G.R. Elton, *The Tudor Revolution in Government: Administrative changes in the Reign of Henry VIII*, Cambridge, 1953. Elton's views are challenged in C. Coleman and D.R. Starkey, eds, *Revolution Reassessed: Revisions in the History of Tudor Government and Administration*, Oxford, 1986, and A.G. Fox and J.A. Guy, *Reassessing the Henrician Age: Humanism Politics and Reform 1500-1550*, Oxford, 1986.

43. See below chapter two, page 33.

44. Richard Hakluyt, *The principle navigation, voyages and discoveries of the English nation, made by sea or land,* 1589, Everyman, 1962, pp 2,3.

45. George Best, *A True Discourse of the late voyages of Discoverie*, 1577, printed in Hakluyt, op. cit..

46. John Dee, *General and Rare Memorials to the perfect Arte of Navigation*, 1577, Advertisement to the Reader.

47. Frances Yates, *The Occult Philosophy in the Elizabethan Age*, 1979, p. 85.

48. See chapter two, pages 45ff.

49. Roy Strong, *Portraits of Elizabeth*, Oxford, 1963, pp 114,73.

50. Frances Yates, *Astraea: The Imperial Theme in the Sixteenth Century*, 1975, p. 58. For a comparison between the Ditchley portrait and the frontispiece to Michael Drayton's *Poly-Olbion*, see page 120, below.

51. William Gaunt, *Court Painting in England from Tudor to Victorian Times*, 1980, p. 40

52. Martin Arthur Breslow, *A Mirror of England: English Puritan Views of Foreign Nations, 1618-1640,* Cambridge, Mass., 1970 argues convincingly that early seventeenth-century Puritans saw foreigners in religious terms and were disappointed that England did not lead the Protestant states in the Thirty Years War.

53. For a more detailed discussion of the ideas of Haller and his critics see below chapter two, pages 45-46.

54. See illustration below chapter two, page 46.

55. William Haller, *Foxe's Book of Martyrs and the Elect Nation*, 1963, p. 140.

56. see below chapter two, page 35.

57. Christopher Hill, 'God and the English Revolution' *History Workshop*, 17, 1984, pp 19-37.

58. Chantel Mouffe, 'Hegemony and Ideology in Gramsci', Chantel Mouffe, ed, *Gramsci and Marxist Theory,* 1979, pp 130.

59. Quintin Hoare and Geoffrey Nowell Smith, eds, *Selections from the Prison Notebooks of Antonio Gramsci*, 1971, p. 130

60. Smith, op. cit. 2000, p. 76.

61. Gramsci, *Prison Notebooks*, pp 130-131, 325.

62. James Goodwin, ed, *The Gospel according to St Matthew and part of the first chapter of the Gospel according to St Mark, Translated into English from the Greek with original notes by John Cheke, Knight, formerly Regius Professor of Greek and Public Orator in the University of Cambridge, afterward Tutor and privy Councillor and Secretary of State to Edward VI*, 1843, pp 11-12.

63. William Fulke, *A Defence of the Sincere and True Translations of the holie scriptures into the English tong, against the manifold cavils, frivolous quarrels and impudent slanders of Gregorie Martin, one of the readers of Popish divinitie in the trayterous seminarie of Remes*, 1583, dedication.

64. George Withers, *A View of the Marginal Notes of the Popish Testament, translated into the English by the English fugitive papists at Rheimes in France*, 1583, dedication.

65. Thomas Elyot, *The Castel of Health*, 1541, Preface.

66. F.J. Furnivall, ed, *The First Book of the Introduction of Knowledge made by Andrew Borde*, Early English Text Society, 1870, pp 119, 118, 120.

67. Benedict Anderson, *Imagined Communities: Reflections on the Origins and Spread of Nationalism*, 1983, p. 44.

68. Norman Davies, *The Isles: A History*, 1999, p. 502.

69. Thomas Seccombe and J.W. Allen, *The Age of Shakespeare*, 1904, 2 vols, I, pp x-xi. Hales was responsible for the introduction to this book.

70. Cumberland Clark, *Shakespeare and National Character*, 1934, pp 19, 20, 15.

71. Graham Holderness, 'Agincourt 1944: readings in the Shakespeare myth', in Peter Humm, Paul Stignant and Peter Widdowson, eds, *Popular Fictions: Essays in Literature and History*, 1986, pp 178, 192.

72. See chapter two, pages 30-31.

73. Holderness op. cit., 1986p. 189.

74. David Bevington, *Tudor Drama and Politics, A Critical Approach to Topical Meaning*, Cambridge, Mass., 1968, p. 187.

75. A.L. Rowse, *The Elizabethan Renaissance*, 1972, p. 5.

76. Derek Traversi, *Renaissance Drama*, 1980, p. 11.

77. Walter Cohen, *Drama of a Nation: Public Theatre in Renaissance England and Spain*, New York, 1985, pp 29, 137.

78. Greenfeld op. cit. p. 67.

79. ibid p. 43.

80. Newman, 1987, p. 55.

81. W.R.D. Jones, *The Tudor Commonwealth*, 1529-1559, 1973, p. 190.

82. 'A Treatise concerning the staple', R.H. Tawney and E. Power, eds, *Tudor Economic Documents*, 3 vols., University of London History Series, 14, 1924, III, pp 90-114.

83. See chapter eight, page 143.

84. Press Association, May 12 1999, www.newsunlimited.co.uk

85. Sarah Teasdale, 'Devolving England' BBC Online March 18 1999. http/news2.thdo.bbc.co.uk/hi/eng.

# II

# 'The comyn wele of the realm of Engelande':
# Patriotism, Politics and the State

Various strands of political thought at the beginning of the sixteenth century were woven to produce a fabric suitable for the development of patriotism. The disintegration of feudal loyalties, the growth of individualism, the increasing secularisation of society and the development of the bureaucracy of the nation state provided an atmosphere in which loyalty to the country was likely to flourish. There was a very gradual change among the educated elite, away from an ethos dominated by the international or provincial, and towards an awareness of the concept of the national interest.

The method of obtaining military service through channels of feudal obligation had been superseded in England long before the sixteenth century. The process of change, which originated in the reign of Edward I, has been traced by Keeney, who recognised a dual impetus to patriotism emanating from changes in warfare:

> Common service in warfare made men aware that they were part of
> something larger than their local community, and stimulated emotional
> attachment to King and Country. The propaganda used to encourage
> service appealed to men's loyalty to the community and, in turn,
> strengthened it.[1]

When Huizinga was discussing the decline of chivalry in France, he suggested that it left a vacuum which was filled by patriotism. He explained the translation as follows:

> All the best elements of patriotism – the spirit of sacrifice, the desire
> for justice and the protection of the oppressed – sprouted in the soil
> of chivalry. It is in the classic country of chivalry that are heard, for
> the first time, the touching sentiments of love of fatherland.[2]

Ferguson reversed the argument in dealing with England, seeing loyalty to the country as one of the factors which made chivalric ideals less appropriate; patriotism in the sense of loyalty to the dynasty, had co-existed with chivalry in the fourteenth and fifteenth centuries but in the 1530s this patriotism had changed into a 'complex and sophisticated loyalty to the nation state, and had in the process largely outgrown the chivalric system of values.'[3] Ferguson perhaps overstates the decisive nature of the change and it may be more appropriate to think of the two sets of ideals continuing to influence the attitudes of the educated classes simultaneously. Judicial and administrative developments before the sixteenth century had also tended to encourage national consciousness. By developing the common law and extending the jurisdiction of the King's court, the monarchy had been turning attention away from feudal and manorial groups and focusing it on the national community.

An important stimulus to the development of patriotism in England came from the ideals of the 'commonwealthmen', with their emphasis on the realm of England rather than on any local or universal commonwealth. The idea that every member of the community had a role to play, and should dedicate his labours to the common good, was often interpreted in terms of dedication to the nation. Edmund Dudley, writing in 1509, pledged duty to the commonwealth of England, and his approach provides an example of the patriotism inherent in the 'commonwealth' position:

> For as much as every man is naturally bound not only most heartily to pray for the prosperous continuance of his liege sovereign lord and increase the commonwealth of his own native country, . . . Because I am an Englishman born . . . and for that I bear my hearty goodwill and love towards the prosperous estate of my native country, I intend to write a remembrance . . . called the tree of commonwealth.[4]

Dudley was expressing his devotion to his sovereign and his country. It is conceivable, however, that duty to the common good could become a creed for rebels if the government of the day could be shown to be jeopardising the interests of the community. This had happened in the mid fifteenth century at the time of the crisis of confidence in the government of Henry VI. The Commons' allegation against the Duke of Suffolk accused him of neglecting the commonwealth, and the rebels led by Jack Cade marched to London 'as they sayde, for the comyn wele of the realme of Engelande'.[5]

The influence of civic humanism on the 'commonwealth' writers of the 1520s and 1530s led them to stress their dedication to the government. They believed that elevated social status and a high level of education carried extra responsibilities towards the welfare of the realm. Thomas Starkey, their most important political theorist, was critical of Cardinal Pole, who chose to live in exile in Italy as he opposed the break with Rome, for deserting his country. He was surprised that Pole had not:

> Applied his mind to the handling of the matters of the commonweal here in you own nation, to the intent that both your friends and your country might now at last receive and take some fruit of your long studies wherein you have spent you whole youth – as ever took it to the same purpose and end.[6]

In *The Governor*, Thomas Elyot referred to a legal training as 'a treasure whereby they shall always serve honourably their Prince and the public weal of their country'. Elyot claimed that in writing *The Governor* he was using his own education for the benefit of the country by describing 'the form of a just public weal'.[7] The ideas of the commonwealthmen and the needs of the government coincided, not only in this dedication to 'civic humanism' but also in an insistence on unity and obedience to the law, as essential to the welfare of the realm. Starkey described devotion to the commonwealth as follows:

> Like as in every man there is a body and also a soul in whose flourishing
> and prosperous state both together standeth the weal and felicity of
> man, so likewise there is in every commonality, a politic man, in whose
> flourishing both together resteth also the true commonweal . . . the
> thing which is resembled to the soul is civil order and politic law,
> administered by officers and rulers. The body is nought else but the
> multitude of the people.[8]

Elyot looked to English history to paint a cautionary picture of a disunited state:

> After the Saxons by treason had expelled out of England the Britons,
> which were the ancient inhabitants, this realm was divided into sundry
> regions of kingdoms. O what misery was the people then in! O how
> this most noble isle in the world was rent to pieces, the people pursued
> and hunted by wolves or other beasts savage; none industry prevailed,
> no strength defended, no riches profited.

He expressed a tactful confidence in the prospects for England under its present
king, referring to Henry VIII as 'equal to the ancient princes in virtue and courage'.[9]

The 'commonwealth' approach coincided with Henry's propaganda needs
at the time of the break with Rome. As he drifted towards an Anglo-centric
approach to his matrimonial problems, in the early 1530s, his appeals for
support were inevitably based on concern for the interests of the nation.
This had not been the case in the 1520s. Henry feared that there would be
civil war were he to be succeeded by his daughter, Mary. He hoped that Mary
could be protected by a powerful husband; and a promise to marry the Princess
from the Emperor Charles V was one attraction of the anti-French alliance of
1521. Throughout the 1520s the approaches to Charles show that Henry still
had a vision of a united Europe. The instructions given to Tunstall and Sir
Richard Wingfield when they were sent to negotiate with Charles, included
suggestions that he and Henry should act together 'for the general weal and
commodity of all Christendom' and the usual plea was made for all Christian
powers to combine against the evils of Luther and the Turks. These were
conventional platitudes, but the instructions as to the incentives to be offered
to Charles, in return for help against France, indicate a willingness to ignore
England's national independence. Charles was reminded that if he honoured
his treaty obligations and married Henry's daughter, he could make England
part of his Empire. A list of his possessions was followed by a reference to the

> possibility apparent to come by my lady Princesse he should thereafter
> have England and Ireland, with title to the superiority of Scotland, and in
> this case all France with its dependencies, so as the said Emperor perform-
> ing his voiage, should in process be owner in all parts of Christendom.[10]

The negotiation of a marriage between Charles and Mary represented the
same kind of linking of the Tudor and Hapsburg families which was to arouse
so much opposition when Mary married Charles's son in 1554. It was only the
fact that Charles preferred to marry Isabella of Portugal that forced Henry
into a strategy to secure the succession which involved opposition to Charles
and a coincidence of English national and Tudor dynastic interests.

By the late 1520s, Henry was convinced that the series of miscarriages, still births and early deaths which Catherine had suffered were a punishment from God for marrying his sister-in-law. He asked the Pope to annul the marriage on the grounds that the dispensation granted by Julius II in 1503 was invalid. Pope Clement VII was not in a position to grant Henry's request as he was a virtual prisoner of Catherine's nephew, Charles V. As late as December 1529, when Henry was still hoping to appease Charles, the Duke of Norfolk made what Brandi regards as a formal offer of suzerainty to Charles in return for approval of the annulment.[11] Yet a little over a year later (January 1531) Norfolk, again in an interview with Chapuys, Charles' ambassador, was using a very different approach to sovereignty in England. He quoted the English national myths associated with King Arthur, Brennus and Constantine as arguments against the Pope's authority:

> The Duke said that he had lately shown the King of France the seal on
> the tomb of King Arthur . . . contained only the words 'Patricius
> Arcturus, Britanniae Gallias, aciae Imperoator' . . . that the King had
> the right of Empire and recognised no superior; that there had been
> an Englishman who conquered Rome, to wit Brennus; that Constantine
> had ruled here and the mother of Constantine was English etc.[12]

Chapuys showed little sign of understanding Norfolk's allusions, much less of being impressed by them, but the change of approach which they represent, marks the start of the use of patriotic propaganda.

The change of approach was taken up in *A Glasse of Truthe* (1532), the first pamphlet written in English to present the case for the King's annulment to as wide an audience as possible. It cited the authority of Scripture, of a church council and of 'ancient authors'; and for the first time the government made a definite statement that the annulment was not needed for Henry's benefit, but for that of the country, as the lack of an heir would not affect him in his lifetime 'but our loss would be permanent'. Something so important should not be 'tossed and turned over high mountains, laboured and vexed at Rome, from judge, but should be dealt with in the realm'. The monarch was identified with the nation and aligned against foreign influences:

> Wherefore I doubt not (God assisting us) but that this his realm will
> rather stick with him in this his manifest right, according to their duty,
> than put their necks under the yoke of the Pope, or his, at pleasure,
> laws; for God commandeth obedience to the Prince.

The anonymous author (possibly Henry, himself) argued that subjects should be loyal to the king because he was taking pains for the commonwealth. The plea for unity for the common good, 'for so long as no member halteth or is in pain, the whole body must needs be the healer',[13] echoed the customary organic imagery, as well as the ideas of the commonwealthmen.

The *Act in Restraint of Appeals to Rome*, which enabled a court in England, presided over by the Archbishop of Canterbury, to declare Henry's marriage to be null and void, was itself a crucial landmark in the development of England's national identity, the opening section of the preamble uses patriotism to justify government action:

> Where by divers sundry old authentic histories and chronicles it is manifestly declared and expressed that this realm of England is an Empire, and has so been accepted in the world, governed by one supreme head and king having dignity and royal estate of the same, unto whom a body politic compact of all sorts and degrees of people divided in terms and by names of spirituality and temporalty be bounden and owe to bear next to God natural and humble obedience.[14]

The statute developed the claim that the Pope's jurisdiction in England should be restricted because he was a foreigner.

Thomas Cromwell, who was by now influential as First Secretary, was able to stress England's interests in measures designed to improve the financial strength of the monarchy. The *Act of Annates* (1534) opened with the exaggerated claim that:

> Forasmuch as it is well perceived by long approved experience that great and inestimable sums of money be daily conveyed out of this realm to the impoverishment of the same. . . .[15]

In the same year, the *Act of the Exoneration of Exaction Paid to the See of Rome* portrayed Henry as having saved his country from ruin rather than his government from bankruptcy, referring to the 'tender love, zeal and affection that you bear and have always born to the wealth of this your realm and the subjects of the same'.[16] A pamphlet justifying the Royal Supremacy, also published in 1534, entitled *A Litel Treatise ageynste the mutterynge of some papists in corners*, included a similar picture of a nation drained of its wealth by the Pope:

> yea whom would it not make right sorrowfull and heavy in heart to remember what riches this cursed caytiffe the Pope hath pulled out of this realm by the space of these three hundred years. . . . What pilleth he yearly, what mischievous means do he invent and seek out to rob us of our wealth.[17]

Cromwell's recognition of the effectiveness of appeals to national consciousness is also apparent in the *Act of Supremacy*'s statement that Henry was made head of the church in England:

> for the conservation of the peace, unity, and tranquility of this realm; any usage, custom, foreign laws foreign authority, prescription or any other thing or things to the contrary hereof notwithstanding.[18]

Thomas Cromwell employed writers such as Thomas Starkey, Richard Morison and William Marshall as propagandists in the 1530s. Their approach was especially useful against the Pilgrimage of Grace rebels, who themselves claimed to be acting to protect the country against the government's employment of commoners as advisors. A letter of encouragement to the rebels, probably written by Sir Thomas Tempest, warned that the stability and welfare of the realm was being threatened as at the time of Edward II and Richard II.[19] An oath taken by the rebels said they were fighting for

> The love that ye do bear unto almighty God his faith and to the holy

church militant and the maintenance thereof, to the preservation of
the King's person and his issue, to the purifying of the nobility and to
expulse all villein blood and evil councillors against the commonwealth
from this grace and his privy council of the same.[20]

The Government replied by sponsoring the publication of two pamphlets by
Morison: *A Lamentation in which it is showed that ruin and destruction
cometh of seditious rebellion* and *A Remedy for Sedition*. The latter provided
the more substantial response and argued that order and obedience were of
paramount importance to the welfare of the country. Again, welfare of the
state was linked to the law:

A commune welth is, as I think, nothing else but a certain number of
cities, towns, shires, that all agree, upon one law and one head, united
and knit together by one observation of the lawes: these kept they
need must flourish; these broken they must needs perish.[21]

In the face of threats from abroad, Henry's humanist friends used a more
ostentatious form of patriotism, bordering on chauvinism, to appeal for a
united effort. Richard Morison's work is typical. In *An exhortation to stir all
Englishmen to the defence of their Country*, he recalled previous victories
and praised English valour at Crecy, Poitiers, Agincourt and the Field of
Spurs. He was proud of the fact that 'As long as Englyshe bodies remein in
England they shall find Englyshe Stomackes, Englyshe handes Englyshe
hartes'. He linked patriotism with the monarch:

Why not may we think, that noble Henry VIII is the lyon, the wynde
ordeyned and sente by God to toss this wicked tyraunte of Rome, to
blame him out of Al christen regions? May we not reioyce that god
hath chosen our king, to work so noble a feat?[22]

An English theme had been introduced alongside the dynastic element of
Henrician propaganda, but to say, as Hastings does, that 'From now on, for
England at least, the national principle would reign supreme' is an
exaggeration.[23] The identification of monarch and nation established so
successfully in the 1530s proved a liability during Mary's reign. Jennifer
Loach expresses surprise at the paucity and lack of effectiveness of
government propaganda pamphlets during her reign. Loach's explanation is
that the literary talent had been used to justify the break with Rome, and,
with the exception of Stephen Gardiner and the Bishop of London, Edmund
Bonner, there was a lack of experience on the Catholic side.[24] But the real
problem was not lack of talent but the difficulty of reconciling the return to
Papal authority and the marriage to Charles V's son Philip with the patriotic
propaganda of the 1530s. It was now possible for patriotism to be used against
the monarch, and pamphleteers and political theorists on the government
side failed to combat this problem.

The most serious opposition to the marriage manifested itself in the
rebellion in Kent, led by Sir Thomas Wyatt. The Wyatt rebellion began as a
wider conspiracy of disgruntled gentry,[25] who planned to replace Mary with
her sister, Elizabeth, who was to be married to Edward Courtenay. Conspirators

in other areas proved ineffectual when the government got wind of the plot and it was activated prematurely. There is controversy as to the relative importance of religion and resentment of the royal marriage as motives for the Wyatt rebellion. In *Two Tudor Conspiracies*, D.M. Loades put forward what became the established interpretation – that Protestantism was not an important consideration of the rebels.[26] This approach has been challenged by Malcolm R. Thorpe, who examined the background of the rebels and concluded that the religious implication of Mary's link with Spain was important to them.[27] The evidence is difficult to evaluate as none comes from disinterested sources; but whatever the motivation behind the objections to the marriage, propagandists on both sides recognised the value of stressing patriotic idealism above the other motives, be they religious, financial or consideration of family or local loyalties. According to a contemporary account by John Proctor, Wyatt himself recognised the propaganda value of playing down religion and stressing dislike of foreigners:

> His proclamation therefore published at Maidstone and so in other places persuaded that quarrels should be taken in hand in defence of the realm from the over-running by strangers.

When a wealthy supporter expressed the hope that he would restore the right religion, Wyatt is said to have replied:

> You may not so much as name religion for that will withdraw you from the hearts of many. You must make your quarrel with the overrunning of strangers. And yet to thee, be it said in cousel as to my friend we mind only the restitution of God's word.[28]

Because of the self-acknowledged bias of Proctor's account, the accuracy of this report is open to question, and it should not be used, as it is by Thorpe, to assess the importance of religion to the rebels. Yet it is significant that for Proctor, patriotism was a more acceptable motive for rebellion than heresy. He was undoubtedly loyal to his Queen and, by implication to his country; but those who stress his patriotism[29] misunderstand his priorities. When Proctor claimed to be writing 'out of duty to my country'[30] he was referring to Kent. He explains that he published the work to make clear the motives of the people of Kent, and in stressing that Wyatt played down the religious aspect, Proctor, although not condoning rebellion, is accusing his countrymen of the lesser crime of rebellion for patriotic rather than religious motives.

Official reaction to the Wyatt conspirators shows fear that their appeals to patriotism might find a wide audience. The government claimed that the rebels' interest in their country was a pretence and that Mary was the one with the country's welfare at heart when she chose a Spanish husband. A proclamation issued at Westminster (27 January 1554), offering a pardon to Wyatt's supporters, stated that they were acting 'under the pretence of benefit of the Commonwealth of the realme to withstande strangers'. The publication of the marriage treaty was designed to reassure opponents that England's interests were being safeguarded. A later proclamation went further in emphasising that it was Mary who was acting in the country's interests:

for as much as her highness hath hitherto always preferred the benefit
of the Commonwealth before any of her own causes and being 1st
married to her realm doth mean by any 2nd marriage anyway to hinder
or prejudice the state of her said realm or the commonwealth of her
good subjects.[31]

The image of Mary's first marriage being to her country was repeated in a
speech at the Guildhall: 'I am your Queen, to whom at my coronation when
I was wedded to the realm. . . .' It was in this speech that reference was made
to religion as the real cause of the rebellion. Objections to the marriage were
seen as 'a Spanish cloake to cover their pretended purpose against our
religion'.[32] The Spanish ambassador was optimistic about the effects of the
proclamation and about the reaction to Mary's Guildhall speech.[33] The defeat
of the rebellion seemed to justify this optimism, but the feeling against the
marriage remained strong.

One should not assume, however, that opposition to a foreign King was
absolute, even among those members of the ruling elite who were genuinely
concerned about the welfare of the country as well as their own careers. This
is illustrated by an examination of the views of Mary's Lord Chancellor,
Stephen Gardiner. Gardiner hoped Mary would marry an Englishman and
had backed Courtenay. Because of early misgivings about the marriage to
Philip, he has been labelled the 'leader of the Catholic patriot opposition' by
Harbison.[34] P.S. Donaldson's discovery of a treatise by Gardiner written as
advice to Philip on taking power in England, and illustrated with historical
parallels, led him to conclude that Harbison's picture of Gardiner as 'myopically
patriotic' would have to be revised.[35] Both judgements assume that a patriot
would automatically resent foreign influences. It is necessary to appreciate
that this was not always the case before one can understand Gardiner's form
of patriotism. Gardiner's original objections to the marriage were based, not
on blind xenophobia but on recognition of the practical difficulties; he feared
that England would be involved in a war against France and that Spaniards
would be resented because of their pride. He was also apprehensive about
being linked with a failed marriage, remembering the fate of Cromwell after the
failure of the union with Anne of Cleves, but the evidence points to the fact
that he believed the marriage treaty to be an adequate safeguard.[36] The nature
of his treatise shows that Gardiner had not compromised these principles by
accepting the marriage to Philip; in fact it is one of the most patriotic
documents written in the sixteenth century. There is an early reference to the
duty to use education for the benefit of one's country in Alphonso's reply to
the question as to why he was eager for knowledge:

my spirit is greedy for all kinds of knowledge and understanding, and
particularly for knowledge of the rule and governance of different
countries and realms, so that, taught by diverse examples I can help
my country when I return, as all men were born to do.

No opportunity was lost to praise Britain, which was referred to as 'superior
to its neighbours in arms and everything necessary to human life' and as a

country which had 'made its mark for posterity in the practise by its men of wit in all ages, of letters and liberal arts'. Gardiner dealt with changes in England such as those brought about by Brutus, the Romans, the Danes and the Normans; and he perceived the arrival of the Hapsburgs in the same context, referring to their succession as 'legitimate' and 'confirmed by all orders for the restoration of religion, the honour of the country and the benefit of the people'.

The hope that Spanish rule would bring peace to Europe as a whole was an important theme, and Gardiner spoke of Philip's inheritance as ordained by divine providence so that 'Christianity after such dark clouds would enjoy the precious and inestimable joy of peace'. But he was also anxious that England's national integrity should be maintained. He warned Philip against using foreign troops or civilians in England because:

> In every age some of their predecessors, their ancestors long dead have
> lost life or property in the service of their country's honour, advantage or
> interest and reason does not permit, nor can nature of man patiently
> suffer unknown foreigners to enjoy the fruits of other men's labour.[37]

Gardiner's outlook is an example of the fact that love for England could still, as late as the mid-sixteenth century, still be combined with hopes of European peace and religious unity, and one must not assume that the patriot was necessarily an opponent of foreign influences.

The organic imagery used by the 'commonwealth' writers in the reign of Henry VIII was mentioned above. The patriotic monarch as physician, protecting the country against the sickness of sedition by upholding the law, provided a useful analogy. But if the monarch was causing the illness in the first place, as the mid-fifteenth century rebels believed, and as the Protestant polemicists asserted during the reign of the Roman Catholic Mary Tudor, the analogy became a dangerous one for the crown. *A Shorte Treatise of Politike Power*, written in Strasburg and published in 1556, is especially significant in this context. Its author, John Ponet, left England because of his Protestant views; and his intention was to justify the overthrow of Mary because of her religion; but he used the argument that the welfare of the country was more important than the authority of the monarch:

> Men ought to have more respect to their country than to their prince
> to the commonwealthe than any one person. For the country and the
> commonwealthe is a degree above the King. Next to God men ought
> to love their country and the whole commonwealth before any member
> of it: as Kings and princes (be they never so great) are members and
> commonwealths may stand well enough and flourish, albeit they are not
> King, but contrarywise without a commonwealth there can be not king.[38]

Ponet was not the only writer to fall back on patriotism as a basis for challenging authority. Christopher Goodman argued from exile in Geneva that the people of England had not only the right but the duty to rebel against an ungodly monarch. In putting forward guidelines for a choice of ruler, his first priority was that the King 'should have the fear of God before his eyes', and he opposed female rulers, referring to an Empire ruled by a woman as 'that monster of nature and disorder among men'. But he also laid great stress on the dangers of a foreign ruler: 'The next rule to be obeyed is that he should be one of their brethren . . . partly to exclude the oppression and idolatrie which cometh in by strangers as our country now is an example'. In opposing foreign rule he was thinking, of course, of Mary's marriage to Philip II of Spain. He appealed to office holders to oppose Mary, accusing them of being ready to sell their subjects 'for slaves to the proud Spaniards, a people without God'. He compared Elizabeth favourably with Mary, not only as the 'kings daughter lawfully begotten, that Godlike lady' but also as 'voyde of all Spanish pride and strange bloude'. Goodman's recognition of the propaganda value of a xenophobic approach is shown by his choice of the quotation for the frontispiece:

The Lord hath brought upon them a strange nation from a farre country, an impudent nation and of a strange language. (Deut. 28)

But he also used more positive appeals to patriotism; he compared the English with the Jews in captivity, recalling God's promise to 'make you a wise people and mighty nation – praised and commended of all nations'. Referring to Mary as an 'ungodly woman who seeks to consume the English nation', he hoped the English 'may yet with God's help and your endeavour promote his glory, underprop that realm and commonwealth which by your falsehood is falling under ruin'.[39] Goodman held that responsibility to overthrow an ungodly monarch lay with the common people, not just with the nobles and magistrates, and used the concept of national sovereignty to guard against individual rebellion. Appeals to the welfare of the country to justify disobedience, made by Ponet and Goodman, although not typical of the Protestant approach, were a dangerous reversal of Henry's VIII's attempts to identify monarch with nation.

Elizabeth tried to emulate her father's identification with the English people; but the possibility of the use of patriotism by opponents, as had happened in Mary's reign, remained a real threat. The struggle to monopolise patriotic propaganda can be seen in the religious domain. Elizabeth's first priority in her religious settlement was to uphold her political authority and this made a return to a Protestant church expedient. By the *Act of Supremacy* Elizabeth became Supreme Governor of the Church of England with control exercised via a government-appointed episcopacy. The *Act of Uniformity* introduced a form of service which was Protestant, but which retained some of the trappings of the old religion, such as the vestments worn by the priests. The latter caused offence to extreme Protestants, especially those who had been in exile during Mary's reign. These Puritans initially attacked the form of service but some were eventually driven to criticise the power of the Bishops and even the Royal Supremacy, preferring a Calvinist form of organisation on Presbyterian lines. Elizabeth's government needed to win as much support as possible for the Church of England by undermining support for both Puritan and Catholic opponents. That this had been achieved and the Church of England had become the 'national church' by the end of the century, was, paradoxically, due to the efforts of Philip II. There was no intrinsic tendency for a popularization between patriotic Protestants on the one hand and international Catholics on the other. When Philip II sent his Armada to invade England in 1588, in an attempt to cut off support for the Dutch rebels, he did so in the name of God and the Catholic Church. This gave Elizabeth the opportunity to link the Church of England with defence of the country.

Appeals to national unity at the time of the invasion threat were necessary as it was by no means inevitable that the response to the landing of Duke Parma's army would have been totally hostile.[40] It is impossible to estimate how many Catholics would have rallied to a Spanish backed government. How many ambitious politicians would have grovelled to new dispensers of patronage? How many 'patriotic' pirates would have jumped at the chance of free access to Spanish colonies for legitimate trade? Because the identification of monarch, nation and the Protestant faith was so strong in propaganda at the time of the Armada, historians have assumed it was in some way inevitable and was established at the beginning of the reign. Hurstfield's comment is typical. He referred to Elizabeth as:

The last monarch whose name and fame were, from the start, intimately
interwoven with the fabric of the English nation.[41]

It would perhaps be more accurate to suggest that the necessity for so much patriotic propaganda was a reflection of the potential weakness of national unity rather than its strength. This impression is heightened by an examination of the struggle by religious groups to monopolise the patriotic approach.

From the beginning of her reign Elizabeth had recognised the value of patriotic propaganda. The speech she made to both Houses of Parliament on 5 November 1566 is an example of the way she used patriotism to manipulate the members:

Was I not born in the realm? Were my parents born in any foreign country?
Is there any cause I should alienate myself from being careful over this
country? Is not my kingdom here? Who have I oppressed? Whom have I
enriched to another's harm? What turmoil have I made in this
commonwealth that I should be suspected to have no regard for the same?

But patriotism could also be used by opponents of government policy. When the House of Commons was demanding the execution of Mary Stuart in 1586 they reminded Elizabeth of her role as protector of the nation:

She is only cousin to you in remote degree: but we be sons of the children
of this land, whereof you be not only the natural mother but the wedded
spouse. And much more is due from you for us all than from her alone.

In the same year Francis Hastings decided to speak in favour of the Puritan 'Bill and Book', a private members Bill introduced by Anthony Cope, in the hope of changing the Elizabethan Prayer Book. He chose to speak as 'considering his duty to God, loyalty to the Queen and love of his country', he could not be silent. He spoke of the danger to the country when 'our ministers are blind'. When introducing his famous questions on privilege, Peter Wentworth, also a Puritan, spoke of the enrichment, strengthening and preservation from enemies of 'this worthy realm of England'.

The imminent danger from Spain meant that the Parliament of 1587 was inclined towards patriotism. Sir Walter Mildmay's statement was typical of the official encouragement of pride in England:

> England, our native country, one of the most renowned monarchies in the world, against which the Pope a spectacular eye and malice: envy for the wealth and peace that we enjoy through the goodness of almighty God.

A speech made by Job Throckmorton in the same debate shows that, not only could patriotism be used by opponents of government policy but that on occasion it could take a more extreme form from supporters. He claimed that 'God had vowed himself to be English' and described the Pope as Antichrist, Catherine de Medici as 'an adder whose brood is left to pester the earth', Philip II as 'idolatrous and incestuous'. His criticism of foreigners was not confined to individuals: he also attacked national stereotypes. A Frenchman was 'as vile a man who lives' and no villainy can make him blush' and he said that 'as a boy I heard it said that falsehood was the very nature of the Scot.' He was dubious about James VI because of his mother, and saw the offer of sovereignty over the Netherlands as 'an evident sign that the Lord has yet once more vowed himself to be English.' This emotional, xenophobic outburst was dangerous in view of the Government's attempts to negotiate against Spain, especially with James, and Throckmorton was criticised for 'speaking sharply of Princes' and then imprisoned in the Tower.[42]

Until Philip II provided assistance by invading in the name of the faith, the English government had not found it easy, or even desirable to brand English Catholics as traitors to their country. It had been possible for the Catholics to argue that they were the ones with England's interests at heart. During the Parliamentary debate on the *Act of Supremacy* of 1559, the Catholic Viscount Montague asserted that he was speaking 'out of duty to my Prince and country' and argued that a Catholic settlement was advisable, not only because it was the true faith but also because of the dangers from abroad which would result from Protestantism: 'I fear my Prince's sure estate and the ruin of my native country: May I then being her true subject see such peril grow to her highness and agree to it?'[43]

As founder of the English national church, one would expect Elizabeth to condemn anyone who challenged her settlement as traitorous to the country, but this approach developed only gradually in response to changing threats. The series of proclamations responding to the Northern Rebellion of 1569 declared the rebels to be traitors to Elizabeth and offered pardons to those who would swear allegiance.[44] There was no implication that they were letting the country down by their behaviour. The proclamation of 1573 was the first to use the patriotic approach that the country was being threatened. It opened:

> Whereas certain obstinate and irrepentant traitors after their notorious rebellion made against their native country, have fled out of the same and remained in foreign parts with the continual and wilful

determination, as it appeareth, to contrive all the mischief that they can imagine to impeach and subvert the universal quietness and peace of this realm (whereof they do behold with deadly envy this their natural country, by God's special grace directing her majesty in her government, to be of a long time most comfortably possessed both inwardly and at home with all the outward countries next adjoining).[45]

One can account for this change of approach by an examination of the work which was the main cause of the proclamation – *A Treatise of Treasons* – published at Louvain in 1572. The importance of the pamphlet has been recognised by Clancy, who regards it as the first political statement to come from the English Catholic exiles.[46] The authors argued that heresy was responsible for disorder which would eventually lead to the overthrow of civilization in England, and that the 'new men' such as William Cecil and the Earl of Leicester were to blame. Cecil was even criticised for allowing too many foreigners into England.[47] The general impression given in the pamphlet was that the Catholic exiles were conservatives, wishing to preserve the order and stability of their native land. It was because of the danger that this approach could have led to a full-scale appeal to patriotism that the government felt obliged to respond by accusing Catholics of treason to their country as well as to the person of their monarch.

Later proclamations, this time against seminary priests and Jesuits, reverted to stressing the danger that they would encourage disloyalty to Elizabeth.[48] The proclamation of 1588 returned to a patriotic approach in view of the increased danger from abroad.

the Pope and other foreign enemies . . . compass the destruction of her majesty and the utter ruin and overthrow of this state and commonwealth . . . preparing them [her subjects] to betray their own natural country and most unnaturally to join with foreign enemies in the spoil and destruction of the same.

Subjects living abroad were accused of planning to:

overthrow our most happy estate and this flourishing commonweal and to subject the same to the proud servile and slavish government of foreigners and strangers to betray themselves, their parents, kindred children and their religion, country and commonweal to be subjects and slaves to aliens and strangers.[49]

A similar pattern emerges when one considers the legislation against Roman Catholics, especially seminary priests and Jesuits. The government wanted to avoid the impression that these people were being persecuted for their religion, having seen the effect of martyrdom in strengthening the resolve of Protestants during Mary's reign. As with proclamations, earlier legislation stressed disloyalty to the Queen. The *Act Against the Bull from Rome* referred to 'diverse seditious and evil disposed people, without respect of their duty to almighty God or of the faith and allegiance which they ought to have and to bear to our sovereign lady Queen.'[50] *The Act to return the Queen's subjects to their lawful Obedience,*[51] had a similar approach. But in 1585, again in response to a more dangerous position abroad, the justification became more patriotic. The purpose of the priests and Jesuits was now to:

> not only draw her majesties subjects from their due to obedience to her majestie but also to move up and stir sedition, rebellion and open hostility within her highnesses realms and dominions, to the great endangering of the safety of her most royal person and the overthrow of the whole of the realm.[52]

As priests and Jesuits at their trials tried to counter government insistence that they died as traitors, and to claim martyrdom for their faith, the trials became propaganda arenas where both sides claimed a monopoly of patriotism. The 'Bloody Questions' put to suspects were designed to trap priests into admitting disloyalty to their country; the government felt the need to justify its actions in reply to such defences as Thomas Alfield's *A True Report of the Death and Martyrdom of M Campion*; William Allen's *A Briefe Historie of the Glorious Martyrdom of XII reverend priests*; and Robert Person's *De Persecutione anglicana libellus* all of which claimed that the martyrs were devoted to England.

As mentioned earlier, the Protestant polemicists Ponet and Goodman had used patriotism in their arguments in favour of the right to depose monarchs on religious grounds. Elizabeth was faced with similar threats from her Catholic opponents, as evidenced by the writings of the leading Catholic exile, Cardinal William Allen. Allen quoted Protestant authorities in his *Defence*, as part of his justification of the Pope's right to excommunicate and depose heretic monarchs.[53] One might expect appeals to patriotism to be less forthcoming from an upholder of the universalist ideal. Indeed, Allen was critical of the principle of a national church, arguing that:

> It maketh one part of the church in different territories to be independent and several from another according to the distinction of realms and kingdoms of the world. And finally it maketh every man that is not born in the kingdom to be a foreigner also in respect of the church.

He believed that the power of the church should be superior to the state.

> By which examples of Holy Scriptures we see, first that anointed and lawfully created kings may be deposed; secondly for what causes they may be deposed; thirdly that as in the creation and consecration of kings, so also in their deprivation God used the ministry of priests and prophets, as either ordinary or extraordinary judges or executors of his will towards them.

He made it clear that he felt this right to depose a monarch rested ultimately outside the country, with 'the supreme pastor of the church.' But a patriotic tone was introduced as Allen tried to stress that Catholics were loyal to England. The Preface to his *Defence* included the following:

> We are not so perversely affected (God be praised) as purposely to dishonour our Prince and country, for whose love in Christ so many have meekly lost their lives; . . . but we set forth the truth of all these actions for the honour of our nation, which otherwise to her infinite

> shame and reproach, would be thought wholly and generally to have
> revolted from the Catholic faith.[54]

He explained his attitude as an attempt to make it possible for English priests executed by the government to be regarded as martyrs for their faith rather than traitors to their country. Allen was replying specifically to William Cecil's *Execution of Justice in England* (1583) in which it was argued that the aim of the exiles was to:

> continue their former wicked purposes, that is to make arms against
> their lawful Queen, to invade her realm with foreign forces, to pursue
> all her good subjects and their native countries with fire and sword,

and that their numbers included people who had left the country because of destitution, bankruptcy or lack of promotion. He claimed that they were only pretending to desert their country for religious reasons as they knew foreigners would not shelter traitors.[55] It was possible for Allen to reconcile love of his native land with a desire to see its religion restored by the Spaniards. His *Admonition to the nobility of England and Ireland concerning the present warres . . .* , published in Antwerp in 1588, was a vicious attack on Elizabeth, designed for circulation after the defeat of the Armada, which urged all good Englishmen to abandon the Queen for the sake of their country.

Roman Catholic exiles, understandably, felt less need to profess loyalty to England than their co-religionists in England; and for the exiles, patriotism was a weapon of rebellion. But for many who hoped that their religion might eventually be tolerated in England, patriotism was an aspect of their loyalty to the government.[56] Anti-Spanish feeling, in the face of invasion threat, was strong among Catholics, despite Allen's pleas that they should support Philip II. The appearance of Lord Montague and his force at Tilbury in 1588 to defend Elizabeth against the Spaniards, indicates the eagerness of some of the Catholic laity to show that they had resolved their dilemma of conflicting loyalties.[57] Wright, an English priest, published a pamphlet justifying the decision made by Catholics who stayed loyal to their country at the time of the Armada. In answer to the question 'whether Catholics in England might take up arms to defend Queen and country?' he replied that resistance to the Spaniards was permissible because they were fighting for their own selfish reasons, not for faith. He warned against the 'intolerable lust and heat towards women,'[58] from which the English would suffer if the Spaniards landed, in a manner worthy of the government's own propaganda. The English Jesuit, Southwell took a similar line in response to the proclamation of 1591, which had accused the College of Rome of training young men to encourage sedition among English Catholics. He insisted that they were loyal to Elizabeth, and while not as extreme as Wright in his xenophobia he promised that

> we do assure your majesty that what army so ever should come against
> you, we would rather yield our breasts to be broached to our countries
> swords, than use our own swords to the effusion of our countries blood.'[59]

Conflict between the different factions of English Roman Catholics in the 1590s was based on a variety of interests and jealousies but patriotism was an important aspect of the growing anti-Jesuit feeling. The quarrels began at Wisbech, the prison for Roman Catholics, with the arrival of William Weston, the leading English Jesuit and Christopher Bagshaw, a secular priest. Bagshaw saw Robert Parsons as a threat to Queen and country: 'for his so vile a rascal to deprave and extenuate the blood royal which is in her majesties sacred person, descending from the renowned King Henry the seventh, what true English heart can endure it?'[60] William Clarke believed that respect for the Jesuits was incompatible with patriotism, as 'everyman is bound more to love his country than a Jesuit, yea the whole order of Jesuits: sith unto the first he is bound by the laws of nature, to the second only by the law of fraternal charity.'[61] Anthony Copely, an appellant[62] priest, warned that if the Jesuits were allowed to establish Spanish influence in England, the loyal Englishman could expect 'the rape of your daughter, the buggarie of your son or the sodomizing of your sow.'[63] The conflicts in England were linked with those involving students in Rome. A letter from Barret to Persons reporting on the quarrels in Rome, indicated that patriotic opposition to the Jesuits because of their links with Spain, was one element in the dispute. He explained that the scholars hated the Jesuits 'as though the fathers were enemies to them, their cause and their country.'[64]

The feuds at Wisbech were exacerbated by the exiles' publication of the *Conference about the next succession to the crown of England*.[65] This was published under the pseudonym of R. Doleman, and although it was attributed to Parsons, it was probably the work of a group of exiles.[66] The author argued that the commonwealth itself had the right to choose the most suitable monarch from potential claimants, and of the nine discussed they came to the conclusion that the Infanta of Spain, daughter of Philip II was best from the Catholic point of view. Anthony Copley's reaction was predictably hostile, given his afore-mentioned opinion on the tendencies of the Spaniards. He noted that the Infanta's claim went back to Edward III, and argued that 'much less may his ghost abide to see England under foreign rule, who subdued foreign powers and crowns to it.'[67] There followed an account of the religious and military exploits of the English nation which owed more to patriotism than to accuracy. Christopher Bagshaw condemned the Jesuits for backing the Infanta and for not being 'loyal to the line of King Henry the seventh, or any one of the Bloud royall of our owne Nation, borne and living within the Isle of Albion.'[68] Agazzari reported from Rome to Parsons that the English students were hostile to the book on the succession and that 'all openly rejoice over Spanish reverses, grieve over their successes. . . . I know not whether they hate the society more on account of the Spaniards, or the Spaniards more on account of the society.'[69]

Hurstfield explained the hostility of the English Catholics to *The Conference* by saying that they had 'imbibed also, along with their fellow countrymen, the insular patriotic emotions which it seems to have been the special task of Philip II to intensify.'[70] Whether the Catholic publicists had actually 'imbibed insular patriotism' is debatable, but they certainly had come to recognise the propaganda value of appearing concerned to protect their native country against Spain. They believed that demonstrations of loyalty to the government may lead to concessions and perhaps even toleration; a belief which was encouraged by Bancroft, who hoped to widen the gulf in the Catholic establishment. When evaluating the importance of the support for Queen and country expressed in Catholic pamphlets, one must remember their patriotism was encouraged by the knowledge that Bancroft's assistance, which included printing facilities,[71] would not otherwise have been forthcoming.

The use of patriotism by the Catholic exiles and martyrs of the 1570s and 1580s had been a dangerous weapon. But when the defeat of the Spanish Armada smashed their hopes and English Catholics turned to using patriotism to ingratiate themselves with the government, the danger had been neutralised.

Greenfeld's contention that 'Protestantism was not only the manifestation of a true faith, but also the manifestation of their being Englishmen'[72] cannot be substantiated. There was no indication that the Protestants would eschew internationalism, and the move towards the identification of the monarchy and a national church was a slow and gradual process.[73] I have already mentioned Thomas Cromwell's role in the patriotic propaganda backing the break with Rome. He did not, however, think in terms of a national church. His hostility to the Papacy was not peculiar to England and his call for church reform on Erasmian lines showed him to be part of an international community of like-minded men. The fact that in 1536, in a letter to Gardiner, Cromwell suggested that a church council would be beneficial to 'the whole unity, state and body of Christendom'[74] is evidence that the ideal of a united Church did not die with the break with Rome. The international hopes of the Protestants were strong throughout Edwards's reign. Cranmer's doctrinal pronouncements were influenced by Continental reformers and a large number of letters survives between English and Continental Protestants. The correspondence shows little awareness of the idea of a national church. When inviting the Strasbourg reformer, Martin Bucer, to London, Cranmer assured him that he would be able to benefit the 'Universal church of God' and he used the term 'Christian Commonwealth' to apply to Protestants of every nation. He believed that a council of the Protestant Church should be held to counteract the international influence of the Council of Trent.[75]

The Church of England became a Protestant and a national church because of the political needs of Elizabeth and not because of the aspirations of the English Protestants. Henry VIII's actions may have precluded membership of the international Catholic church but the idea of a universal brotherhood remained strong. In 1559, John Aylmer, who had been a Protestant exile during Mary's reign and was to become Elizabeth's Bishop of London, wrote a book entitled *An harborowe for faithful and true subjects*, wherein appeared the phrase 'God is English'.[76] This is usually taken to represent an assumption of a special relationship between Protestantism and the nation. It was traditional, however, to call for God's assistance for one's country or to thank God for deliverance from one's enemies. Commentators during the Hundred Years' War put successes against France down to the fact that God must be English,[77] so the tendency to nationalise God was not necessarily a Protestant trait.

Until recently William Haller's views, as expressed in his *Foxe's Book of*

*Martyrs and the Elect Nation,* were influential. He saw the sixteenth-century writers, John Bale and John Foxe as the originators of the idea that England was as elect nation, especially chosen by God for a role in His providence. Hastings follows the same line, referring to *The Book of Martyrs* as follows: 'the book as a whole became for generations of ordinary Englishmen their national history *par excellence*, an explanation of why they were indeed a 'perculiar' people set apart for divine purposes'.[78] Haller's view has been challenged by V. Norskov Olsen in his study of Foxe's theology and by Katherine Firth's work on the apocalyptic tradition.[79] The Protestant dramatist, John Bale believed that it was possible to correlate detailed historical research with apocalyptic prophesies. He tended to concentrate on English examples and his call for a rewriting of English history was made in patriotic language:

> I would wish some learned Englishman . . . to set forth the English
> chronicles in their right shape, as certain other lands hath done before
> them, all affectations set apart. I cannot think a more necessary thing
> to be laboured to the honour of God, beauty of the realm, erudition of
> the people and commodity of other lands next to the sacred scriptures
> of the Bible than that work would be.[80]

But elsewhere he explained why he used English examples. In *The Image* he referred to the image in the Apocalypse of the Beast's wounds being healed. He associated this with the 1540s in England, when Bishop Bonner and his conservative colleagues were proving a disappointment to those who hoped that the break with Rome heralded a reformed church. He made it clear, however, that this was part of an international process and he had only chosen English examples as he was writing for Englishmen.[81] Antichrist was a worldwide problem and he preferred English examples because they were familiar to him.

Both Bale and John Foxe were exiled during Mary's reign and were part of an international community of Protestant scholars. The martyrologist, Foxe made an important contribution to the building of a national Protestant faith in England. His *Actes and Monuments*, more popularly know as *Foxe's Book of Martyrs,* provided a history of the English Church as well as those who died in its defence. But Foxe did not see England as an 'elect nation'. He was concerned with the universal application of the apocalyptic prophecies and used England as an example to illustrate wider patterns. In *Eicasmi*, written in 1587, Foxe identified ten periods of persecution under the pagan Emperors. The ninth was the Marian persecution in England and the tenth, Philip's oppression of Protestantism in Spain and Flanders. The respite from persecution brought about by accession of Elizabeth was irrelevant to Foxe as the faithful were still being harassed on the Continent.[82]

Olsen and Firth are right to doubt whether Bale and Foxe thought of England as an 'elect nation'. Haller, however, was also concerned with the reception of the book by its sixteenth-century and early seventeenth-century audience. As well as considering the book itself Haller wanted:

> To explain what the book appears to have conveyed to the people of
> its own time, and to suggest what seems to have been its effect on the

public mind in that and the immediately succeeding age.[83]

There is no doubt that Foxe's work was extremely influential. It was first published in Basle in 1559 and the first English edition was in 1563. In 1570 a second edition appeared which included more martyrs and an extended account of ecclesiastical and national history. A copy of *Foxe's Book of Martyrs* was put alongside the Bible in churches and in other public places. Two further editions were published in the year of the Armada and one in 1596, the year of Foxe's death. There were four more editions in the seventeenth-century. Various extracts and abridgements were also published and the work influenced other writers.[84] Foxe's use of English examples and his providential approach to history did give the impression that God had a special interest in England, whether or not this was Foxe's intention. It is impossible, however, to estimate whether this interpretation was prevalent among his contemporaries. Protestant writers continued to see their Church in an international context. William Fulke, chaplain to the Earl of Leicester, turned to the Book of Revelation for sermons in response to the Rising of the Northern Earls in 1569 and the material was later published as a commentary. His concern that the rebellion would have restored a Catholic government in England is seen as a threat to European Protestantism:

> in our age, what tumults (Antichrist) hath raised up in France, in Germanie, in Spain and in Flanders, who is there throughout all Europe which knoweth not? and in England what hath he practised and wrought even this present year that we write these things, I would to God it were as ready avoided as it is easy to remember.[85]

In the 1570s and 1580s the popular expectation that the world was about to end was fuelled by the nova of 1572, the comet of 1577 and the earthquake of 1580 all believed to herald the Second Coming. A famous prophecy attributed to the 15th century mathematician, Regiomontanus, suggested 1588 as 'annus mirabilis' – the 'wonderful year'. Similar calculations were made by a German lawyer, Sheltco a Geveren. He preferred 1593 as the date of the final coming but saw 1583 and 1588 as years of danger.[86] The majority of Protestant writers poured scorn on attempts to date the end of the world so precisely. Nevertheless the Armada preparations were seen in the context of these prophecies, as described by Thomas Dekker in *The Wonderful Year:*

> Octogesimus, Octavus Annus, that same terrible 88, which came sayling hither in the Spanish Armado, and made mens hearts colder than the frozen zone, when they heard but an inkling of it: that 88, by whose horrible predictions Almanack-makers stood in bodily feare their trade would be utterly overthrowne . . . in that same 88 which had more prophesies wating at his heeles, that ever Merlin the Magitian had on his head.[87]

The Protestants, of course, believed that the Armada had been defeated by divine intervention. Anthony Marten wrote in 1588 'God himself hath stricken the stroke and yee have looked on'[88] and this was reflected in the official celebrations.[89] But again the defeat of the Armada was not the end of the

struggle for the faith and the Protestants still looked to the fight against
Antichrist. Arthur Dent in *The Ruine of Rome* (1603) discussed the revival of
the Catholic Church and the work of the Jesuits, seeking to reassure his
readers that their efforts were doomed to fail. He saw the defeat of the Armada,
not as a once and for all defeat of the Catholic faith but as part of the
continuing European struggle:

> As in part we see fulfilled in 1588, when the great and invincible
> Armado of the Spaniards, as they thought, which was long in preparing
> against us, and at last, by the instigation of the Jesuits, brought upon
> us, came to Armageddon. . . . And in all time to come, in the like case
> let them looke for the like success.[90]

He emphasised the role of Elizabeth in this struggle referring to her as 'God's
greatest instrument in the whole world, for the weakening and overturning of
Rome, the defence of his most glorious gospell (which is her crown and
glory in all the Churches and her great renowne in all Christian kingoms)'.
But the role was a personal one, for Elizabeth, rather than a national one. As
diplomatic circumstances changed early in the 17th century the mantle of
saviour of Protestantism was transferred to Gustavus Adolphus of Sweden,
who was also referred to as 'God's greatest instrument in all the world.'[91]

In the 1590s, the need for patriotic propaganda was as great as ever from
the government's point of view. The urgency to persuade Englishmen to repel
the invaders may have gone, though there were further armadas in 1599 and
1601;[92] but recruits were needed for the long and tedious campaigns in the
Netherlands in support of the Dutch; in France in support of the Huguenot
leader, Henry of Navarre, who had become Henry IV in 1589; and in Ireland
against the rebel Earl of Tyrone. Deserters and traitors continued to be a
problem. In 1583 a complete garrison deserted to the Spaniards when Captain
Pigot sold Alost to the Duke of Parma; and Gertruidenberg was sold to the
Spaniards by unpaid English troops.[93] In 1588 the Catholics Sir William
Stanley and Sir Rowland Yorke surrendered Deventer and Zutphen
respectively and the former was part of the army preparing to invade in 1588.[94]
The Council had to take measures to prevent desertions from Ireland. They
ordered the execution of two of the six men from Essex who refused to fight
and the Warders of the Border were told to look out for deserters from Ireland
who were escaping via Scotland.[95] The men who were employed on the ships
defending England against the Armada were not paid for some time and many
died of disease and starvation on their boats in port. After the 1589 Portuguese
Expedition about 500 men, who were forced to beg by lack of pay, congregated
at Westminster and were attacked by the trained London bands.[96] It was
common for leaders, both military and at sea, to disobey their orders and
pursue courses which were more profitable or more likely to lead to glory.
Curtis Breight points out that the late 1590s witnessed 'an ongoing battle
between exploitation and popular resistance'. His detailed study of
contemporary documents reveals many examples of corrupt captains, harsh
conditions and mass desertions.[97] The realisation that Shakespeare's audience

was not only divided by wealth and status, but also included men who had fought in disastrous campaigns and suffered deprivation and repression changes the perception of national unity taken for granted by many critics.

Unlike common soldiers, members of the aristocracy may have revelled in the opportunity for military adventure but it was difficult to exclude them from political power on their return to court, as is indicated by the rebellion of the Earl of Essex. Essex's supporters sponsored a performance of Shakespeare's Richard II on the eve of the rebellion and the significance of this in understanding the nature of cultural nationalism is discussed in chapter six. Literary responses to the conflict with Spain are also discussed in later chapters. The government did its best to glorify deaths in war. The demise of Sir Philip Sidney in the Netherlands was a Godsend in this respect. Here was a member of the feudal elite who had shown some promise as a poet. All that was needed was an anecdote about his giving his last water to a dying soldier, a state funeral, and he was made a national hero. Sidney's fellow poets, however, responded with elegies lamenting the loss of a great poet and friend without mention of the loss to the country.[98] The death of Sir Richard Grenvile while taking on 74 Spanish ships single-handed did, however, receive a patriotic response in verse. The variety of expressions of national awareness in poetry is discussed in chapter seven.

## Notes

1. Keeney, 'Military Service' p. 538.
2. J. Huizinga, *The Waning of the Middle Ages*, 1955, p. 102.
3. Arthur B. Ferguson, *The Indian Summer of English Chivalry*, Durham, N. Carolina, 1960, p. 102.
4. D.M. Brodie, ed *Edmund Dudley's The Tree of Commonwealth* 1509, Cambridge, 1948, p. 22.
5. J. Gardiner, ed *The Historical Collections of a Citizen of London in the Fifteenth Century,* Camden Society, New Series 17 (4), 1876 p. 191.
6. Kathleen M. Burton, ed *Thomas Starkey's A Dialogue between Reginald Pole and Thomas Lupset* 1948 pp 21-2.
7. S.E. Lehmberg, ed *Thomas Elyot's The Governor*, 1962, p. 56.
8. Starkey, op. cit., p. 55.
9. Elyot, op. cit., p. 11.
10. *S.P. Henry* VIII, vol, vi pp 416, 421.
11. Karl Brandi, *The Emperor Charles V*, 1939, p. 307.
12. *L. & P.* vol v, 45 Chapuys to Charles V.
13. Nicholas Pocock, ed, *Records of the Reformation* 2 vols, Oxford, 1870, vol II p. 389,410, 399.
14. 24 Henry VIII c 12 1533.
15. 25 Henry VIII c 20 1534.
16. 25 Henry VIII c 21 1534.
17. Pocock, op. cit., p. 549.
18. 26 Henry VIII c 1 1534.
19. *L. & P.*, vol, xi 1244.
20. *L. & P.*, vol, xi 705.

21. Richard Morison, *A Remedy for Sedition*, 1536 sig B iii.
22. Richard Morison, *An Exhortation to stir all Englishmen to the defence of their country*, 1539, sig C iii-iv, sig D vii-viii.
23. Adrian Hastings, *The Construction of Nationhood: Ethnicity, Religion and Nationalism*, 1997, p. 53.
24. Jennifer Loach, 'Pamphlets and Politics 1553-88' *Bulletin of the Institute of Historical Research*, 48, 1975, pp 31-2.
25. The Duke of Suffolk, Lady Jane Grey's father, planned to raise a force in Leicestershire and Sir James Croft and Sir Peter Carew were to organise risings on their estates in Herefordshire and Devon.
26. D.M. Loades, *Two Tudor Conspiracies*, Cambridge, 1965, pp 16, 17.
27. Malcolm R. Thorpe 'Religion and the Wyatt Rebellion of 1554' *Church History*, 47, 1978, pp 363-380.
28. John Proctor, 'The History of Wyatt's Rebellion' (1554) in A.F. Pollard, ed *Tudor Tracts*, 1930, pp 209, 210.
29. Anthony Fletcher, *Tudor Rebellions*, 1968, p. 156.
30. Proctor, op. cit., p. 203.
31. *T.R.P.* II 399, 398, 401.
32. Josiah Pratt, ed *Acts and Monuments of John Foxe* 8 vols, pp 415, 414.
33. *Cal. S.P., Sp.* 1554 January 29, Ambassadors to the Emperor and Renard to the Emperor.
34. E. Harris Harbinson, *Rival Ambassadors at the Court of Queen Mary*, Oxford 1940 p. 90.
35. P.S. Donaldson, ed *A Machiavellian Treatise by Stephen Gardiner*, Cambridge, 1975,p. 25.
36. *Cal. S.P., Sp.* vol xi 338.
37. Donaldson, op. cit., pp 104, 107, 149, 150.
38. Winthrop S. Hudson, *John Ponet Advocate of Limited Monarchy*, Chicago, 1942 p. 61. (This volume contains the full text of Ponet's *A Shorte Treatise of Politike Power*).
39. C. Goodman, *How Superior Powers ought to be Obeyed*, Geneva, 1558, pp 51, 96, 100, 193, 129, 140.
40. Geoffrey Parker 'If the Armada had Landed' *History* vol 61 no 203, Oct 1976 pp 358-368.
41. Joel Hurstfield, *Elizabeth I and the Unity of England*, 1971 p. 146.
42. J.E. Neale, *Elizabeth and her Parliments, 1584-1601*, 1957, pp 116, 168, 169-73.
43. Timothy J. McCann, 'The Parlimentary Speech of Viscount Montague Against the Act of Supremacy 1559', *Sussex Archaeological Collections*, 108, 1970, pp 50-57.
44. *T.R.P.* II 567, 568, 569.
45. *T.R.P.* II 598.
46. Thomas H. Clancy, *Papist Pamphleteers: The Allen-Persons Party and the Political Thought of the Counter-Reformation in England 1572-1615*, Chicago, 1964 p. 18.
47. *A Treatise of Treasons against Q Elizabeth and the croune of England* Louvain, 1572, pp 86a, 148a, 148b, 97b, 104.
48. *T.R.P.* II 660; cf 672, 665.
49. *T.R.P.* III 699.
50. 13 Eliz I c 2, 1571.
51. 23 Eliz I c 1, 1581.
52. *An Act against Jesuits, seminary priests and other such like disobedient persons*, 27 Eliz I c 2, 1585.
53. Robert M. Kingdom, 'William Allen's use of Protestant Political Argument', in

Charles H. Carter, ed *From the Renaissance to the Counter-Reformation: Essays in Honour of Garrett Mattingly*, 1966, pp 164-178.

54. Robert M. Kingdom, *William Allen's A True Sincere and Modest Defence of English Catholics*, New York, 1965, p. 69.

55. Robert M. Kingdom ed *William Cecil's The Execution of Justice In England*, New York, 1965, p. 5.

56. Arnold P. Pritchard, *Catholic Loyalism in Elizabethan England*, 1979, is a useful account of Catholic attitudes, but does not distinguish between loyalty to England and loyalty to the government.

57. *The Copie of a letter Writtten out of England to Don Bernardin de Mendoza*, pp 24-25. Burghley's authorship of the letter is proved by Conyers Read in 'William Cecil and Elizabethan Public Relations' in S.T. Bindoff, ed, *Elizabethan Government and Society: Essays presented to Sir John Neale*, 1961. There is some doubt as to the accuracy of the story but Manning's comment is opposite: 'the story may or may not be true. Certainly Burghley knew it was plausible', Roger B. Manning. 'Anthony Browne, 1st Viscount Montague: The influence in County Politics of an Elizabethan Nobleman', *Sussex Archaeological Collection*, 106, 1968, pp 103-112.

58. J. Strype *Annals of the Reformation and Establishment of Religion and other various Occurences in the Church of England, During Queen Elizabeth's happy reign*, Oxford 1824, III, ii pp 583-97, cf Christopher Bagshaw, *A Sparing Discoverie of our English Jesuits and of Fa. Persons proceedings under pretence of promoting the Catholike faith in England*, English Recusant Press series, 39, 1971, p. 51.

59. R.C. Bald ed *An Humble Supplication to her majestie by Robert Southwell* (Cambridge 1953) p. 11. This work was circulated in manuscript form but published by the Appellants in 1600.

60. Bagshaw, op. cit., p. 56.

61. William Clarke, *A Reply to a certain libel, lately set forth by Father Persons* English Recusant Press Series, 115 (London 1972) p. 28b.

62. The Appellants were so called because of their appeals to Rome against the Jesuits, which first took place in 1598-9.

63. Anthony Copely, *Another Letter from Mr A C to his dis-Jesuited Kinsman* (1602) quoted in Clancy, op. cit. p. 162.

64. M.A. Tierney ed *Dodd's Church History of England* III Appendix pp lxiii.

65. *A Conference about the next succession to the crowne of England . . . whereunto is also added a new and perfect geneologie of the descents of all the Kings and Princes of England.* (1595) S T C 19398.

66. For a discussion of authorship see L. Hicks, 'Father Parsons and the Book of Succession', *Recusant History,* IV (1957) pp 104-137.

67. Anthony Copely, *An Answer to a letter of a Jesuit Gentlemen* (1601) p. 46, quoted in Pritchard, op. cit., p. 163.

68. Bagshaw, *A Sparing Discoverey*, The Epistle to the Reader.

69. Tierney, op. cit., p. LXXV.

70. Joel Hurstfield, *Freedom, Corruption and Government in Elizabethan England*, 1973, p. 121.

71. Gladys Jenkins, 'The Archpriest Controversy and the Printers', *The Library*, 5th series, vol 2. 1948, 180 ff.

72. Liah Greenfeld, *Nationalism: Five Roads to Modernity*, 1992, Cambridge, Mass., p. 57. Her suggestion that 'The Protestant insistence on the priesthood of all believers reinforced the nationalist individualism in which the idea of the nation

in England was grounded', p. 52, is undermined when one realises that 'the priesthood of all believers' was a Lutheran tenet, while the Edwardian and Elizabethan settlements were doctrinally Calvinist.

73. Hastings agrees that 'There was nothing inherently nationalist about Protestantism', Adrian Hastings, *The Construction of Nationhood: Ethnicity, Religion and Nationalism*, 1997, Cambridge, 55.

74. Arthur J. Slavin, ed, *Thomas Cromwell on Church and Commonwealth: Selected Letters*, New York, 1969, p. 96.

75. *Original Letters Relative to the English Reformation*, Parker Society, 1846, pp 20, 23, 24, 25.

76. John Aylmer, *An harborowe for faithful and trewe subiectes*, 1559, sig. P4v.

77. John W. McKenna, 'How God became an Englishman' in DeLloyd J. Guth and John W. McKenna, eds., *Tudor Rule and Revolution: Essays for G.R. Elton from this American Friends,* Cambridge, 1982, pp 25-43.

78. Hastings, op. cit., p. 59.

79. V. Norskov Olsen, *John Foxe and the Elizabethan Church*, 1973; K.R. Firth, *The Apocalyptic Tradition in Reformation Britain, 1530-1645*, Oxford, 1979.

80. John Bale 'Sir John Oldcastell', sig. Avv cited in Bauckham, op. cit., p. 72.

81. John Bale 'The Image of bothe Churches after the most wonderfull and heavenlie Revelacion of Saint John 1550', H. Christmas, ed., *Select Works of John Bale,* Parker Society, 1849.

82. John Foxe, 'Eicasmi seu meditationes in sacram Apocalypsin', 1587, cited in Bauckham, op. cit..

83. William Haller, *Foxe's Book of Martyrs and the Elect Nation*, 1963, p. 15.

84. Haller, op. cit., p. 228.

85. Bauckham, op. cit., p. 113.

86. ibid, pp 162-163.

87. Thomas Dekker, *The Wonderful Year*, 1603, p. 27.

88. Anthony Marten, 'An Exhortion to stirre up the mindes of her majesties faithful subjects . . . 1588' in T. Park, ed., *The Harleian Miscellany*, 10 vols, 1808-13, II, pp 85-108.

89. See chapter six.

90. Arthur Dent, *The Ruine of Rome*, 1603, pp 218, 253.

91. B.S. Capp, *The Fifth-Monarchy Men*, 1972, pp 34 ff.

92. The first was driven back by storms and the second landed forces to help the rebels in Ireland.

93. Arthur Clifford, ed., *The State Papers and Letters of Sir Ralph Sadler*, 2 vols, Edinburgh, 1809, II, pp 220-1.

94. Albert J. Loomie, *The Spanish Elizabethans: The English Exiles at the Court of Philip II*, New York, 1963, p. 151.

95. J.R. Dasent, ed. *Acts of the Privy Council of England*, 32 vols, 1890-1907, XXX, 589, 612.

96. Curtis C. Breight, *Surveillance, Militarism and Drama in the Elizabethan Era,* 1996, p. 230

97. ibid pp 225-227.

98. e.g. Lodowick Bryskett, 'A Pastoral Eclogue upon the death of Sir Philip Sidney Knight', Emrys Jones, ed., *The New Oxford Book of Sixteenth-Century Verse*, Oxford, 1992, pp 413-417. Sir Fulke Grenville, 'An Epitaph upon the Right Honourable Sir Philip Sidney', Gordon Campbell, ed., *Macmillan Anthologies of English Literature*, 1989, II p. 105-106. 'The Phoenix Nest Elegies,' 1593, Katherine Duncan-Jones, ed., *Sir Philip Sidney,* Oxford, 1989. pp 319-328.

# III

## From 'barbarous tongue' to 'copious and pithie language': The Educated Elite and the Vernacular

It was noted in chapter one that some members of the intellectual elite were fighting a rearguard action against the vernacular, seeing Latin as a means of protecting their status and power. This chapter is concerned, however, not with those who continued to write only in Latin but those who used English, often alongside continued output in a classical language.

Before the eleventh-century Norman Conquest, Anglo-Saxon had been used for administrative and literary purposes. For the next 150 years most government documents were in Latin and this was superseded by Norman French. From 1200 to 1350 the fusion of the Norman of ruling classes with the Anglo-Saxon of the subject population produced early English, which was adopted as the language of the courts and for the opening of Parliament during the reign of Edward III. Throughout the fourteenth century English became the language of the state but not of the nation as at various times the state had jurisdiction over people who spoke Welsh, French, Cornish and Irish. Moreover, Latin continued to be used by the intellectual elite for religious and scholarly purposes, partly because of the international nature of these activities. The decision by a growing number of writers in the sixteenth century to use their mother tongue, represented an important stage in the development of the English language.

Some of the educated elite who chose to write in English were professional writers or scholars but others came from a range of backgrounds such as the law, publishing, administration and the Church. Many had direct or indirect links with the government. I will return to the subject of official policy in chapter five. Many of the publications were translations and these will be considered in chapter four. It is possible to consider attitudes to the vernacular as writers were at pains to justify their use of English, either in prefaces or separate essays. One would not be so naive as to assume that they were always honest about their reasons but these justifications do indicate what they thought would be acceptable either to patrons or readers, so tell us something about contemporary attitudes.

A number of factors influenced members of the classically educated elite to write in English. The Protestant insistence on using the vernacular inevitably increased the prestige of the English language as did the interest of Protestant scholars in Anglo-Saxon culture, language and history. This interest arose because they wanted to emphasise the continuity of the English church from its early origins and to portray the use of Latin for ecclesiastical purposes as innovative and corrupting. For example, Matthew Parker, Elizabeth I's first Archbishop of Canterbury, tried to popularise Anglo-Saxon writings and his household became a centre for antiquarian studies. His secretary, John Joscelyn, published an Anglo-Saxon version of the gospels and the editor, John Foxe, justified the work, partly on the grounds that it would convince people that Protestantism was returning the Church to its true origins and partly to prove wrong those who 'judged our native tongue unmeete to expresse God's high secret mysteries being so barbarous and imperfect a language'.[1] The growth of secular literacy produced an expanded market for didactic as well as religious material and encouraged governments to step up their output of printed propaganda.[2] The spread of printing itself led to increased publication in English as printers sought to expand their markets to include those who did not have a classical education. Elizabeth Eisenstein has suggested that the printers contributed to growing national sentiment.[3] This does not mean, however, that national awareness was a further factor in stimulating the use of the vernacular, although this is assumed by Charles Barber, who listed 'national feeling' as one of the influences and later commented that 'national feeling led to pride in the national language and to attempts to create a vernacular language to vie with that of Greece and Rome'.[4] The main theme of this chapter is to discuss whether sixteenth-century writers were in fact influenced by national consciousness in their perception of the mother tongue or whether this assumption is anachronistic.[5]

Many of the members of the intellectual elite whose attitudes are reviewed exhibited patriotic tendencies. They were proud of England's countryside, architecture, scholarship and in some cased the prowess of her soldiers in battle. Some twentieth-century writers, mistaking this patriotism for nascent nationalism, have assumed that their attitude to language would mirror that of the nineteenth and twentieth-century nationalist. That this was not the case can be illustrated by a consideration of the development of views on the English language throughout the sixteenth century, which will be the subject of the next section and especially by examining how they felt about diversity of language and foreign influences on English, which will be dealt with in the final section of this chapter.

The ideas of the Commonwealthmen, that education should be undertaken, not for the benefit of the individual but for the common good, and of civic humanists, who believed scholarly talent should be dedicated to the state, provided the basis for the development of patriotism. But in the early sixteenth century there was no tendency for educationalists to show pride in the English language. Thomas Elyot's *The Governor* described the ideal education for the lesser magistrates, who were to dedicate their lives to the 'common weal' and it was written out of 'the duty that I owe to my natural country'. Elyot's patriotism was evident throughout and he even sanctioned death for one's country. Although he wrote *The Governor* in English, Elyot showed no pride in the English language. A combination of patriotism and awareness of the inadequacy of English was shown in his discussion of the value of poetry where he quotes from Plautus's first comedy an example of sentiments of which he approved:

> Verily virtue doth all things excel
> For if liberty, health living and substance
> Our country, our children, our parents do well
> It happened by virtue; she doth advance all

But he continued 'I could recite a great number of good sentences out of other wanton poets, who in Latin could express with more grace and delectation to the reader than our English tongue may yet comprehend'. He referred to legal training as 'a treasure whereby they shall always be able to serve honourably their prince and the public weal of their country'. He did not envy the students of law because of the 'barbarous language' in which the law was written. Elyot called for improvement, but for him the language used was irrelevant, providing the style was up to standard. He advocated that the laws 'be brought to a more certain and compendious study and in either English, Latin or good French, written in a clear and elegant style'. Children (he was speaking, of course of the children of the nobility – the future governors) must use the time under seven years old to rid themselves of the disadvantage of having English as their mother tongue:

> Some old authors hold opinion that before the age of seven years a child should not be instructed in letters, but those writers were either Greeks or Latins, among whom all doctrine was in their maternal tongues . . . therefore that infelicity of our time and country compels us to encroach somewhat upon the years of children that they may sooner attain wisdom and gravity.[6]

Educationalists saw English merely as a prerequisite for a sound classical education. The reference by John Colet in his statutes for St Paul's School (1518) to the need for English as a grounding for Latin is typical:

> I would they were taught always in good literature, both Latin and Greek . . . And for that intent I will the children first learn above all the catechism in English and after the accidence that I made, to induce children more speedily to learn the Latin speech.[7]

Many authors choosing to write in English did so with apologies to the learned and stressed that they were writing for the benefit of the uneducated. In Roger Ascham's works one encounters the familiar theme of devotion to the national cause and his use of English contributed to this prestige, but he had no illusions about the nature of the language. In the preface to *Toxophilus* (1545) he explained that he was writing for the benefit of the 'unlatined gentlemen of England', even though using Latin would have been easier and better for his reputation. His claim to be writing 'This English matter, in English, for Englishmen', is often quoted as an example of Ascham's patriotism[8] but, taken out of context, it gives a false impression of his attitude to his mother tongue. His patriotism was combined with distaste for the vernacular which he condescended to use for the benefit of the unlearned.

The preface continued:

> And as for the Latin or Greke tongue, everyone is so excellently done
> in them that none can do better. In the English tongue contrary,
> everything in a manner so meanly, bothe for the manner and the
> handelynge that no man can do worse.[9]

When he wrote *The Schoolmaster* in 1568 Ascham no longer felt the need to
justify writing in English and was full of praise for English literature and
learning. He was highly critical of the Italians, against whom he launched a
prolonged and scathing attack, largely on religious grounds. But he still
preferred their language to his own, referring to the 'Italian tongue which,
next to the Latin and Greek tongue I like and love above all other'. His
praise for the wisdom in England included criticism of the language:

> Yet nevertheless, the rudeness of the common and mother tongue is
> no bar to wise speaking. For in the rudest countrie and most barbourous
> mother language, many be found (who) can speke verie wiselie.[10]

A striking example of the way in which patriotism and pride in the national
language were not necessarily linked is found in the work of the doctor and
travel writer, Andrew Borde. His *Fyrst Booke of the Introduction of
Knowledge,* written in 1547, oozes with patriotism. He is extravagant in his
praise of England and the English: 'English men be bolde, strong and mighty:
The women be full of beauty and they be decked gayly. They fare
sumptuously', and he believed his countrymen to be superior: 'The people
of England be as goode as any other land and nation that every I have travelled
in, yea and much better in many things'. For Borde, England's capital, her
universities, her ports, gold and silver and various wonders from baths to
Stonehenge far surpassed anything other countries had to offer. Yet his only
reference to language was derogatory: 'The speche of England is a base speche
to other speches as Italian, Castilian and French'.[11]

It is well known that the prestige of the English language had increased by
the end of the sixteenth century, but when did the transition take place?
Richard Mulcaster, who was headmaster of Merchant Taylors School from
1561 to 1586, and whose *Elementarie* (1582) is discussed below, is usually
referred to as the first advocate of the teaching of English for its own sake
and not just as a medium for instruction in Latin and Greek, but William
Thomas had expressed similar views some thirty years earlier. In his preface
to a translation of Sacrobosco's treatise *De Sphera*, he regretted that it was
'harde to find any good Author in our own mother tongue' and blamed the
fact that 'as a child had learned his A B C straight waies his master putteth a
Latine grammer in his hande'. His plea for schoolmasters to put more emphasis
on the teaching of English ends with an appeal to the needs of the nation:

> Wherefore if our nation desire to triumphe in civil knowledge, as other
> nations do, the meane be that each man first covett to flourish in his
> owne naturall tongue: w'out whiche he shall have much ado to be
> excellent in any other tongue.[12]

Thomas was a Protestant, but his concern for the vernacular developed from secular rather than religious interests. He had spent some time in Italy in the late 1540s.[13] His *Historie of Italie* was first published in England in September 1549 and his *Principal Rules of Italian Grammar* in 1550. Paradoxically, it was his appreciation of Italian which led him to stress the importance of English as a written language. In the letter preceding *Principal Rules of Italian Grammar*, he emphasised the importance of Italian and the valuable works written in it, and this led him to believe that English could achieve a similar success.

Thomas was not an isolated example of interest in the English language. He was made Clerk of the Council in 1551 and became one of Edward VI's closest advisers. His views were shared by a group with close connections to the Court, of whom the most influential were Sir John Cheke, Edward's tutor, Thomas Wilson, tutor to the sons of the Duke of Suffolk, and Sir Thomas Smith, a Secretary of State. Thomas Wilson's explanation for writing *The Rule of Reason* (1551) in English shows more faith in the ability of his audience than had earlier apologists for the vernacular:

> Weighing also that capacity of my countrymen the English nation is
> so pregnaunt and quick to achieve any kind of Arte of knowledge,
> whereunto wit may attayne, that they are not inferior to any other . . .
> I thought that logique among other people being as Arte as apt for the
> English wittes and as profitable for their knowledge as any other
> sciences are, might with a good grace be set forthe in the Englishe, as
> the other Artes here to for have been.[14]

His *Arte of Rhetorike* (1553) was one of the first attempts to deal with that subject in English. Sir Thomas Smith's *De Recta et emendata Linguae Anglicae Scriptione*[15] worked towards the improvement of English spelling. An even more ambitious attempt, although not published until 1569, was based on an unpublished treatise which had been dedicated to Edward VI in 1551.[16]

Sir John Cheke's interest in the vernacular was based on a desire to ensure comprehensibility of the English Bible, which led to a campaign for the use of compound rather than borrowed words. Cheke did not discuss his views on spelling, but Strype indicated that he tried to use a simplified system in his works:

> And whereas the writing and spelling of our English tongue was in
> those times very bad, even scholars themselves taking little heed of how
> they spelt, he endeavoured the correcting and regulating thereof . . .[17]

Many ideas expressed by these would-be reformers of English differed in detail from those of Mulcaster, who disapproved of attempts to change spelling or alphabet, but this group of scholars associated with court circles during the reign of Edward VI represents an increase in interest in the study of English for its own sake. As well as being linked through government service, Cheke, Wilson and Smith were colleagues at Cambridge. As Regius Professor of Greek from 1540 to 1551, Cheke led a campaign for a purified pronunciation of Greek against a conservative group led by Gardiner. Thomas Smith, who also lectured at Cambridge, after a period of study abroad from 1540 to 1542, was a leading supporter of Cheke in this controversy. Thomas Wilson first went to Cambridge in 1531 and later came under the influence of Cheke and Smith.

Wilson's *Arte of Rhetorike* was part of a trend towards writing in English on subjects previously considered unsuitable for the vernacular, and George Puttenham's *Arte of English Poesie* falls into the same category. If the editors of the twentieth-century version of the latter are correct in claiming that sections of the work were written much earlier than the publication date (1589), it is a pioneering example of the view that 'Arte' was not incompatible with the English language. In a chapter entitled 'That there may be an Art of our English Poesie as well as there is in Latin and Greek', Puttenham argued:

> Our language being no lesse copious, pithie and significative than theirs, our conceipts the same and our wits no less apt to devise and imitate than theirs were? . . . our language admitting no fewer rules and nice diversities than theirs.

He even pointed to the advantages English possessed, 'by reason of our rime and turnable concords or simphonie which they never observed', a theme which he expanded in detail in Book II. In Puttenham's work pride in language was combined with pride in his country. He wrote of the honour due to English poets:

> For having by their thankful studies so much beautified our English tong, as at this day will be found our nation is nothing inferior to the French or Italian for copie of language, subtiltie of device, good methode of proportion in any forme of poems, but that they may compare with the moste and perchance pass a great many of them.

Puttenham's patriotism was not xenophobic and he welcomed the Italian influence on Wyatt and Surrey. In explaining his use of 'our own natural termes' rather than borrowed Latin or Greek, he apologised to the learned and explained that he was writing, not for 'clerks' but for 'courtiers'. Earlier in his chapter on language, Puttenham suggested that the poet should use the English spoken 'in the King's court, or in the good towns and cities' but not in 'marches and frontiers', ports, 'any uplandish village or corner of the realm'; nor should he use 'speech beyond the river Trent', or at the universities, where 'scholars use such peevish affection of words out of primative languages'.[18] The distinction between the classical scholar and the unlearned had been replaced by the distinction between clerk and courtier and with this change English was escaping from its exclusive association with the 'inferior classes'. But the association was equally narrow, and, although patriotism was being expressed as pride in language, there was still no equation of language and nationality.

Richard Mulcaster's views are important to the study of patriotism and language as his approach automatically linked the two. His plea for the adequacy of English came from his criticism of Hart and Wilson for trying to impose artificial reform on language:

> Their dispare, which thought, that the tung was incapable of anie direction came of wrong cause, that fact rising indeed not of the thing

which theie condemn, as altogether rude and unrulie but of the parties themselves, who mistook their waie.

He believed that languages developed naturally to a peak of perfection as in the Greek of Demosthenes, the Latin of Cicero, and the English of his contemporaries. He saw the value of a language as a reflection of the people using it, arguing on the basis of four essentials 'the antiquity of our tongue, the people's wit, their learning and their experience' and because of this view, pride in the English language was linked inexorably with pride in the English nation and people. In suggesting that Latin should be displaced by English, he made one of the most patriotic statements of the sixteenth century concerning the English language:

> For is it not a marvellous bondage to become servants of one tongue for learning sake, the most of our time, with loss of most time? Our own bearing the joyfull title of our libertie and freedom, the Latin tongue remembering us of our thraldom and bondage? I love Rome, but London better, I favour Italie but England more, I honour the Latin but I worship the English. If we should cleave to the eldest and not the best we should be wearing old Adam's pelts. But why not all in English? I do not think that any language, be it whatsoever, is better able to utter all our arguments with more pith or greater plainness than our English tongue is.[19]

Mulcaster's idea that English should become the centre of the educational system was too revolutionary to have any real impact on the dominance of classical scholarship, and Adair made the point that his work 'fell almost still-born from the press'.[20] But Mulcaster was headmaster of Merchant Taylors' school when Spenser was a pupil there and the influence on him gives Mulcaster a critical place in the history of the development of the English language.

Although Mulcaster's ideas on teaching English had little impact, expressions of pride in the superiority of the language were becoming commonplace in the last decade of the sixteenth century. In suggesting that the English language no longer needed to borrow foreign words, Stanyhurst referred to it as 'copious and fluent.'[21] Sidney compared English favourably with classical languages:

> But for the uttering sweetly and properly the conceits of the mind, which is the end of speech, that hath it equally with any tongue in the world: and it is particularly happy in compositions of two or three words together, neere the Greeke, far beyond the Latine; which is one of the greatest beauties can be of any language.[22]

In fact poets and their critics regarded the advancement of the English language as one of the justifications for their work. Spenser deliberately wrote the *Faerie Queen* in archaic language using dialect and foreign words, because he wanted to elevate English and give it the dignity of a classical tongue.[23] Thomas Nashe's pamphlet, *Pierce Penilesse*, includes a section on 'The Fruits of Poetry' in which he mentioned contributions to the language:

> First and foremost, they have cleansed our language from barbarism

and made the vulgar sort here in London which is the fountain whose rivers flow round about England, to aspire to a richer purity of speech than is communicated with the commonality of any nation under heaven.[24]

It was noted above that a group of Elizabethan Protestants studied Anglo-Saxon culture as a way to undermine Catholic doctrines. The first historian to study the Saxon period in detail without religious motivation was William Camden. His *Britannia*, first published in 1586, gave an account of the history of England from the arrival of the Saxons to the Norman Conquest, and he said that he was writing out of 'a common love for our country, and the glory of the British name'. He believed that the 'English Saxons', as he called them, virtually dominated Britain and that the native population 'embraced their laws, name and language'.[25] Camden stressed the Germanic origins of the Saxons and saw this as a source of great pride. He was familiar with the work of the German Humanist scholars, especially Konrad Celtis, Ulrich von Hutton and Joannes Becanus, who enthused about the greatness and antiquity of the German nation and its language. Both they and Camden lay great store by Tacitus's essay *On the Origins and Geography of Germany*, written in 98 BC, which compared the Germans favourably with the Romans. The pride in the Germanic origins of the English people comes out more strongly in a later work by Camden – his *Remaines Concerning Britain*. He noted with approval that the Saxons were a 'warlike, victorious, stiff, stout and vigorous nation', and the English should be especially grateful to the Germans for their language: 'The English tongue is extracted, as the nations, from the Germans, the most glorious of all now extant in Europe, for their morall and martiall vertues, and preserving the liberty entire'.[26] Camden also described the way the English language had been developed and enriched since Henry VIII's time: he concluded 'our tong is as copious, pithie and significative as any other tong in Europe'; and later he referred to English as 'fluent as Latine, as courteous as the Spanishe, as courtlike as the French, as amorous as the Italian, as some Italianated amorous here confessed'.[27]

The status of the English language among the intellectual patriots was growing by the end of the century, but this does not necessarily mean that they saw language as an aspect of national consciousness. Camden may have admired the English language but he saw nothing incongruous in writing in Latin. He was proud of the variety of languages in which Englishmen greeted the defeat of the Armada, writing in the *Annals*:

The learned both at home and abroad, congratulated the victory with hearts leaping for joy, wrote triumphal poems in all languages.[28]

Marshall McLuhan argued that there was a connection between print and national consciousness through the medium of language:

It may well be that print and nationalism are axiological or co-ordinate, simply because in print a people sees itself for the first time. The vernacular in high visual definition affords a glimpse of social unity co-extensive with vernacular boundaries . . . Manuscript culture had

> no power to fix a language or to transform a vernacular culture into a
> mass medium of national unification.[29]

This statement is an over-simplification of what was a very slow process.
Certainly in the sixteenth century, to which McLuhan was referring, there is
little evidence that patriots believed it to be essential to work for a unified
language for their nation. Borde did not associate national unity with
uniformity of language, as is shown by his description of the variety of
language as part of his discussion of the 'manye wonderfull thynges of
England'. There is French used in Englande, specyally at Calys, Gensey and
Jersey. In Englande the Walshe tongue is in Wales, the Cornishe tongue in
Cornwall and the Iryshe in Irelande and the Frenche in the Englysse Pale.[30]
Towards the end of the century, pride in the English language was still being
expressed as pride in the diversity of the mother tongue. Richard Carew wrote:

> Moreover the copiousness of our dialect appeareth in the diversity of
> our dialects, for we have court and we have country Englishe, wee
> have northern and southern, grosse and ordinary.[31]

There are many examples of writers who retained an affection for the
northern dialect. Alexander Gil made the point that many poets still used the
northern dialect for the sake of rhyme and poetic effect 'since it is most
pleasant, the most ancient and the purest, seeing it is the closest to the speech
of our ancestors.'[32] Although forbidding poets to use any dialect from north of
the Trent, Puttenham recognised the northern form as the purest English Saxon.[33]

The mid-century attempts to impose phonetic spelling failed because of
the need for written English to represent a variety of dialects but,
paradoxically, the writers themselves saw the preservation of dialects as one
of their aims. In a poem prefacing one of Baret's dictionaries, Golding asked
how the difference between north and south could be established except
through proper spelling.[34] John Hart, also an advocate of phonetic spelling,
argued that his system had the advantage that it allowed people to write in
their own dialect, and referred especially to the far north and west.[35]

Writers using English, for either translations or original works were
conscious of the inadequacy of the vocabulary, especially for sophisticated
or technical subjects. Various methods were tried to repair this inadequacy,
such as the use of foreign words, compounds of monosyllabic English, or
archaic English words. There is a tendency for historians to link hostility to
'inkhorn' (Latin) and foreign terms in general with a patriotic love for the
mother tongue. In a chapter on nationalism, Einstein discusses 'literary
nationalists' who had a desire to purge their language of borrowing.[36] In
discussing the opposition to inkhorn, the editors of Puttenham's *Arte of
English Poesie* suggest that the 'easy link with patriotism gave it an
unexpected currency among the poets'.[37] Barber argued that purists who
objected to foreign influences tended to 'appeal to patriotic feeling'.[38] A
similar line had been taken by Jones who stated that 'The nationalistic spirit
with its pride in things native, resented the imputation of verbal deficiency
and the appearance of foreigners among good native citizens'. Jones was

aware, however, that the attribution of hostility to foreign words to nationalism does not fit the facts, as he makes a passing comment in a footnote:

> When we note that the period that witnesses the most favourable attitude to borrowing also entertained the strongest national feelings we are warned from attributing to nationalism any great part of the opposition to neologizing.[39]

In fact a closer examination of reactions to foreign words shows a complex interaction of a desire to improve the language and a wish to remain easily comprehensible and free from affectation. Not all writers were critical of foreign words and those who wished to improve the language by that method were often more patriotic than those who rejected inkhorn out of hand.

That Thomas Elyot's love of his country did not lead to pride in its language has already been noted. At the time *The Governor* was published Elyot saw no need to explain why he was writing in English, but some years later he wrote that the choice of English was to 'augment our English tongue, whereby men should as well express most abundantly the thing they conceive in their hearts'. Elyot favoured borrowing foreign words where no English word existed but was careful to explain the meaning and derivation, as in his use of the word 'magistrates', when he explained: 'Albeit they be named in Latin 'magistratus' and hereafter I intend to call 'magistrates' lacking another convenient work in English'. In explaining his use of the word 'maturity' he showed that he was aware that the choice of strange words might be criticised:

> . . . an excellent virtue whereunto we lack a word in English. Wherefore I am constrained to usurp a Latin word calling it maturity: which word, though it be strange and dark, yet by declaring the virtue in a few more words, the name once brought into custom, shall be facile to understand as other words late coming out of France and Italy and made denizens among us.

Elyot was simply exhibiting a scholar's care in choosing the most appropriate word. He preferred the word 'understanding' to the Latin 'intellectus' as 'intelligence' is now used for an elegant word where there is mutual treaties or appointments . . . between princes and noblemen' and his preference for the word 'public' rather than 'commonwealth' was based on the fact that the words had been mistranslated.[40] Elyot's acceptance of foreign words was part of his concern for the English language, and was separate from but in no way incompatible with his patriotism.

Elyot's contribution to the enrichment of the language was recognised by Richard Sherry, himself an excellent example of a patriot who welcomed inkhorn. He praised the contribution made to the language by our 'auncient forewriters Gower, Chaucer and Lydgate', and by more modern writers:

> In especiall of the right worshipful knight, Syr Thomas Elyot, which first in his dictionary as it were generallye searchinge out the copie of our language in all kinde of words and phrases . . . hath hereby declared the plentyfullness of our mother tongue . . .

Sherry's own patriotism was reflected in the way he continued by praising

Elyot for his 'love of his country, hyse time spent not in vanytie and tryfles'. Earlier in the same preface Sherry had defended his own use of foreign words:

> I doubt not that the title of this treatise all straunge to our English ears, wil cause some men at syghte to marvayle what the matter of it should mean. These words Scheme and Trope are not used in our English tongue neither are they English words. Nor more be many which nowe in our time be made by continual use . . . that as well is known among us the meaning of them, as if they had been in our native blood.[41]

George Pettie provides a later example of the same outlook. His love of his country is exemplified by his criticism of those who underestimate the mother tongue 'for they count it barren, they count it barbarous . . . but for our country I am persuaded that those who love it will report it for the civilest country in the world', and he then went on to justify the use of foreign words to enrich the language:

> And as for the barbarousness of our tongue, I must likewise say that it is much the worse for them and such curious fellows as they are: who if one chance to derive any word from Latin, which is insolent to their ears . . . they forthwith make a jest of it and call it an Inkhorne term. And though for my part I use these words as little as any, yet I know no reason why I should not use them . . . for it is indeed a readie way to inriche our tonge and make it copious, and it is the way which all tongues have to inriche themselves.[42]

Thomas Nashe replied to those who criticised him for using compound and 'Italionate coyned verbes' as follows:

> Our English tongue of all languages, most swarmeth with the single money of monosyllables, which are the onely scandall of it. Bookes written in them and no other seeme like shopkeepers bookes, that containe nothing else save halfe-pence, three-farthings, and wo-pences. Therefore what did me I, but having a hugh heap of thse worthlesse shreds of small English in my 'pia maters' purse, to make the royaller show with them in men's eyes, had them to the compounders immediately, and exchanged them foure into, one, and other into more, according to the Greek, French, Spanish and Italian.[43]

George Gascoigne was unenthusiastic about the use of foreign words:

> Next to this I have always bene of opinion that it is not impossible eyther in Poemes or in Prose too write both compendiously and perfectly in our English tongue. And therefore although I challenge not unto myselfe the name of English poet, yet may the reader finde in keeping the olde Englishe words than in borrowing of other languages, such Epithetes and Adjectives as smell of Inkhorne.

But he accepts that borrowing may be inevitable on occasion and apologises in advance to anyone who may be offended:

> although I be sometimes constreyed for the cadence of rimes, or per licentiam Poeticam, to use an yknehorne terme or straunge word; Yet

> I hope it shall be apparent I have rather regard to make our native language
> commendable in itselfe, than gay with the feather of straunge birdes.[44]

Hostility to foreign invasions which did exist was not necessarily on patriotic grounds. Opposition to inkhorne was on the basis of style rather than nationality as many of the early translators retained a high level of Latinity in their English. John Skelton was one of the worst culprits. His translation of the *Biblioteca Historia* of Diodorus Siculus based on Poggio's Latin version of the original Greek, was one of the first attempts to make a Greek work available to those who understood only English. The editors aptly describe Skelton's prose as:

> Characterised by a high degree of Latinity in vocabulary and syntax,
> as full of tautology, periphrasis and alliteration, decorated with
> conventional diction and aiming chiefly at ornamental volubility.[45]

Objections to this kind of prose did not necessarily involve hostility to foreign words in general and had nothing to do with patriotism.

Thomas Wilson is usually grouped with the opposition in the inkhorn controversy on the evidence of his views as expressed in *The Art of Rhetorike*: 'Emong al other lessons this should first be learned that we never affect any straunge ynkehorne terms but speak as commonly received'. But his attack was on affected rather than foreign words. He attacked travellers who aped the languages and clothes encountered in the countries they visited. Wilson criticised the jargon of the lawyers and auditors; and the courtiers and clerks for delighting in the obscurity of their references. He was especially scathing about pretentious scholars who peppered their speech with Latin so the uneducated, unable to understand, would assume the speaker had something of significance to reveal. However, he came out decisively in favour of borrowing foreign words where necessary:

> Now whereas wordes be received, as well Greke as Latine to set furthe
> our meaning in the Englishe tongue, either for lacke of store, or else
> because we should enriche the language; it is well doen to use them,
> and no man therein can be charged with affectation when all others
> are agreed to follows the same waie.[46]

That Ascham has been misleadingly referred to as a 'literary nationalist' was discussed above, where it was suggested that his undoubted patriotism did not encompass pride in the English language. His comments on Hall's *Chronicle* have been similarly misinterpreted. He argued that 'much good matter is quite marred with indenture English', and suggested that it would be a worthwhile exercise to 'change strange and inkhorne terms into proper and commonly used English', but his objections were only on the grounds of verbosity. He continued: 'cutting away words and sentences and diminishing nothing at all of the matter, should leave the man's use of a story twice as good as it was both for pleasure and comodity'.[47]

Objections to foreign words, then, were based on hostility to affectation and verbosity rather than patriotism. Equally strong opposition came from translators or writers of original works in English, who were conscious that they were writing for the uneducated and wanted to be sure that their works would be easily understood. John Cheke advocated the use of compound words where English vocabulary was inadequate. His contribution to the English language was recognised by Strype:

> And, moreover, in writing and discourse he would allow no words but such as were true English or of Saxon origin, suffering no adoption of any foreign words into English speech, which he thought was copious enough. . . .

But Strype was mistaken when he assumed a patriotic motivation in adding:

> That indeed was Cheke's conceit, that in writing in English, none but English words should be used, thinking it a dishonour to the English tongue, to be beholden to other nations for their words and phrases to express our minds.[48]

As mentioned above, Cheke's work on the vernacular originated in his interest in the English Bible. He objected to the number of Latin words retained in the Bible translation and accused Gardiner of a conscious attempt to keep the Scriptures unintelligible to the common people. It was for this reason that his own Scripture translation was undertaken,[49] and he made an effort to use compound English rather than foreign words. Cheke's comments on Thomas Hoby's translation of Castiglione's *The Courtier* are often quoted as an example of his opposition to foreign words:

> I am of this opinion that our tongue should be written cleane and pure, unmixt and unmangled with borrowing of other tongues wherein if we take not heed of tyme, ever borrowing and never paying, shall we be fain to keep our house as bankrupt.

But he went on to make it clear that he was only against unnecessary borrowing:

> And if she want at ani tiym (as being unperfight she must,) yet let her borrow with such bashfulness, that it may appear that if either the mould of our own tong could serve us to fascion a word of our own, or if the old denizened words could content and ease this need, we would not boldly venture into unkown words.[50]

Isolated comments criticising inkhorn terms can give a false impression of total rejection when quoted out of context, and this has led to an overestimation of the opposition to foreign influences. Puttenham complained that:

> We find in our English writers many words and speeches amendable, and yet shall see in some, many ink-horne termes so ill affected brought in by men of learning such as preachers and schoolmasters.

But he went on to say that he was himself guilty of 'using many strange and unaccustomed words' and gave a lengthy explanation of why he found it appropriate to use specific foreign words, concluding: 'I cannot see how we can spare them, whatsoever fault we find with inkhorne terms; for our speach wanteth words to such sense as well to be used.'[51] Jones quotes a long passage from Daniel's *Defence of Ryme*, ending with:

> And I cannot but wonder as the strange presumption of some men,
> that dare so audaciously adventure to introduce any whatsoever
> forraine words, be they never so strange, and of themselves as it
> were, without a Parliament, without any consent or allowance to
> establish them as free-denizens in our language.

He refers to the passage as one of the examples of opposition to neologising
in the last quarter of the sixteenth century, and attributed it to Daniel's
'outraged nationalistic spirit'.[52] But the comment which followed changed
the whole tone of the discussion and showed his acceptance of the inevitability
of foreign influences on the language:

> But this is but a character of that perpetual revolution
> which we see in all things that never remain the same;
> and we must be herein content to submit ourselves to
> the law of time whiche in a few years will al of that of
> which we now contend nothing.[53]

As pride in the vernacular developed towards the end of the century one
might expect an increase in hostility to foreign words, either based on a feeling
that they were no longer necessary, or in line with a growing awareness of
nationality; but instead one finds evidence of pride in the diversity of the
origins of language. Richard Carew named copiousness as one of the four
essentials for an adequate language and was proud of the copiousness of
English which he explained was based on past borrowing:

> seeing then we borrow (and that no shamefully) from the Dutch, the
> Breton, the Dane, the French, the Italyane, and the Spaniard, how can
> our stock be other than plentiful?[54]

Sir Philip Sidney's *An Apologie for Poetry* included a similar defence: 'I
know some will call it a mangled language. And why not so much better
taking the best of both the other'.[55]

There is, then, little evidence of a xenophobia of words, but rather a
tendency among sixteenth-century writers to welcome foreign influences to
enrich their language, provided comprehensibility was maintained and
affectation avoided. From the attitudes considered in this chapter it is clear
that linguistic patriotism was increasing as affection for, and pride in, the
vernacular replaced the idea that English was only for the unlearned and that
the language itself was unsophisticated. However, the views of the intellectual
elite were a long way from linguistic nationalism.

## Notes

1. John Foxe, *The Gospel of the Fower Evangelists*, 1571, quoted in A. McDougall,
   *Racial Myth in English History*, New England, 1982, p. 40.
2. The publication of propaganda in English was especially prevalent during the
   1530's as Thomas Cromwell orchestrated his campaign to win support for Henry
   VIII's stand against Rome. See above chapter two, pages 31-33.
3. Elizabeth L. Eisenstein, 'Some Conjectors about the Impact of Printing on Western

Society and Thought', *Journal of Modern History*, 40, 1968, pp 1-56.

4. Charles Barber, *Early Modern English*, 1976, pp 68, 69.

5. Not all commentators assume that the use of vernacular languages was motivated by national consciousness. Benedict Anderson's comment that there is no evidence of a 'proto-national impulse' underlying vernacularisation was quoted above, chapter one p. 26.

6. S.E. Lehmberg, ed Thomas Elyot's *The Governor*, 1962, p. 1.

7. Quoted in Nicholas Carlisle, *A Concise Description of the Endowed Grammar Schools*, 1878, III, p. 79.

8 E.g. G.G.C. Smith, ed, *Elizabethan Critical Essays*, Oxford, 1904, p. lvi. Lewis Einstein, *Tudor Ideals*, New York, 1921, p. 304. Liah Greenfeld, *Nationalism: Five Roads to Modernity*, 1992, Cambridge, Mass., p. 43.

9. Roger Ascham, *Toxophilus*, preface.

10. Roger Ascham, *The Schoolmaster*, 1570, Cassell's National Library, 1888, pp 76-92, 72, 113.

11. F.J. Furnivall, ed *The First Book of the Introduction of Knowledge made by Andrew Borde*, Early English Text Society, 1870, pp 119, 118, 120.

12. E.R. Adair, 'William Thomas – A forgotten Clerk of the Privy Council', R.W. Seton Watson, ed, *Tudor Studies*, 1924, pp 159-160.

13. His departure was caused by a combination of Protestantism and gambling debts.

14. Quoted in H.S. Bennett, *English Books and Readers, 1475-1605*, 2 vols, Cambridge 1952, I p. 92.

15. Published in Paris in 1568. Smith indicated that his ideas had been worked out much earlier when he was at Cambridge. See R.F. Jones, *The Triumph of the English Language*, Oxford, 1953, p. 145.

16. *An Orthographie, The Opening of the unreasonable writing of our English tong,* Adair, op. cit. p. 158.

17. J. Strype, *The Life of the Learned Sir John Cheke*, Oxford, 1821, p. 221.

18. G.C. Willcock and A. Walker, eds, *George Puttenham's The Arte of English Poesie*, Cambridge, 1936, pp xiix, 5, 59, 60, 144.

19. R.C. Alston, ed Richard Mulcaster's *The First Part of the Elementarie which entreateth chefelie the right writing of our English tong*, 1582, Menston 1970, pp 78, 79, 254.

20. Adair, op. cit. p. 160.

21. Richard Stanyhurst, dedication to his translation of *The Aeneid*, in G.G.S. Smith, ed *Elizabethan Critical Essays*, Oxford 1904, I, p. 138.

22. Sir Philip Sidney *An Apologie for Poetry*, ibid, p. 204.

23. Edmund Spenser, *The Faerie Queene*, introduction.

24. G.R. Hibbard, ed, 'Thomas Nashe's Pierce Penilesse – His supplication to the Devil', 1592, *Three Elizabethan Pamphlets*, 1951, p. 109.

25. Edmund Gibson, trans, *Camden's Britannia*, 1772, p. xxx.

26. Cited in MacDoughall, op. cit., p. 46.

27. William Camden, ' The Languages: Remaines Concerning Britain', W.F. Bolton, ed *The English Language, Essays by English and American Men of Letters 1490-1839*. Cambridge 1966, pp 29, 30.

28. William Camden, *The History of the most renowned and virtuous Princess Elizabeth, late Queen of England, composed by way of Annals,* 161, pp 136-44.

29. Marsh McLuhan, *The Gutenburg Galaxy: The Making of Typographical Man,* 1962, p. 120.

30. Andrew Borde op. cit., p. 120.

31. Richard Carew, 'The Excellency of the English Tongue', 1595, in Bolton, op. cit., pp 285-294.
32. Alexander Gill, *Logonomia Anglica*, 1619, p. 18 quoted in Bennett, op. cit., I, p. 234.
33. Puttenham, op. cit., p. 145.
34. Jones, op. cit., p. 152.
35. John Hart, *Orthographie*, 1569.
36. Einstein, op. cit., p. 304.
37. Puttenham, op. cit., p. xli.
38. Barber, op. cit., p. 90.
39. Jones, op. cit., pp 68, 115.
40. Quoted by Lehmberg in the introduction to his edition of *The Governor*, Elyot's *The Governor*, pp 13, 80, 225, 2.
41. Richard Sherry, *A Treatise of Schemes and Tropes*, 1550 Preface.
42. George Pettie, trans, *The Civile Conversation of M Stephen Guazzo*, 1586.
43. Thomas Nashe, Preface to 'Christ's Teares', 1594, in B.B. McKerrow, ed, *Thomas Nashe, the Complete Works*, vol IV, p6.
44. J.W. Cunliffe, ed, *George Gascoinge: Complete Works*, 2 vols, Cambridge, 1907-10 I, pp 5,6.
45. F.M. Salter and H.L.R. Edwards, eds, *John Skelton's Translation of Biblioteca Historia of Diodorus Siculus*, Early English Text Society, 1957, p. xxxii.
46. Thomas Wilson, *The Arte of Rhetorike*, 1553, fol 86i – 87 ii in J.L. Moore, *Tudor-Stuart Views on the Growth, Status and Destiny of the English Language,* 1910, reprinted 1970, New York, pp 91-3.
47. Ascham, op. cit. 1570, p. 126.
48. Strype, op. cit. p. 162.
49. James Goodwin, ed, *The Gospel according to St Matthew and St Mark, translated from the Greek, with original notes by John Cheke*, 1843.
50. John Cheke, Letter of July 16, 1557, appended to Sir Thomas Hoby's translation of *The Courtier* 1561.
51. Puttenham, op. cit., p. xli. The editors see Puttenham as an opponent of foreign words!
52. Jones, op. cit., p. 202.
53. Samuel Daniel, ' A Defence of Ryme' 1603, in *Elizabethan Critical Essays*, pp 356-384.
54. Richard Carew 'The Excellency of the English Tongue', ibid, pp 285-294.
55. Sir Philip Sidney, 'An apologie for Poetry', in ibid, pp 148-207.

# IV

# 'Casting pearls before swine':
## Translation into the English Language

A wide range of historical, legal and religious texts was translated into English in the sixteenth century. Why were the translations undertaken? What was the translators' attitude to their native tongue and to their uneducated audience? I will suggest that awareness of English as a national language should not be exaggerated. The ruling elite saw the vernacular as the language of the lower classes and publication into English as a means by which those orders could be controlled.

The main source of information on the outlook of the translators comes from their prefaces and their correspondence with their patrons. Dedications were based on literary convention, but any change in that convention represents a change in their judgement on audience receptiveness, or on the approach which would impress potential patrons and publishers. Any analysis of the market for translations is more problematic. We do not have reliable information on numbers who were literate but who did not have a classical education. David Cressy has tried to estimate literacy rates and to link them with social groupings, but, despite the title of his book his results are based on seventeenth-century figures.[1] Margaret Spufford's *Small Books and Pleasant Histories* examines lower-class literacy but again concentrates on the seventeenth century while offering some fascinating glimpses of sixteenth-century reading habits. She argues that historians of literacy have probably been too conservative in their estimates of the spread of reading ability.[2] There is, however, no evidence for Liah Greenfeld's contention that 'Literacy was exceptionally widespread in sixteenth-century England; only the bottom of the social ladder remained unaffected.'[3] Even if we could estimate literacy rates more accurately we would be only part of the way to understanding the audience for translations. The readership varied considerably with the nature of the text. More importantly, the size of the readership was determined not by the numbers who could read but by the extent of oral dissemination.

Translators of historical texts often used patriotism to explain their choice of subject matter. Lord Berners claimed to have translated Froissart because the present generation of Englishmen would benefit if they read of the glories of the nation's past:

> I judged it necessary and profitable to be had in English since they treat of famous acts done in our parts, that is to say in England, France, Spain, Portugal, Scotland, Brittany and other places joining: especially they redound to the honour of Englishmen. . . . What pleasure it shall be to the

noble gentlemen of England to see behold and read the high enterprises
famous acts and glorious deeds done and achieved by their ancestors?[4]

Berners was encouraged by Henry VIII, who presumably felt that it would
be useful to remind his subjects of the successes of Crecy and Poitiers at a
time of aggression towards France. John Brende felt that translation of history
would prevent England from slipping behind other countries. He translated
Quintius Curtius' *History of Alexander the Great* 'that we Englishmen might
be found as forward in the behalf of other nations which have brought all
worthy histories into their natural languages.'[5] When he translated
Demosthenes' *Three Orations* in 1570, Thomas Wilson believed that they
would provide a useful example to 'all them that love the country's liberty
and desire to take warning for their better avail by the example of others.'[6]

The subject matter did not have to be explicitly patriotic, however, for
translators to claim to be working for their country, and this was becoming
more common by the middle of the sixteenth century. In the early 1530s,
typical dedications hoped to 'answer question of wisdom, both moral and
natural', 'to benefit the health of the reader', 'to help the reader patiently to
suffer the death of a friend'.[7] By the end of the 1530s a widening of the
didactic purpose was apparent to encompass translation for the good of the
country. Taverner translated Erasmus's *Adages* 'for your sakes and for the
love I bear to the furtherance and adornment of my native country.'[8] Thomas
Elyot referred to the 'profit of the commonwealth' in one of his translations
in 1533.[9] By the 1550s the patriotic preface had become commonplace. Claims
such as that of Ralph Robinson that he was translating *Utopia* 'out of love of
God and my country' became usual.[10] Humphrey Lloyd gave a more detailed
account of the translator's duties in his preface to his translation of John XII's
*Treasury of Healthe* in 1550, giving priority to duty to one's country:

> I, calling to memory the notable sentence of Cicero that everyman is
> not born for himself but chiefly to benefit his native country, then his
> parents, afterwards his children and friends, seeking a means whereby
> I might profit my native country, thought it might be best to translate
> this little treatise. . . .[11]

Even though these scholars included patriotic sentiments in their prefaces,
they did not necessarily see the vernacular as a national language of which
they could be proud. In the same way as the people choosing to write in
English, the translators were conscious that they were addressing the
'uneducated classes' and that the language was 'inadequate'. Richard Taverner's
dedication of a translation to Henry VIII contained the following comparison:

> The selfe prayers, no doubt, be excellent, pure, sincere, godly and
> christian. But my translation I fear, is rude, base, unpleasant, gross
> and barbarous. I fear, I say, lest according to the proverb I shall render
> pro aureis ferrea, lest I have wine into water.[12]

In many cases, prefaces to translations were designed to further the
author's career by attracting government attention. When Thomas Paynell
translated a work of Constantius 'to teach the unlearned that rebellion against

the King did not pay'[13] he was aware that this would impress his patron, Thomas Cromwell. Elyot had lost his job as senior clerk to the council as a result of Wolsey's downfall and he dedicated *The Governor* to Henry VIII in the hope of regaining favour.[14] Taverner's publications included propaganda for Cromwell as well as translations. William Marshall advocated the publication of translations useful to the government cause and he produced the only two undertaken – Valla's *Donation of Constantine* in 1534 and Marsiglio of Padua's *Defensor Pacis* in 1534 – both of which were anti-Papal tracts.[15]

The government also took an interest in translations of law treatises and statutes and these made an important contribution to the number of texts published in English in the 1520s and 1530s. John Rastell published his abridged version of the statutes in 1518 and *Littleton's Tenures* in 1525. The translation process culminated in three major publications in the 1530s: The *Great Boke of Statutes*, covering 1327-1483, (1530-33): The *Boke of Magna Carta*, which was George Ferrer's translation of the statutes 1225-1327, (1534): and Lynwood's *Constitutions prouicialles*, an English canon law, were published by Robert Redman. Howard Graham has argued that the government may have been directly involved in these publications, and he stressed the family connection between Redman and the Inns of Court circle of lawyers and suggested that Ferrers may have been subsidised by Cromwell.[16] Evidence of official involvement is somewhat circumstantial, but the publication of English translations of Statues was in line with government policy of the 1530s, and printers would be encouraged by the prospect of government approval.

Translation of the law into English was stimulated by the rift between the secular and religious legal establishments. *The Commons Supplication against the Ordinaries* (1532) attacked church 'laws, constitutions and ordinances' not only because they were made without royal consent, but because:

> your said humble subjects nor their predecessors could never be privy
> to the said laws, nor any of the said laws have been declared unto
> them in English or otherwise published, by knowledge thereof might
> have eschewed the penalties, dangers and censures of the same.[17]

The break with Rome brought additional pressure for use of the vernacular because of appeals to precedent in official propaganda. Graham has suggested that the order of the printing of the *Great Boke* is significant in this context. It was in reverse order except for 1-28 Edward III, thus giving priority to the *Statutes of Provisors* and *Praemunire*, which were used to justify anti-Papal legislation.[18] Cromwell reminded a colleague of the opening article of the *Magna Carta* – 'Anglicana Ecclesia libera sit' – 'The English Church shall be free' – so would have approved of Ferrers' translation.[19]

The fact that printers and translators were responding to increased demand for law in the vernacular and had an eye to government approval, does not rule out the possibility of wider motivation, and it has been suggested that they had a patriotic concern for their native tongue. Graham refers to the 'mutual reciprocating impact' that law translation had on 'national ideals and feelings throughout the brilliant Tudor century'[20] and Eisenstein stressed Rastell's patriotic motivation.[21] However, if Rastell's 'Proheme' to his statute abridgement can be taken as indicative of his views, he was primarily concerned with order and stability. He felt that translation was 'needful to be made for the order of this realm.'[22] George Ferrers justified his translation of *The Boke of Magna Carta* by claiming that he wished to bring enlightenment to the unlearned:

> me thought it necessary to set forth in such sort as men might have best knowledge of them . . . and how should they understand the meaning that understand not the text? For this cause I say, was this book translated into English which, though perhaps it shall not satisfy the learned, yet shall it be a good help for the unlearned.[23]

The campaign for law in the vernacular became part of the general demands made by the 'commonwealth' writers. That their ideas on the importance of unity and obedience to the law coincided with those of the government was discussed in chapter one, where reference was made to Thomas Starkey's views. Starkey's statement on the language of the law introduced an element of patriotism in his condemnation of the law in French:

> Our common law is written in French and therein disputed and taught, which besides it is against the commonweal, it is also ignominious and dishonour to our nation forasmuch as thereby is testified our subjection to the Normans.[24]

Although patriotism was only one facet of the drive towards the translation of statutes, the process itself was vital, both to the use of the vernacular and to England's development, and the triumph of common law over international canon law provided a focus for national awareness.

The translators and their patrons so far discussed have been concerned to enlighten the unlearned in the hope that this would make them more likely to obey the law. The prospects of success were, however, restricted by the limits of the market. High illiteracy rates, combined with a taste among the literate for more interesting subject matter would inevitably mean that the audience was narrow. Graham suggested that there was 'substantial demand' for the translations of the statutes. The *Great Boke of Statutes* ran to four or five large editions – about 3,000 copies. The *Magna Carta* section was reprinted singly at least three times.[25] But the demand would be specialised and there were enough people with some experience of, or a direct interest in the law, to account for these sales. Rastell's 'Proheme' to his statute abridgement cited the wishes of both Henry VII and Henry VIII that 'the universal people of the realm' who gave themselves 'greatly to the reading of the English vulgar tongue' would soon 'have knowledge of the said statutes and ordinances.' But this was hardly practical and later in the 'Proheme', Rastell gave the more realistic advice that anyone who wanted information on the law should consult an expert.[26] *Defensor Pacis* may have been a crucial text in the government's propaganda campaign, but it did not sell. In fact it seems that Marshall had difficulties in giving away copies of his English translation.

In a letter to Cromwell, he explained that he had sent 24 copies to the monks at Charterhouse only to have them returned three days later. John Rochester took a copy but burnt it after five days. Marshall desperately needed the money Cromwell had promised him to cover the costs of printing.[27] Paradoxically, the wider the audience for any English translation – whether based on greater interest in the text or on its suitability for oral dissemination – the more apprehensive the government became. This applies especially to the religious translations discussed in the next section.

Despite Thomas Cromwell's approval of English translations of the statutes and his use of English pamphlets in his anti-Papal propaganda, the government in the 1530s remained dubious about publication in the vernacular. This ambivalent attitude towards the national language is no better exemplified than in the official approach to the translation of the Bible. Adrian Hastings places the vernacular Bible in a central position in the development of national consciousness. He argues that by the 1580s:

> The mass impact of this English Bible in strengthening a common
> language, installing in all its hearers and readers the idea of nationhood
> and actually shaping the English of all classes into an awareness of
> their own nationhood cannot be overstated.[28]

Since Lollard times the English Bible had been a symbol of opposition to authority. John Wycliffe, the Oxford scholar who inspired the Lollard movement, believed that the individual should have access to the Bible without the need for the mediation of the clergy. John Purvey, one of Wycliffe's associates, led a group who produced a literal translation of the Bible into English in 1382 and a more readable version in 1392.[29] The social implications of some of Wycliffe's ideas, especially as popularised by his more radical followers, led the authorities to associate Lollardy with lower class dissent,[30] and the emphasis on preaching – especially the idea that any men or women inspired by God should be allowed to preach – made control difficult. The extent of the government's fear of Lollardy is indicated by the fact that the death penalty was introduced for impenitent heretics in 1401, and in 1414 laymen were introduced into the surveillance system as secular courts were authorised to receive indictments for heresy and justices were given powers to look into the activities of those who may have been spreading heresy in sermons as well as in writing. The Synod of Oxford of 1408 forbade the reading of the English translation of the Bible without official sanction and in the early sixteenth century possession of the English Bible still conjured up fears of Lollard dissent in the minds of the lay and ecclesiastical establishment.[31]

Official hostility to the English Bible was increased by its connection with Lutheranism, as is indicated by the strength of official antagonism to Tyndale. His English New Testament was published in Worms in 1526 and was immediately distributed in England. It was one of the works from the Continent whose import was banned and the difficulty of enforcing the ban is indicated by the need for a further proclamation, where the reasons for government opposition were explained.

> It was not necessary that the said scripture be in the English tongue
> and in the hands of the common people. . . . The translation of the
> New Testament and the Old Testament into the vulgar tongue of the
> English should rather be the continuance or increase of errors among
> the said people.[32]

Yet by 1534 the climate of opinion had changed so much that Convocation, hardly a progressive institution, felt sufficiently confident of a less than hostile response to petition the king for an official translation of the Bible into English. The Archbishop of Canterbury, Thomas Cranmer, played an important part in the change of opinion within the church hierarchy and there can be no doubt of the influence of Cromwell, whose interest can be traced back to the 1520s.[33] The change does not represent a volte-face in Establishment thinking, as the English Bible was still perceived within the context of the maintenance of order. McConica stresses that Cromwell's reforms at this time such as the Ten Articles, his Injunctions to the Clergy and the Coverdale Bible, represented his attempt to put his Erasmian ideas into practice.[34] Whether one agrees, or goes along with Elton's view that Cromwell's ideas were similar to but not actually Erasmian,[35] the reforms definitely represent the practical religious equivalent of Starkey's views on order within the commonwealth. There was no reference to the vernacular bible in Cromwell's *First Injunction* of 1536, but item V specified that children and servants should be taught their 'Pater Noster', the articles of faith and the Ten Commandments in their mother tongue:

> that the said youth be in no manner or wise kept or brought up in
> idleness, lest any time afterwards they be driven by lack of some
> mystery or occupation to live idly or to fall back on stealing.

The provision made in the second set of Injunctions that each church should have an English Bible, reminded the clergy that their parishioners should be exhorted to:

> avoid all contention and altercation therein, and to use honest sobriety
> in the inquisition of the true sense of the same, and refer the explication
> of obscure places to men of higher judgement in scripture.[36]

Cranmer's preface to the second edition of the Great Bible contained a similar warning against 'frivolous disputation'. He discoursed at some length about how good things might be abused 'and turned from fruitful and wholesome to hurtfull and noisesome'. He made specific reference to the Bible as a source of an ordered society:

> Herein may Princes learn how to govern their subjects: subjects
> obedience, love and dread to their princes; husbands how they should
> behave to their wives; how to educate their children and their servants;
> and contrary the wives, children and their servants may know their
> duty to their husbands, parents and masters.[37]

The proclamation ordering the Great Bible to be placed in every church echoed this theme of order and obedience:

That every of the King's majesty's loving subjects minding to read therein, might by occasion thereof not only consider and perceive the great and ineffable omnipotent power promise, justice, mercy and goodness of almighty God but also thereby, learn to observe God's commandments and so obey their sovereign lord and high powers and to use themselves according to their vocation. . . . without murmuring and grudgings.[38]

Limitations on the readership of the Bible, in an act of 1543, are usually seen as part of the reaction which included an increase in the persecution of heretics and culminated in the *King's Book* in May of the same year. But in fact the *Act for the Advancement of true religion and for the abolishment of the contrary* attacked the Bible, not so much out of doctrinal conservation, as out of a fear that the English Bible was leading to disorder among the uneducated. The Act limited the reading of the Bible on a class basis: nobles and gentlemen were allowed to read to their families at home; substantial merchants, noblewomen and gentlewomen were trusted to read by themselves; while reading of the Bible was forbidden under any circumstances to 'the people of the lower sort' who were listed as follows: 'no women, nor artificers, apprentices, journeymen, serving men of the degree of yeomen or under, husbandmen nor labourers.'[39]

A further comment on this subject comes from Henry VIII, in a speech to Parliament, during which he expounded the theme of 'discord' and 'dissention'. He gave the abuse of the privilege of being permitted to read the Bible as one of the causes of these problems, adding; 'I am very sorry to know and hear, how unreverently that most precious work of God is disputed, rhymed sung and jangled in every alehouse and tavern.'[40]

Government concern for order and unity carried over to primers. In 1535 John Rastell appealed to Cromwell for permission to print 'certain prayers in English . . . I have devised . . . some are printed already in a primer I have sent to court,'[41] and, in 1534, Redman printed 'prayers of the Bible taken out of the Old Testament and the New.'[42] Twenty-seven different primers were published in England between 1534 and 1545.[43] The government's response to this proliferation was to authorise an official primer which was published by Grafton,[44] the use of which was made compulsory by proclamation. Again the emphasis was on uniformity 'for avoiding of the diversity of primer books throughout our dominion.' Publication in English was for the benefit of the uneducated, not for the English people as a nation: for 'our people and subjects which have no understanding of the Latin tongue and yet have knowledge of reading' and youth 'until they be competent in understanding to perceive it in Latin.'[45]

The development of the official view of the English translation of the Bible shows that Henry VIII's government did not see language as a focus of national identity. English was the language of the uneducated lower orders and was seen as an aspect of control – initially as a threat to stability but increasingly as a means of enforcing order. For the next two reigns the unity of theology and politics was broken. During the reign of Edward VI, religious statements reflected Protestant theology without the same emphasis on order and obedience. This is not to say that the religious settlement was not politically motivated on the part of Dukes of Somerset and Northumberland and their advisers, only that they did not attempt to use the vernacular Bible as a means of asserting their authority. A comparison of statements made by Cranmer with those already mentioned indicate this change. His preface to the *First Prayer Book* referred to St Paul's views that language in church should be understood by all. He regretted that:

> the service of this church of England (these many years) had been read in Latin to the people which they understood not; so that they heard with their ears only and in their hearts spirit and mind have not been edified thereby.[46]

Comprehension was also the main issue in the conflict over the use of language in Cornwall. The participants in the Western Rebellion of 1549 objected to the use of English in the Prayer Book, item eight of their demands reading:

> We will not receive the new service because it is but like a Christmas game, but we will have our own service of matins, mass and evensong, and the procession in Latin not in English as it was before. And so we Cornishmen (whereof certain of us understand no English) utterly refuse this new English.

Their demands were based on concern for familiarity rather than any form of linguistic separatism and no attempt was made to make the Prayer Book available in Cornish. The rebels also rejected the English Bible on the following grounds:

> We will have the whole Bible and all the books of the Scriptures in English called in again, for we be informed that otherwise the clergy shall not of long time confound the heretics.[47]

Somerset's response showed his concern for comprehensibility. He asked how people had learned their prayers in Latin when they did not understand it, and whether it was really impossible to teach their children basic prayers in English, adding 'we are informed there were very few towns in Cornwall but that shall find more in them that understand English than understand Latin.'[48] There is no evidence that the government was trying to suppress minority languages – in fact the *Prayer Book* was translated into Welsh; and in 1560 permission was given for the use of Welsh and Cornish, as 'It may be useful for such Welsh and Cornish children who speak not English to learn the promises in the Welsh and Cornish languages.'[49]

Mary's repeal of the *Act of Uniformity* automatically restored the Latin of orthodox Catholicism, but by the time of Elizabeth's religious settlement it seemed equally to be taken for granted that the English services would be returned. The *Thirty-Nine Articles*, in one of the few changes from Cranmer's *Forty-Two Articles*, included a strongly worded defence of the vernacular, again on the grounds of understanding:

'Of speaking in the congregation in such a tongue as the people understand.' It is a thing plainly repugnant to the word of God and the custom of the primitive church, to have public prayer in the church or to minister the sacraments in a tongue not understood by the people.[50]

But there was no attempt made by the government to make the English language into a symbol of the Anglican Church,[51] and its ambivalent attitude to the mother tongue was retained. A proclamation of 1559, 'Prohibiting unlicensed interludes and plays especially on religion or policy', indicated a continuing tendency to associate English with lower class disorder and sedition. 'Common interludes in the English tongue' were criticised as being 'not convenient in any good ordered Christian commonwealth to be suffered.'[52]

One of the reasons why mid sixteenth-century governments were careful to control translation of religious texts into English was the fact that the audience was potentially wider than for historical or legal works. There is evidence, albeit sketchy, that people learned to read in order to gain access to the English Bible. Claire Cross discussed the importance of literacy among Lollard women and commented:

It may be that considerably more women than churchmen suspected acquired the ability to read in order to pursue Lollard books. Certainly a reverence for books characterise women in a majority of communities; and in several Lollard women took a major part in organising book distribution.[53]

An account by William Malden described the impact of Henry VIII's decision to put the Bible in all churches. He told of how his father's disapproval of Bible reading sessions gave him an incentive to learn to read and of how he clubbed together with his father's apprentice to buy a copy of the New Testament.[54] A description by the Jesuit, William Weston, of a Puritan gathering which he witnessed from his prison at Wisbech suggests lower class literacy among Puritan groups:

From the very beginning a great number of Puritans gathered here. Some came from the outlying parts of the town, some from villages round about, eager and vast crowds of them flocking to perform their practices – sermons, communions and fasts . . . each of them had his own Bible and sedulously turned the pages and looked up the texts cited by the preachers, discussing the passages among themselves to see whether they had quoted them to the point and accurately, and in harmony with their tenets.

One should be wary of generalising from isolated incidents as the urge to read did not always lead to success. Earlier in the same autobiography, Weston was scathing about a Puritan fellow prisoner, this time in the Clink, who had spent eight years poring over one book, found to be 'an A.B.C. containing elements of the alphabet' without being able to 'decipher one word, let alone a sentence.[55] The appearance of the Bible was sometimes greeted with apathy rather than a rush to learn to read. The Protestant, Thomas Becon, writing in 1541, lamented the lack of interest in the English Bible in some churches:

The most sacred and Holy Bible is now had among us in our vulgar tongue, and freely permitted to be read of all men universally . . . but how many read it? Verily a man may come into some churches and see the Bible so inclosed in dust and cobwebs, that with his finger he may write on the Bible this epitaph: ecce nunc in pulvere dormio, that is to say, I sleep now in the dust, such little pleasure have these filthy swine and currish dogs in that sweet and most singular treasure.[56]

Whatever the extent of literacy and interest in reading the Bible, one should remember that the audience for religious translations was not limited to those who could read. Oral dissemination, through preaching and through domestic and public Bible reading, meant that the audience far outstripped the numbers of the literate. In the account mentioned above, Walden told of how 'divers poor men in the town of Chelmsford in the county of Essex brought the New Testament and many would flock to hear the reading.'[57] It is common for descriptions of Bible readings to refer to violence. Weston continued his account of the Puritan meeting as follows:

Also they would start arguing among themselves about the meaning of passages from the scriptures – men women, boys and girls, rustics labourers and idiots – and more often than not, it was said, it ended in violence and fisticuffs.[58]

Weston was hardly a sympathetic witness and he seems to be relying on hearsay for his comments on violence – but there is enough evidence from the time before Henry VIII's government limited Bible readership to suggest that the decision may have been influenced by disorderly Bible reading sessions. Edmund Bonner, Bishop of London, had provided six Bibles at St Paul's for public use, but had forbidden crowds to gather. In 1540, John Porter, a tailor, was imprisoned by Bonner for reading the Bible out loud.[59] In 1541 Humphrey Grynshill, a weaver from Stonehurst in Gloucestershire, provoked a public disturbance by reading aloud from the English Bible and declaring masses for the dead to be worthless.[60]

In their attitude to the translation of histories, statutes and religious texts into English the governing elite showed that they were concerned to control the uneducated, either by censorship or enlightenment. The government's use of precedent in propaganda for the break with Rome stimulated the publication of statutes. Official approval increased the chances of profit for the publishers, but this does not rule out the possibility of other motives and their prefaces show an awareness of the importance of the law for a stable society. Concern for stability was also apparent among patrons of religious translations. Initially members of the Establishment were worried that the English Bible was a threat to an ordered society, but the ruling elite gradually came round to the idea that, if uniformity was carefully maintained, religious works in English could provide a means of control over the lower classes. Many of the translators and their patrons had 'commonwealth leanings'.[61] It is not surprising, therefore, that their views on language paralleled the commonwealth view of the community. Their continued association of the vernacular with the lower classes was appropriate to their belief in a hierarchically structured society.

One should not assume that the Protestant push for all to be familiar with the word of God gave them democratic credentials or that their concern for the English language made them patriotic, although this connection has been made by Eisenstein who states that 'the same combination of democratic and patriotic themes accompanied Protestant Bible translation. It is no accident that nationalism and mass literacy developed together.'[62] It is more useful to think of a split in the intellectual elite between the conservatives, who wanted to preserve their monopoly of access to knowledge through the use of classical languages, and the progressive thinkers, who realised it would be easier to control the ideas of the masses by using the vernacular. The need for the Bible to be available in the vernacular had been recognised by Catholic reformers. Erasmus's hope that 'the farmer sing some portion of them at the plough, the weaver hum some parts of them to the movement of his shuttle, the traveller lighten the weariness of his journey',[63] was justified with the egalitarian argument that, as baptism and other sacraments were available to all, there should be no monopoly in the hands of 'theologians and monks' of the understanding of the word of God. Erasmus was the archetypal international scholar, and for him support for the vernacular could have no links with patriotism. The same applies to Thomas More, whose rejection of national autonomy was the basis of his stand against Henry VIII, and who also approved of the vernacular Bible. But More shared the government's fear of dissent resulting from the availability of the Bible in English and advocated strict control over translation and distribution. He felt that the Scriptures should not be 'disputed in taverns, for every lewd lad to keep a pot Parliment on.'[64] More's interest in the English Bible had neither democratic nor patriotic implications.

The following comments were made by the clergymen Thomas Harding and John Standish as part of their campaigns against the English Bible:

> Yee [the Protestants] prostitute the Scriptures . . . as baudes do their Harlottes, to the ungodly, unlearned, Rascal people. . . Prentices, Light Personnes, and the rifferaffe of the people. . . . The unlearned people were kept from the Readings of the Scriptures by special providence of God, that pretious stoanes should not be thrown before swine.[65]
>
> Christ does not wish the herd to handle his mysteries. . . . Translating scripture is like casting pearls before swine. . . the rude and unlearned, not being able to understand the mysteries, stick to the letter which killeth.[66]

These statements indicate the strength of their disdain for the lower classes whom they regarded as unworthy to have access to the word of God. Harding remained a Catholic and was exiled to Louvain in Elizabeth's reign.[67] His views on the vernacular emerged as part of his controversy with Bishop Jewel in the 1560s. Standish, however, was a Protestant so his hostility to the

English Bible cannot be explained by doctrinal orthodoxy.[68]

It could be suggested that the continued hostility to the vernacular from within the state-dominated Anglican Church did not reflect the true reformed doctrine. But work on the attitudes of the German reformers to the vernacular Bible has indicated that, despite initial enthusiasm, Protestants began to fear that free access to the Bible might be socially disruptive. Richard Gawthorp and Gerald Strauss have questioned the assumption of a 'progression from Protestantism to literacy through the vernacular Bible' by pointing out that, after about 1525, Luther 'failed to actively encourage an unmediated encounter between Scripture and the untrained mind.' He no longer believed that it would be enough for the understanding of Scripture to read the Bible in German 'because no-one can really know what the Scripture says without first having studied it in the original tongues.' Instead, he recommended that those who could only read the vernacular should be taught the catechism. Protestant reformers and teachers in Germany feared that the availability of the Bible in the mother tongue might lead to unorthodox beliefs and result in an unstable society. Luther's statement that 'one must steer and drive the common crowd to learn what counts as right and what counts as wrong in the land where they live and earn their daily bread', made in the preface to the shorter catechism in 1529, indicates that he saw vernacular publication as a means of social control.[69]

This survey of motives behind the patronage of translation into English has suggested that the governing elite did not perceive English as a national language. They were a long way from Gramsci's vision of 'expansive hegemony' based on 'intellectual, moral and cultural unity.'[70] They did, however, understand the manipulation of language as a form of power.

## Notes

1. David Cressy, *Literature and the Social Order: Reading and Writing in Tudor and Stuart England*, Cambridge, 1980.
2. Margaret Spufford, *Small Books and Pleasant Histories: Popular Fiction and its Readership in Seventeenth Century England*. Cambridge, 1981, Preface p. xviii.
3. Liah Greenfeld, *Nationalism: Five Roads to Modernity*, Cambridge Mass., 1992, p. 54.
4. C.H. Williams, ed., *English Historical Documents*, V, 1967, pp 138-140.
5. John Brende, *Quintius Curtius' Historie of the Acts of the Great Alexander, 1553,* preface.
6. Thomas Wilson, *Demosthenes' Three Orations*, 1570, To the Gentle Reader.
7. Hugo of Campden, *Kynge Boccus and Syndrake,* 1530; Sir Thomas Wyatt, *The Governaunce of goode helthe, beynge Erasmus interpretoure*, 1530; Sir F. Poyntz, *The table of Cebes the philosopher*, 1530.
8. R. Taverner, *Proverbs and Adages of Erasmus*, 1539.
9. Sir Thomas Elyot, *Plutarch's How to make a profit of his enemies.*
10. Ralph Robinson, *More's Utopia*, 1551.
11. Humphrey Lloyd, *John XXI's Treasury of Health*, 1550, Preface.
12. R. Taverner, trans., *An Epitome of the Psalmes, or brief meditations on the same,* 1539. This example and many others are cited in R.F. Jones, *The Triumph of the English Language*, Oxford, 1953, p. 29.

13. Thomas Paynell, *Constantius Felicius' The Conspiracy of Lucius Catiline*, 1541 Preface.

14. S.E. Lehmberg, ed, *Thomas Elyot's The Governor*, 1962, p. 2.

15. G.R. Elton, *Policy and Police, The Enforcement of the Reformation in the Age of Thomas Cromwell,* Cambridge, 1972, p. 186.

16. Howard Jay Graham, 'Our Tongue Maternall, marvellously amendyd and augmented: the first Englishing and Printing of the Medievel Statues at Large. 1530-33.' *U.C.L.A. Review*, 13, 1965, pp 66-7.

17. Henry Gee and W.J. Hardy, eds., *Documents Illustrative of Church History*, 1896, p. 146.

18. Graham, op. cit., p. 85.

19. R.B. Merriman, ed., *The Life and Letters of Thomas Cromwell*, Oxford, 1902, p. 102.

20. Graham, op. cit., p. 62.

21. Elizabeth L. Eisenstein, *The Printing Press as an Agent of Change*, Cambridge, 1979, p. 362.

22. John Rastell's *Statutory Abridgement*, The Proheme.

23. Quoted in H.S. Bennett, *English Books and Readers, 1475-1557*, p. 80.

24. Kathleen M. Burton, ed, *Thomas Starkey's A Dialogue between Reginald Pole and Thomad Lupset*, 1948, pp 55,117.

25. Graham, op. cit., p. 77.

26. Rastell, op. cit., The Proheme.

27. *L. & P.*, III, no 523.

28. Adrian Hastings, *The Construction of Nationhood: Ethnicity, Religion and Nationalism,* Cambridge, 1997, p. 24.

29. Greenfeld seems to be under the impression that part of the Bible was translated into English for the first time in 1525 and that a full version appeared for the first time in 1535 (op. cit., p 53). This misconception undermines her argument that English nationalism was born in the 1520s.

30. Margaret Ashton, 'Lollardy and Sedition, 1381-1431', *Past and Present*, 17, April 1960, pp 1-44.

31. Possession of English versions of the Bible was used as evidence in trials of 74 suspected Lollards in Coventry in 1511, Claire Cross, *Church and People*, 1976, pp 38-40.

32. *T.R.P.*I. 69, 122, 129.

33. *L. & P.*, vol, XIV, 214.

34. J.K. McConica, *English Humanists and Reformation Politics*, Oxford 1965, p. 151.

35. G.R. Elton, *Reform and Reformation*, 1977, p. 172.

36. Gee and Hardy, eds., op. cit., pp 270, 277.

37. J.E. Cox, ed., *Miscellaneous Writings and Letters of Thomas Cranmer*, Parker Society, 1846, pp 121-2.

38. *T.R.P.*, I 200, 6 May 1541.

39. J.F. Mozley, *Coverdale and His Bibles*, 1953, pp 283-4. A Comment by Elton in *Reform and Reformation*, p. 300, that Bible reading was forbidden to 'women and the lower orders' as both groups were 'too ill-instructed and volatile to be exposed to such heady stuff' is misleading. The proscription applied only to lower class women, not to women in general.

40. Edward Hall, *The Union of the two noble and Illustrie families of York and Lancaster,* 1548, facsimile reproduction, Scolar Press, 1970, p. cclxii.

41. *Letters and Papers*, op. cit., vol.VII, 1073.

42. C.C. Butterworth, 'Robert Redman's Prayers of the Bible', *The Library*, 279, 5th series, 1948.

43. W.A. Jackson and F.S. Ferguson, eds *A Short Title Catalogue of Books Printed in England, Scotland and Ireland, and of English Books Printed Abroad, 1475-1642.* Vol II, 1976.

44. *The Primer set forth by his Kinges maiestie and his clergy . . . and none other to be used throughout his dominions.*

45. *T.R.P.* I, 248.

46. *The First and Second Prayer Books of Edward VI,* 1913, p. 3.

47. Anthony Fletcher, *Tudor Rebellions,* 1968, pp 135-6.

48. Julian Cornwall, *Revolt of the Peasantry, 1549,* 1977, p. 117.

49. H. Jenner, *A Handbook of the Cornish Language,* 1904 p. 13, see chapter five, p. 5.

50. Edgar C.S. Gibson, ed., *The Thirty-Nine Articles, Explained with an Introduction* 1896, Article XXIV.

51. The use of Latin in church music by Thomas Tallis and William Byrd had government support. The publication of their Cantiones Sacrae, a semi-official project dedicated to the Queen, was rewarded with the lucrative monopoly for the sale of printed music.

52. *T.R.P.* II, 458.

53. Claire Cross, 'Great Reasoners in Scripture, Women Lollards 1380-1530', in D. Baker, ed., *Medieval Women, Studies in Church History,* 1978 Oxford Subsidia I, 378, cited in Spufford, op. cit., p. 43.

54. J.G. Nichols, ed., *Narratives of the Days of the Reformation,* Camden Society, lxxvii, pp 349-351.

55. Philip Caraman, trans. & ed., *William Weston's Autobiography of an Elizabethan, 1611,* 1951, pp 164-5. No date given for his description of the Puritan meeting, but Weston was at Wisbech from 1588 to 1598. p. 117.

56. John Ayre, ed., *Thomas Becon's Works,* 3. vols, 1843-4, I, p. 38.

57. Nichols, op. cit., p. 350.

58. Weston, op. cit., p. 165.

59. Mozley, op. cit., pp 265-269.

60. This incident is referred to in Imogen Luxen, 'The Reformation and Popular Culture', in Felicity Heal and Rosemary O'Day, eds. *Church and Society in England, Henry VIII to James I,* 1977, p74.

61. McConica, op. cit..

62. Eisenstein, op. cit., P.363.

63. 'The Paracelsis' in John C Olin, ed., *Desiderius Erasmus, Christian Humanist and the Reformation: Selected Writings,* New York, 1965.

64. W.E. Campbell and A.W. Reed, eds., *The English Works of Sir Thomas More,* 2 vols, 1927-31, pp 244, 246.

65. John Jewel, *A Defence of the Apologie of the Churche of Englande,* To the Christian Reader, 1567. Jewel had written his *Apologie of the Churche of England* in 1562 and Harding replied with *A Confutation of a book by Bishop Jewel entitled An Apologie of the Church of England,* Antwerp, 1565.

66. John Standish, *A Discourse wherein it is debated whether it be expedient that Scripture be in English for all men to read at will,* 1554, quoted in R.F. Jones, op. cit., Oxford, 1953, p. 63.

67. *Catholic Encyclopedia,* III, 135a.

68. *Dictionary of National Biography.*

69. Richard Gawthorp and Gerald Strauss, 'Protestantism and Literacy in Early Modern Germany', *Past and Present,* 104, 1984, pp 31-5.

70. See chapter one.

# V

# 'Diversity in tongue, language, order and habit': Tudor Governments and Minority Languages

In chapter three I suggested that members of the intellectual elite who expressed patriotic views did not necessarily equate national consciousness with a common language. In chapter four, I demonstrated that language was an aspect of power rather than a badge of nationality. These conclusions have been based on an examination of perception of the English language by members of the classically educated elite. But what of attitudes to linguistic diversity within the state? Language policies were part of the movement to increase the power of the Tudor monarchy by centralisation of government, but were not an attempt to indulge in linguistic imperialism. They and later English governments have been accused of this by a number of writers. For example, Anthony Buckley has pointed out that the English government has been popularly blamed for the 'decline of the Irish culture found in the Irish has language, in ancient texts and in folklore'.[1] It is outside the scope of this study to consider the reasons for the subsequent decline of the Celtic vernaculars. The subject has been covered by a number of writers such as Durkacz and Hechter.[2] It is, however, possible to defend sixteenth-century monarchs against the accusation of having a conscious policy to eradicate the Welsh, Cornish and Irish languages.

In the twentieth century, minority languages have been seen as dangerous in leading to nationalist demands as in the case of the Welsh, Breton and Basque separatists. This outlook can be traced back to the German Romantics of the late eighteenth and early nineteenth centuries. For example, Johann Herder in a 1772 essay *Ueber den Ursprung der Sprache*, saw language as a valuable collective inheritance, the survival of which was essential for the survival of the nation. Johann Fichte went further in his prejudices. He too saw language as a determinant of nationhood, defining a people as 'men whose organs of speech are influenced by the same external conditions, who live together in continuous communication with each other'. He also argued that, as the German language was superior because of its antiquity and purity, the German nation must be superior.[3] Elie Kedourie included a linguistic criterion in his definition of nationalism: 'A group speaking the same language is known as a nation and a nation ought to constitute a state.'[4] Kedourie was not condoning this viewpoint: he disapproved of nationalism and believed that it was wrong to claim the right to independence because of a common language. More recently, writers have questioned the centrality of language for nationalism. Anthony Smith has pointed out that language is not an essential part of national identity in Africa and that in countries such as Greece, Burma and Pakistan religion is more important.[5] John Edwards had argued on a theoretical level that language is not essential for national identity.[6]

Because of the possible link between linguistic and political separatism, the assumption is often made by social historians of language that the Tudors had a deliberate policy of suppressing minority languages and that, because Henry VIII and Elizabeth wanted to increase the power of the crown throughout their territories, they must also have wished to eradicate Welsh, Cornish and Irish. Dick Leith even accuses them of an "historic blunder" in allowing worship in vernaculars other than English.[7] The following generalization from Victor Durkacz is typical of this approach:

> Language policies in Ireland, Wales and Gaelic Scotland have tended
> to vary according to the prevailing political and cultural situations in
> each nation: only in the sixteenth and seventeenth centuries can it be
> said that they were brutally repressed by central government which in
> this period followed a rigid policy of linguistic uniformity in the Celtic
> periphery.[8]

The perception of 'brutality' is echoed by Gwyn Williams in discussing the Welsh language. He made the point that the Welsh language culture which 'had been buoyant and innovatory in the fifteenth century stammered before the Renaissance' and this coincided with the period when 'it [the Welsh language] was brutally expelled from political life in the first attack by the English state on the Welsh Language'.[9] However, the evidence outlined below does not support a verdict of 'brutal repression'.

When analysing Tudor language policy it is essential to be aware of the differences between sixteenth-century and modern attitudes towards the patchwork of administrative and judicial divisions within the jurisdiction of the English crown, as well as towards vernacular languages in general. At first glance it may appear that the administrative systems in Cornwall, Wales and Ireland indicated that they were perceived as in some way alien. But in fact London and the South East dominated government to such an extent than any outlying region could be treated with suspicion and regarded as in need of additional supervision. Hugh Kearney stresses the dominance of London in terms of law courts, the Commons and the Lords, trade and education.[10] Norman Davies acknowledges Kearney as 'one of the very first historians to view the history of the Isles as a whole' and agrees with him that what was developing as a result of administrative changes in the sixteenth century was an empire based on the wealth, population and resources of southern England over the rest of the British Isles.[11]

Wales was governed by a Council acting as a regional governing board, but so was the North of England. The South West had a similar system only briefly in 1539-1540. The jurisdiction of the Council of the Marches of Wales extended to Shropshire, Worcestershire, Hereford and Gloucester and, until 1569, Cheshire. A second section of Wales, the Principality, was governed differently from the Marches and England.[12] Hugh Kearney argues that although the use of the terms 'Wales' and 'Welsh' is unavoidable in the sixteenth century, 'Wales' was very much a 'geographical expression' lacking cultural and social unity.[13] The Duchy of Cornwall was administered separately, but so was the Duchy of Lancaster; and the palatinates of Durham, Chester and Lancaster retained their special courts. There was a variety of jurisdictions within Ireland: The Pale, a small area around Dublin where the Royal writ ran; Anglo-Irish earldoms; and the Gaelic chieftainships. The attitude of Tudor rulers to all the peripheral areas of their realm was that of feudal overlord seeking to curb the ambitions of the overmighty subject. The policy of increased centralisation begun in the 1530s under the influence of Thomas Cromwell, which is discussed below, should be seen in this light rather than as the beginnings of English imperialism within the British Isles. It should not be surprising, therefore, that government attitudes to minority languages were not imperialistic.

Henry VIII's reputation as an opponent of minority languages is partly based on his statute designed to bring Welsh justice and administration in line with that of the English – *An Act for the Laws and Justice to be administered in Wales in like form as it is in this realm.*[14] Clause 17 of the Act specified that:

All Justices, commissioners sheriffs, coroners escheators, stewards and
their lieutenants and all other officers and ministers of the law shall proclaim
and keep the sessions courts and all other courts in the English tongue,

and that all office holders had to speak English. There is no doubt that this provision had a detrimental effect on the Welsh language by confirming that English was to be essential for the advancement of all those who wished to hold office. But it would be a mistake to assume that the Act was designed to 'deliberately suppress the language and break the spirit of the Welsh people.'[15]

The changes in Wales should be seen as part of a wider reconstruction of local government undertaken by Henry VIII's Council in the 1530s, under the guidance of Thomas Cromwell. The aim of the policy was to increase the control of the Privy Council in Wales, the North of England and in private Lordships where legal jurisdiction was still under the control of bishops, abbots, or territorial magnates, rather than the crown. The Council of the North was remodelled in 1537 so that it could oversee northern administration of justice on behalf of the Privy Council; and the Act for *Recontinuing of Certain Liberties and Franchises* of 1536[16] curtailed local anomalies so that feudal or ecclesiastical officials could no longer prevent the assize judges, sheriffs or J.P.s from carrying out their duties. Before 1536 jurisdiction in Wales was complex. Some lands belonged to the English crown and some to the Duchy of Lancaster. In addition marcher estates were held by feudal lords in chief of the crown. Conflicts of jurisdiction enabled criminals to avoid justice and remedies of common law were not available. The Act of 1536 and further legislation in 1543 ensured that the common law was enforced uniformly throughout Wales.[17] To achieve this, proceedings had to be in the hands of English speakers but, as most aspirants to official posts were bilingual anyway, there was little difference in practice. Interpreters were allowed for Welsh speaking witnesses and Royal Proclamations and Orders of the Council were to be read out in Welsh.[18] These were actions of a government intent on enforcing the law not on suppressing minority languages.

With the development of Protestantism in the second half of the sixteenth century, the emphasis on vernacular worship gave the government an incentive to encourage the use of the Welsh language. By a statute of 1563[19] bishops in Wales were empowered to supervise the translation of the Bible and the Prayer Book into Welsh. The work was to be completed by St David's day 1566, after which services were to be conducted in Welsh. The government hoped that by making the Bible available in churches in both languages they would encourage people to learn English, but the priority was to encourage a uniform faith, not to insist upon a uniform language. Translation was undertaken by William Salesbury with assistance from Bishop Richard Davies of St David's. They managed only the New Testament and the Prayer Book, but their work was completed by Bishop William Morgan, who published his Welsh Bible in 1588. All three translators were appreciative of Welsh language and culture. For example Davies, in his epistle attached to the Prayer Book, wrote of his pride in the ancient origins of the true church in Wales before the corrupting influence of Rome had been felt. He appealed to his fellow-countrymen – 'do not de-nationalize yourself, do not be indifferent, do not look down but gaze upwards to the place where you belong.' Their enthusiasm for Welsh culture was not incompatible with their dedication to the Anglican church and their admiration for the Tudors, whom they praised for returning the ancient unity of Britain.[20] The Welsh Bible produced a text which ensured the survival of the Welsh language.

Leith has suggested that the decline of the Cornish language in the sixteenth century was due to a conscious policy decision by the government.[21] The issue arose early in the reign of Edward VI when the government of Protector Somerset introduced an *Act of Uniformity* to make the new Protestant Prayer Book compulsory. In line with reformed doctrine, services were to be in the vernacular which of course meant English. The legislation provoked The Western Rebellion of 1549. The participants' objection to the use of English in the Prayer Book, was discussed in chapter four, where it was suggested that the rebels wanted to retain a familiar form of service which they associated with the Catholic doctrine. There was no suggestion of linguistic separatism. After all, the rebels wanted the services to be conducted in Latin, not in Cornish.[22]

Hostility to Irish Gaelic was stronger than towards Welsh or Cornish. An *Act for th'Englishe Order* was passed in the Dublin Parliament in 1537 which included the following:

there is nothing which does more contain and keep many of (the

King's) subjects of this saide lande in a certaine savage and wilde kind and manner of living, than the diversity between them in tongue, language, order and habit, which by the eye deceiveth the multitude and persuadeth unto them that they should be as it were of sundry sorts, or rather of sundry countries, where indeede they bee wholly together one body whereof his highness is th'only head under God.[23]

In this statement the assumption is made that loyalty to a country and hence obedience to the state would be in doubt if people did not speak the same language. To explain this it is necessary to look at the circumstances behind the legislation and especially the nature of the Kildare rebellion of 1534. Before the 1530s the Fitzgeralds, Earls of Kildare, had acted as Lord Deputy in Ireland. The system worked in the interest of both sides on the whole but there had been some conflict: when Lambert Simnel had been crowned in Dublin in opposition to Henry VII in 1487; and when Wolsey had attempted to build up an alternative power base to the Kildares in the 1520s, an attempt which was only abandoned because of the expense. The rebellion came about because of developing mistrust on both sides.[24] Kildare was summoned to England in 1533. He expected support from the Duke of Norfolk but his rivals looked to Cromwell who was now at the height of his influence. In May 1534, Kildare was accused of 'manifold enormities' and his son, 'Silken Thomas' was summoned to court. The rebellion, led by Thomas, was sparked off when the Earl was put in the Tower, where he died. Thomas's attempts to gain wider support for opposition to Henry provide the key to the nature of the 1537 legislation. He had some clerical support which gave the impression that the protest was directed against the break with Rome but, more importantly, he turned to the Gaelic chiefs and transformed the revolt into a Gaelic war of independence. It would appear, then, that the cultural imperialism, implicit in the English government's response to the rebellion was triggered off by fear of separatist agitation, rather than being an example of an aggressive desire to ensure linguistic unity.

Henry was crowned King of Ireland in 1541, and this has been interpreted as part of a policy of aggressive imperialism.[25] His motivation was, however, more limited and practical. Henry's headship of the Church in Ireland, which the Irish Parliament had established in 1536, could not be enforced as long as he remained 'Lord' – a title which implied he was viceroy to the Pope.[26] Under the new arrangements a Kingdom of Ireland was to embrace the whole of the island and its people would speak English and be governed by English law.[27] John Guy has suggested that the legislation:

even militated *against* the idea of a unitary state, for a subordinate superstructure had been created for Ireland: the later Tudors ruled technically two separate kingdoms, each with its own bureaucracy. In future ideological terms, it became possible to conceive of Anglo-Irish nationalism, as opposed to English or Gaelic civilization.[28]

The Lord Deputy, Sir Anthony Leger, who devised the regnal policy, actually hoped to reconcile English, Anglo-Irish and Gaelic interests; but after Henry's death any hope of peaceful co-existence was ruined. In 1557 the Lord Deputy, the earl of Sussex confiscated Leix and Offaly, to the west of the Pale and 'planted' them with English settlers. Ireland was influenced by the Counter Reformation so increasingly resented the English as Protestants as well as conquerors. During Elizabeth's reign, relations between England and Ireland became increasingly hostile. Sir Henry Sidney, Lord Deputy 1565-1578, attacked the power of the Gaelic Lordships and tried to increase the authority of the Crown by establishing presidencies in Munster and Connaught. Ireland became a magnet for soldiers and adventurers, wishing to enhance their personal influence and fortune. A serious rebellion in 1579-83 involved Papal and Spanish help for the rebels. Rebellion also broke out in Ulster in 1593 and became more dangerous in 1595 when Hugh O'Neil, Earl of Tyrone, assumed leadership. Order was eventually restored between 1600 and 1603 by Lord Mountjoy, but it had been at the cost of growing religious and cultural alienation of the Gaelic Irish and the Anglo-Irish population.[29]

Despite growing hostility towards the Irish peoples, there was no discernible attempt to limit the Irish language in the second half of the sixteenth century. As in Wales and Cornwall, language policy was influenced by the need to enforce the Protestant Reformation which involved encouragement of the vernaculars. As early as Henry VIII's reign the Government's religious policy came up against the stumbling block of language differences. George Browne was appointed Bishop of Dublin in 1536 and had instructions to carry out the same reforms as had been introduced in England, including an English version of the common prayers. In 1538, however, the requirement to provide an English Bible translation for every parish had to be waived because of the prevalence of Gaelic.[30] The more extreme Protestant measures of Edward VI's reign also faced problems. The first printing press in Ireland was set up in 1551 to provide religious texts for the English-speaking areas of Galway and Limerick but the Gaelic-speaking areas remained problematic. The English Council authorised Gaelic services where a "convenient number" did not speak English and a Latin version of the Prayer Book was allowed.[31] When Elizabeth I's Uniformity legislation was introduced into Ireland a special clause allowed ministers who could not speak English to continue using the Latin version of the Prayer Book.[32] Given the strong views of the Protestants on the use of the vernacular, such measures could only be temporary expedients, however, and a campaign was undertaken to increase the use of Gaelic for religious purposes. Some appointments of conscientious bishops were made; bishops such as Hugh Brady of Meath (1563 to 1584) and Robert Daly of Kildare (1564 to 1583), were able to preach in both English and Gaelic. The campaign for the use of Gaelic for sermons, prayers and religious texts was backed by English councillors Thomas Lancaster, Bishop of Armagh from 1568 to 1583 and by John Lang, who took over in the same diocese from 1583 to 1589.

Brendan Bradshaw has drawn attention to a conflict of strategy between these reformers who thought that the Irish people could be converted to

Protestantism by education and persuasion and those who advocated force.[33] The reformers faced a slow struggle in the face of intransigence from the more repressive elements and indifference from the complacent, but gradual expansion of the use of Gaelic resulted from their endeavours. The first book to be printed in Gaelic originated in Scotland. In 1567 Bishop John Carswell's translation of John Knox's *Book of Common Order* was published in Edinburgh. Carswell specified in the introduction that his translation was 'especially for the men of Scotland and Ireland'. He also regretted that 'we suffer greater want than any other, that we have no the Holy Bible printed in Gaelic, as it has been printed in Latin and English…and likewise that the history of our ancestors has never been printed, although a certain amount of the history of the Gaedhil of Scotland and Ireland has been written in manuscripts'.[34] Because of its intended audience, the translation was made into classical common Gaelic, not the Scottish and Irish dialects that became predominant.

In 1571 a catechism, compiled by John Kearney, Treasurer of St Patrick's, became the first Gaelic book to be printed in Ireland and this had been made possible by a gift of Irish types from Elizabeth. A Gaelic New Testament was completed in 1587 and printed in 1603. Brady, Lancaster and Lang fought for a University to be established in Dublin to help with the development of a vernacular ministry. They campaigned for thirty years until Trinity College was finally established in 1595. The delay was not caused by critics of the motives of the reformers, but by a succession of Archbishops of Dublin who were determined to prevent the use of St Patrick's, one of Dublin's cathedrals, to finance the project.

As well as differing views among the reformers there was also a variety of approaches from the would-be colonists during the period of the plantation of Munster. Declan Kiberd quotes hostile references to the Irish language from Edmund Spenser and Sir John Davies as examples of the politicisation of language. He refers to the way that Sir George Carew, President of Munster, had Gaelic manuscripts of the province cut up to make covers for English language primers being put into circulation for school children.[35] However, Kiberd makes no attempt at contextualization. An explanation for the hostility to the Irish language lies not in inherent racism or nationalism but in a policy split between the Old English whose interests lay in avoiding confrontation, and the New Irish planters such as Spenser whose interests lay in military conquest and colonisation. Spenser first went to Ireland in 1580 as secretary to the Deputy, Lord Grey. Because of his status as England's foremost Renaissance poet, Spenser's *View of the Present State of Ireland*, has, perhaps, received more attention than it deserves in the light of its contemporary reception. The *View* was written in the early 1590s. When it was submitted to the Munster Stationer in 1598 it was refused registration and proscribed by the Government. According to Ciaran Brady the influence of the manuscript version was limited.[36] When it was eventually published in 1633 the editor, Ware, expressed his regret at Spenser's extremism, cut out words such as 'savage' and 'barbarous' and omitted many attacks on the Anglo-Irish.[37]

Spenser advocated starving the population of Ireland, transporting any survivors, confiscating lands and a general policy of repression as a forerunner to conversion to Protestantism. He did not associate language and nationality, in that his hostility applies equally to the 'Old English', the term he uses for the descendants of the Anglo-Norman settlers of the twelfth century, as well as to the Gaelic speakers.[38] In 1581 Sir Nicholas White, the 'Old English' councillor, had warned Elizabeth's minister, Lord Burghley, that: ' innovation hath in all ages been accounted dangerous, and the busiest men that way be not the profitablest ministers . . .'; he urged the merits of 'temperate and peaceable government' against 'the rooting out of ancient nobility by violent and warlike government'.[39] It was to counter this approach, which was after all in line with the English government's instinctive conservatism, that Spenser and his allies developed their arguments that the Irish people were savages who had to be rescued from their barbarity.

The hostility to the Irish language shown by some of the planters was rhetoric designed to further their interests at court. The activities of Sir William Herbert, who was involved with Spenser in the plantation of Munster, indicate that the hostility was not necessarily typical. Herbert's theories on how the Irish could be subdued were explained in his political treatise, *Croftus, sive De Hibernis*.[40] He shared some of Spenser's views, advocating colonisation, the transporting of the native population and the use of force. He was more moderate, however, in not recommending a scorched earth policy. He compared Ireland with his native Wales and believed that it was in the interests of both regions to have native laws and culture superseded by English. He was, however, sympathetic to the use of Gaelic for religious purposes. In *The Croftus* he argued that the Bible and the Common prayers should be read to the Irish in their own language, with the singing of Gaelic hymns and psalms to be accompanied by the harp.[41] His activities in Ireland mirrored these suggestions. In his work in North Kerry, Herbert made the promotion of religious reform his priority. He arranged to have popular prayers translated into Irish and distributed among the native population. He appointed Irish speakers as curates in his estates and secured the appointment of an Irish-speaking bishop to the local diocese of Ardfert.[42]

The failures of those who wished to bring the Protestant faith to the Irish people should not lead one to overlook the fact that their approach involved an encouragement rather than repression of the Irish language. It is also misleading to assume, as some modern historians are prone to do, that Spenser's hostility to the Irish people and their culture was more in line with official government policy than that of the reformers who believed that it was crucial to encourage education in the vernacular.

In this survey of Tudor language policies, I have suggested that government attitudes towards Celtic languages were bound up with the consolidation of power. In the 1530s this led to restrictions on the use of Welsh and Irish. In the second half of the sixteenth century, however, religious change meant that considerations of power provided motivation for the encouragement of vernaculars. In the 1530s the consolidation of Tudor power involved the extension of the use of the English language in Wales for judicial purposes. However the provision of interpreters for court proceedings and the instructions that the Proclamations and Orders of the Council were to be read out in Welsh suggests that there was no attempt to suppress the vernacular. The Protestant Reformation ensured the survival of the Welsh language as the Bible and Prayer Book were translated into Welsh.

There was no need for the Tudors to be hostile to Welsh culture and language. After all Henry VII spent his first 14 years in Wales and himself spoke Welsh.[43] Their propaganda, based on the myth of British Imperial identity, used the narratives of Brutus as the Trojan progenitor of Britain and of Arthurian legend as popularised through Geoffrey of Monmouth's *History of the Kings of Britain*.[44] The connections between these narratives and Wales gave respectability to its culture. Gwyn Williams has emphasised the role played by Welsh humanists at the Tudor court, describing them as follows:

> They were deeply Welsh, Welsh patriots who knew no conflict of languages. They used English as centrally as Latin. They were particularly European in formation.[45]

Paradoxically, the greater the success of Welsh cultural influences on a wider stage, the less likely writers were to use their own vernacular, preferring Latin when writing for the scholarly elite or English for a wider audience.

Protestant changes in the reign of Edward VI brought language issues to the forefront in Cornwall, when the Western Rebels objected to the use of English instead of Latin for church services. The boundaries of Cornish speaking areas were receding in the sixteenth century, not because of any hostility from England, but because of economic factors such as wider commercial links and the increased importance of ports consequent upon naval developments and the war with Spain.[46] Wakelin also emphasises the importance of the Protestant Reformation in influencing he language decline. This was not only as a result of the failure to translate the Bible into Cornish, but also an effect of the eventual ending of the mystery plays and the severing of links between Cornwall and Brittany.[47]

Throughout the sixteenth century, hostility towards Ireland grew and some English administrators and settlers were disdainful of the Irish language and culture. However, as in Wales, government policy in the second half of the sixteenth century was determined by the hope of spreading the Protestant faith, and this involved encouraging, not suppressing, vernacular languages.

Tudor rulers were concerned to consolidate their power in the Celtic peripheries by working with local landed, bureaucratic and clerical elites and it was these groups who were encouraged to use English. In the second half of the century, language policy was dominated by religious factors and in this sphere the language of the masses became a consideration. The audience for printed religious texts was not limited to the literate as there was wide oral dissemination through preaching, domestic and official Bible reading and attendance at services where the Prayer Books were used. In the reigns of Edward VI and Elizabeth government power was inextricably linked to the success of the Protestant faith, which was disseminated through the vernacular languages. It is important to remember that this applied to English as well as to the Celtic languages. Policies such as Bible and Prayer book translations, the provision of Irish type and the appointment of Gaelic speaking Bishops by Elizabeth helped to ensure the survival of the Celtic languages in Wales and Ireland.

# Notes

1. Anthony Buckley, 'We're trying to find our own identity: Uses of History among Ulster Protestants' in Elizabeth Tonkin, Maryon McDonald and Malcolm Chapman, eds, *History and Ethnicity,* 1989, p. 185. In this context the author refers to J.H. Delargy. 'The Gaelic story-teller: with some notes on Gaelic Folk-tales', *Proceedings of the Irish Academy.* Oxford, 1945 ; J.W. Foster. 1982. 'Yeats and the folklore of the Irish Revival', *Eire/Ireland* xvii, 1945, 6-18; P. Kennedy'. 1891. *Legendary Fictions of the Irish Celts*, Detroit: Singing Tree Press; S. O'Sullivan.1966. *Folktales of Ireland*, Chicago: University of Chicago Press.
2. Victor Edward Durkacz, *The Decline of the Celtic Languages*, Edinburgh, 1983. Michael Hechter, *Internal Colonialism: The Celtic Fringe in British National Development, 1536-1966*, 1975.
3. Cited in Elie Kedourie, *Nationalism,* 1960. p. 64.
4. ibid p. 68
5. Anthony Smith, *Theories of Nationalism*, 1971, pp 18-19.
6. John Edwards, *Language, Society and Identity*, 1985, p. 22.
7. Dick Leith, *A Social History of English*, 1983, p. 165.
8. Victor Edward Durkacz, *The Decline of the Celtic Languages*, Edinburgh, 1983, p. 1.
9. Gwyn A. Williams, *The Welsh in their History*, 1982, p. 26.
10. Hugh Kearney, *The British Isles, A History of Four Nations*, Cambridge, 1989, p. 110.
11. Norman Davies, *The Isles, a History*, 2000, p. 485.
12. Alan G.R. Smith, The *Emergence of a Nation State, 1529-1660*, 1984, p. 12.
13. Kearney, op. cit. p. 117.
14. 27 Henry VIII, c.63, 1936.
15. Durkacz, op. cit. p. 3.
16. 27 Henry VIII, c.24.
17. John Guy, *Tudor England*, Oxford, 1990, pp 175-8.
18. P.R. Roberts, 'The Union with England and the Identity of Anglican Wales', *Transactions of the Royal Historical Society*, 1972, pp 61ff.
19. 5 Elizabeth, c.28, 1963.
20. Roberts, op. cit., p. 65.
21. Leith, op. cit. p. 165.
22. See chapter four, page 33.
23. *L. & P.* vol. X, no.1030.
24. Steven G. Ellis, 'Tudor policy and the Kildare Ascendancy in the Lordship of Ireland, 1496-1534', *Irish Historical Studies*, xx, pp 245-250.
25. R.B. Wernham, *Before the Armada: The Emergence of the English Nation,1485-1588*, New York, 1972, p. 149.

26. J.J. Scarisbrick, *Henry VIII*, 1966, p. 549.

27. Steven G. Ellis, *Tudor Ireland: Crown, Community and the Conflict of Cultures, 1470-1603*, 1985, pp 137-140.

28. Guy, op. cit. p. 359.

29. Alan G.R. Smith, op. cit. pp 246-248.

30. Brendan Bradshaw, 'George Brown, first Reformation Archbishop of Dublin1536-1554,' *Journal of Ecclesiastical History*, xxi, 1970, pp 312-313.

31. Ellis, 1985, op. cit., p. 207.

32. A.G. Dickens, *The English Reformation*, 1964, pp 405-15.

33. Brendan Bradshaw, 'Sword, Word and Strategy in the Reformation in Ireland', *The Historical Journal*, 1978, pp 475-502.

34. Steven G. Ellis, *Ireland in the Age of the Tudors, 1447-1603*, 1998, p. 258.

35. R.F. Foster, ed *The Oxford Illustrated History of Ireland*, 1991, p. 282.

36. Ciaran Brady, 'Spenser's Irish Crisis: Humanism and experience in the 1590s', *Past and Present*, 1986, 111, pp 17-49, p. 25.

37. Edmund Spenser, 'A View of the Present State of Ireland' in Rudolf Gottfried, *The Works of Edmund Spenser*, A Variorum Edition, 11 vols, Baltimore, 1932-1949, ix, pp 519-523.

38. ibid. ix, lines 3319-3350.

39. Ellis, 1985, op. cit., p. 291.

40. W.E. Buckley, ed, *William Herbert's Croftus Sive de Hibernia*, iii.

41. Ellis, 1998, op. cit. p. 331.

42. Bradshaw, op. cit., p. 487.

43. Gwyn A. Williams, *The Welsh in their History*, 1982, p. 17.

44. Sydney Anglo, 'The *British History* in Early Tudor Propaganda' *Bulletin of the John Rylands Library*, 44, pp 17-48.

45. Williams, op. cit., p. 27.

46. A.L. Rowse, *Tudor Cornwall*, 1941, pp 23-24.

47. Martyn F. Wakelin, *Language and History in Cornwall*, Leicester, 1975, p. 98.

# VI
## 'Albion's Champions':
## Patriotism in Elizabethan Drama

There's virtue in the name
The Virgin Queen, so famous through the world
The mighty Empress of the maiden isle
Whose predecessors have o'er-run great France
Whose powerful hand doth still support the Dutch
And keeps the potent King of Spain in awe, . . .

Why, England's Queen
She is the only phoenix of her age
The pride and glory of the Western Isles
Had I a thousand tongues, they all would tire
And fail me in her true description.[1]

This combination of eulogy on the Queen and pride in England's role on the Continent was the kind of patriotism which the dramatist Thomas Heywood believed would appeal to his popular audience. However, this approach was not typical and an examination of expressions of loyalty to England in Elizabethan drama shows a complexity of facets and polemical uses which reflect a disparate rather than integrated society.

The tone of patriotism in Elizabethan drama varied with the political circumstances and with the audience. Thomas Norton and Thomas Sackville's *Gorboduc* was first acted in 1560, as part of the Christmas celebrations for the Queen by the gentlemen of the Inner Temple. The play reflects concern for the welfare of the country against internal division which was especially important at a time when the succession was still uncertain. Both dramatists were MPs during the sessions of 1559 and 1563 when the Commons was putting pressure on Elizabeth to marry or name an heir. The warning against a foreign monarch[2] had contemporary relevance when the hostility towards Mary's marriage to Philip II was still a recent memory. *Gorboduc* was, in a less flamboyant way, as patriotic as the more aggressively anti-Spanish literature of the 1580's. The plot revolved around the disasters, including fratricide, murder, rebellion, uncertainty of succession and civil war, which resulted from the decision made by Gorboduc, King of Britain to divide his kingdom between his two sons in his own lifetime. This gave the authors the opportunity to expound the virtues of order and loyalty, as the wise advisers warn the king against abdicating his responsibilities:

> Only I mean to show by certain rules,
> Which King hath graft within the minds of man;
> That nature being her own order and her course,
> Which (being broken) doth corrupt the state
> Of mind and things, ev'n in the best of all.
>                                    [Act I, Sc. ii, 287-291]

> To that part of the realm my lords, your sons,
> I think not good for you, ne yet for them,
> But worst of all for this our native land.
> Within one land, one single rule is best:
> Divided reign do make divided hearts.
>                                    [Act I, Sc. ii, 326-330]

The play includes further examples of the good of the country being presented as a royal responsibility. In the same scene Gorboduc asked for advice:

> And think it good for me, for me, for you,
> And for your country, mother of us all:
>                                    [Act I, Sc. ii, 139-40]

and the answers he received emphasised 'benefit of country' and 'welfare of the realm.' Later Eubulus warned:

> Think not, my lords, the death of Gorboduc;
> Nor yet Videna's blood will ease their rage:
> Ev'n our own lives, our wives and children dear,
> Our country dearest of all, in danger stands,
> Now to be despoiled, now made desolate.
>                                    [Act V, Sc. i, 152-154]

The play came out strongly against rebellion and even included a suggestion that Parliament should decide on the rightful monarch.

The work of George Peele provides an example of the way patriotism was tailored to fit the occasion. His poem, *The Tale of Troy,* probably written about 1581 did not have a noticeably patriotic content, but by 1589 when Peele wrote his pamphlet *A Farewell* to mark the departure of Drake and Norris to Portugal circumstances had changed. The expedition was designed to turn the defensive success against the Armada into a more aggressive anti-Spanish campaign. It seemed appropriate to remind the English audience of their national heritage and *The Tale of Troy* was printed with it in the hope that 'good minds inflamed with honourable reports of their ancestry may imitate their glory in highest adventure.'[3] *A Farewell* encouraged them:

> . . . to Armes, to Armes, to glorious Armes,
> With noble Norris and victorious Drake,
> Under the sanguine Crosse, brave England's badge,
> To propagate religious piety,
> And hewe a passage with your conquering swords
> by land and sea.
>                                    [Lines 23-28]

Needless to say the *Eclogue Gratulatorie*, written on the return of Essex from the same expedition had a different tone as the loss of 11,000 men through desertion, disease and inadequate supplies was hardly the stuff of national glory.

*The Battle of Alcazar*, also written immediately after the defeat of the Armada, was anti-Spanish and anti-Catholic, with Philip II being blamed for the various misfortunes in the play, which included the death of the Portuguese King Sebastian. Peele also emphasised England's invincibility, which was given as the reason why Stukeley should abandon his treacherous ambition.

*Edward I* survives only in fragments and is full of inconsistencies, which arise from Peele's efforts to turn Queen Elinor into a cruel and proud parody of everything Spanish. The patriotic tone was set when the Queen mother welcomed Edward home from Jerusalem

> Illustrious England, ancient seat of Kings,
> Whose chivalry hath royallised thy fame:
> Thus Europe rich and mighty in her kings,
> Hath feared brave England dreadful in her kings,
> And now to eternise Albions Champions,
> Equivalent with Trojans ancient fame
> Comes lovely Edward from Jerusalem.
>                                    [Sc. i, 11-12, 25-29]

Queen Elinor wished to dominate the English people:

> Indeed we count them headstrong Englishmen
> But we shall hold them in a Spanish yoake.
>                                    [Sc. i, 156-7]

Edward was critical of the Queen's pride, which was regarded as typically Spanish. She was made to make cruel demands that the men's hair and women's breasts should be cut off and she herself met with a nasty end when heaven punished her for the murder of the mayoress.

The fact that Peel's patriotism was adaptable to different circumstances is shown by the themes of two pageants. The Lord Mayor's pageant, written in 1585 for Sir Woolstone Dixi, made London rather than England the focus of the patriotism, with the latter only existing to provide for the former:

> New Troye I hight whome Lud my Lord surnam'd
> London the glory of the Western side:
> Throughout the world is lovely London fam'd,
> So farre as any sea comes in with tide,
> Whose peace and calm under her Royal Queen:
> Hath long been such as like was never seen.[4]

In the 1591 pageant for Sir William Web, the Queen is represented as Astraea guarding her flock. Elizabeth had just escaped a conspiracy and the danger to England from internal instability must have seemed more pressing than the now stagnant war.

The opening of the first public theatre by Burbage in 1576 had led to a widening of the audience for drama. Before this time plays such as *Gorboduc* had been limited to the universities; schools such as Westminster and Merchant Taylors; the Inns of Court; and the Court itself. After the opening of the public theatres the audiences still only included a minority of the population – it has been estimated that about 20% of the people of London would be able to afford a ticket,[5] but it was a minority which included a wider cross-section than had been the case with earlier outlet restrictions. It would be plausible to suggest that the dramatists writing for the public theatres catered to popular xenophobia, which had been heightened by the hostility to Spain in the late 1580s. But this does not necessarily mean, as Bevington suggests, that 'For a brief time the crisis [the Armada] produced a rare fusion of interests in private and public drama in England.'[6]

The three extant plays of Robert Wilson serve to illustrate the diverse nature of patriotism in plays written for the public theatre at the time of the Armada. Wilson was a comic actor who was involved with the Earl of Leicester's Company from its founding in 1574. He was one of the 12 actors who formed the Queen Elizabeth's company in 1588 and later was involved with the Lord Chamberlain's men. *The Three Ladies of London*, probably performed in 1581, is a morality play with four knaves – Fraud, Simony, Dissimulation and Usury being used to attack corruption in contemporary London. The sequel, *The Three Lords and Three Ladies of London*, first performed in 1589, introduced an anti-Spanish element. The three ladies are to marry three Lords, but first they have to fight off three Spanish Lords who are intent on invasion:

> I need not tell thee they are poop and proud,
> Vaunters, vainglorious, tyrants, truce-breakers,
> Envious, ireful and ambitious,
> For thou hast found their failings and their brags
> Their backs, their coffers, and their wealth, their rags.
>
> [F.4v]

There is, however, no hint of national unity in response to the threat from abroad, and any patriotism in the play is based on London rather than England. It is the London authorities who bring about the defeat of the Armada. Three additional Lords are introduced from Lincoln, and these characters are as much the enemy as the Spaniards. The author looks down on the people of the countryside whom he sees as unworthy to share the glory of the defeat of the Armada and whom he accuses of Catholic sympathies. Wilson's *The Cobler's Prophesy* also has a patriotic content but this time it is part of a wider theme of class, as opposed to regional conflict. The professional soldiers and citizens of London are the saviours of the Commonwealth and there is a great deal of antagonism towards politicians and scholars.

Peele's anti-Spanish caricature of Queen Elinor mentioned above was designed to appeal to the xenophobia of the audience but there are examples of dramatists writing either for an elite or a popular audience who could portray foreigners without hostility. John Lyly wrote plays for private audiences. He was patronised by Burghley and moved in court circles. David

Bevington's suggestion that in producing Midas in 1589 Lyly 'changed his exclusive concern with court life to respond to the quickening tempo of patriotic fervour'[7] is misleading. Most of his plays were fantasies based on mythical themes, which provided the opportunity for allegorical references to contemporary events as well as spectacle and entertainment. In *Endymion* Cynthia is Elizabeth and Endymion is Leicester; in *Sapho and Phao* Sapho is Elizabeth and Phao is Alencon; similarly *Midas* is based on Phillip II. The dominating theme is the personal humiliation of Philip rather than hostility to Spaniards in general. The plot is based on the legend of the ass's ears. Philip grows ass's ears in response to his shame when the Armada is defeated and the ears fall off as soon as he agrees to leave England alone. The play ends on a note of reconciliation with Philip becoming a good neighbour. The Spanish women in the play are treated with sympathy and Celia and Midas' daughter, Sophronia, are models of virtue. This is partly to provide a dramatic foil to Midas, and partly because Lyly was careful of female sensibilities, especially after offending some with *Eupheus*. Sisterly solidarity must have been more important for the women in the audience than national prejudice!

It was also possible for dramatists catering to a wider audience to introduce Spaniards into their plays without stooping to xenophobia, as in Robert Green's *Friar Bacon and Friar Bungay*, which was first performed in 1590. The play is in fact a patriotic one but the foreign characters are not ridiculed. The Earl of Lincoln, promises to marry the heroine Margaret, but becomes briefly engaged to a Spanish lady-in-waiting. The character does not appear on stage and is introduced as a method of testing Margaret. The contrast is made, not between English and Spanish ladies, but between Margaret as a typically virtuous rustic and the ladies of the court. Prince Edward's marriage to Elinor of Castile is used to introduce the traditional eulogy to Elizabeth with which the play ends. The play's patriotism takes the form of pride in England's universities and scholars. The Emperor praised Oxford:

> Trust me Plantagenet, these Oxford schools
> Are richly seated near the river-side:
> The mountains full of fat and fallow deer,
> The battling pastures lade with kine and flocks,
> The town gorgeous with high-built colleges,
> And scholars seemly in their grave attire.
>
> [1100-1105]

When Friar Bungay claims that Oxford scholars are superior to the German the challenge is taken up by Vandermast and there follows a spectacular duel which involves conjuring fire breathing dragons and fiends disguised as Hercules. Bungay is getting the worst of the exchange when Friar Bacon steps in to save English pride by intimidating Vandermast's Hercules. He is congratulated by King Henry:

> Bacon, thou hast honour'd England with thy skill,
> And made fair Oxford famous by thy art:
>
> [1266-7]

It is also a source of national pride that the English court can put on a celebration worthy of honouring their royal visitors:

> But, glorious commanders of Europa's love,
> That makes fair England like that wealthy isle
> Circled with Gihon and swift Euphrates,
> In royalising Henry's Albion
> With presence of your princely mightiness,
> Let's march: the tables are all pread,
> And viands, such as England's wealth affords,
> Are ready set to furnish out the boards.
> You shall have welcome mighty potentates:
> It rests to furnish up this royal feast,
> Only your hearts be frolic; for the time
> Craves that we taste of naught but jouissance,
> Thus glories England over all the west.

2106-2118.

Thomas Heywood's *The Fair Maid of the West*, the first part of which was probably performed by Worcester's Men around 1599 combined patriotism with praise for Elizabeth. The play is a light-hearted adventure in which the hero, Bess, sails to the Azores to bring back the body of her lover whom she erroneously believes to have been killed fighting alongside the Earl of Essex. Her travels include brushes with hostile Spaniards and capture by the Moroccan King, Mullisheg. Before the first conflict with a Spanish ship Bess exhorts her crew with a mixture of patriotism and self-interest:

> Then, for your country's honour, my revenge,
> For your own fame, and hopes of golden spoil,
> Stand bravely to't.

The ship is captured in true swashbuckling fashion and Bess comes face to face with the Spanish captain. She is dressed as a man so when she makes reference to 'English Bess' the captain assumes she means the Queen, giving rise to the praise for Elizabeth quoted above. The reference to the Queen as the 'phoenix of her age' comes in the following scene when a similar device is used during an exchange between Bess and Mullisheg. Despite the patriotism of the play, the relations with the various foreigners in the cast are not xenophobic. Bess's servant, Clem, is able to identify with a French and a Florentine merchant because both are Christian. Clem's sincerity is in doubt. He merely wanted an excuse to accept a bribe from the merchants. Mullisheg is portrayed as fair, honourable and merciful in dispensing the law. Again there is an ulterior motive as the King is trying to make a good impression in order to seduce Bess. Perhaps the most heartfelt plea against prejudice comes from Clem during a conspiracy with Tota, Mullisheg's wife:

> Our countrymen eat and drink as yours do; open their eyes when they
> would see, and shut them again, when they would sleep:
> gape when their mouths open, as yours: and scratch when it itcheth.[8]

The portrayal of other nationalities in English drama is a complex topic. I have suggested below that the many foreigners introduced to Tudor audiences for comic effect or as stereotyped morality figures, were not treated in such a way as to reflect any cultural nationalism.[9]

Shakespeare's plays also echo the complexity of Elizabethan patriotism. His concern for order is an extension of the political thought of the Commonwealth writers of the first half of the sixteenth century, especially Thomas Starkey.[10] Their notion that every member of the community had a role to play and should dedicate their labour to the common good was often interpreted as dedication to the 'commonwealth' of England. The influence of civic humanism led them to stress their dedication to the government and to insist that unity and obedience to the law were essential to the welfare of the realm. Starkey described devotion to the commonwealth as follows:

> Like as in every man there is a body and also a soul in whose
> flourishing and prosperous state both together standeth the weal and
> felicity of man, so likewise there is in every commonality, a politic
> man, in whose flourishing both together resteth also the true
> commonweal . . . the thing which is resembled to the soul is civil
> order and politic law, administered by officers and rulers. The body
> is nought else but the multitude of the people.[11]

Just as the commonwealthmen's concern for the common good led them to consider the interests of the nation, so Shakespeare's obsession with order was a facet of his patriotism. In one of the earlier plays Titus Andronicus, the last scene includes a plea for unity:

> O let me teach you how to knit again
> This scattered corn into one mutual sheaf,
> These broken limbs again into one body,
> Lest Rome herself be bane unto herself,
> And she whom mighty kingdoms curtsy to
> Like a forlorn and desperate castaway
> Do shameful execution on herself.
>                                        [Act V, Sc. iii. 69-75]

The following statement echoes the commonwealth view of the role of the individual in society:

> Therefore doth heaven divide
> The state of man in divers functions,
> Setting endeavour in continual motion;
> To which is fixed, as aim or butt,
> Obedience. . . .
>                                        [Act I, Sc. ii, 196-200]

This was part of a speech by the Archbishop of Canterbury in *Henry V.* In the same play Henry was shown to respect the law in a way reminiscent of the attitude of Starkey:

> Touching our person we seek no revenge;
> But we our kingdom's safety must so tender

whose ruin you have sought, that to have her laws
We deliver you. . . .
[Act II, Sc. ii, 185-9]

Richard II, on the other hand, was condemned by Gaunt for not upholding
the law:

Landlord of England thou are not King;
Thy state of law is bondslave to the law.
[Richard II Act II, Sc.i, 113-4]

Patriotism was used by Shakespeare, not only as a warning to the 'overmighty subject' against the danger to the country arising from their ambitions,
but also as an argument against rebellion. Clifford's speech to Jack Cade's
supporters, which succeeded in restoring their loyalty to Henry VI, included
the following appeal to their concern for their country:

Better ten thousand base-born Cades miscarry
Than you should stoop unto a Frenchman's mercy.
To France, to France, and get what you have lost;
Spare England, for it is your native coast.
[The second part of King Henry VI, Act IV, Sc. viii, 44-47]

The play King John was based on the familiar theme of the damage caused to
the country by disunity and disloyalty to the government, in this case emphasising
the vulnerability to foreign enemies. John's defiance of Rome reflected English
suspicion of foreigners as shown by his speech to the Papal Legate:

Tell him this tale; and from the mouth of England
Add this much more, that no Italian priest
Shall tythe or toil in our dominions;
[Act III, Sc. i, 154-6]

But he had to come to terms with the Pope because of opposition at home
as well as problems with the French:

Our discontented countries do revolt;
Our people quarrel with obedience
Swearing allegiance and the love of soul
To stranger blood, to foreign royalty.
[Act V, Sc. i, 9-12]

The play ended with the patriotic claim that:

This England never did nor never shall,
Lie at the proud foot of a conqueror,
But when it first did help to wound itself,
Now these her princes are come home again,
Come three corners of the world in arms,
And we shall shock them. Nought shall make us rue,
If England to itself do rest but true.
[Act V, Sc. vii, 116-22]

The Bastard Faulconbridge in *King John* was one of the most loyal and
consistently patriotic of Shakespeare's characters. His honour was established
in the first scene:

> Brother by my mother's side, give me your hand:
> My father gave me hour, yours gave land.
>
> [Act I, Sc. i, 164-5]

When John asked for support against the French, the plea was repeated by the Bastard in the following scene:

> The life, the right the truth of all this realm
> Is fled to heaven; and England now is left
> To tug and scramble and to part by the teeth
> The unowned interest of proud swelling state.
>
> [Act IV, Sc. iii, 108-111]

The speech made to the Dauphin on behalf of the King was typical of the way the Bastard combines loyalty and patriotism:

> No: know the gallant monarch is in arms
> And like an eagle o'er his aery towers;
> To souse annoyance that comes near his nest.
> Any you degenerate, you ingrate revolts.
> You bloody Neroes, ripping up the womb
> Of our dear mother England, blush for shame.
>
> [Act V, Sc. ii, 149-54]

Hastings suggests that:

> To deny the nationalism of Gaunt's 'This blessed plot, this earth, this
> realm of England' or Henry V's speech 'on, on you noblest English'
> before Harfleur . . . is absurd.[12]

Rather than being 'absurd' it is highly productive to consider these two plays in more detail and to question the nature of the patriotism in them.

The cliché that Shakespeare is reinvented by each generation applies particularly to Henry V. Graham Holderness' comparison of the two twentieth century film versions was discussed above.[13] In 1944 Laurence Olivier's King was a martial hero to appeal to a country at war. In 1984 Kenneth Branagh's Henry V was more introverted and full of self doubt and the tone of the film was anti-war in response to the English public's ambivalent response to the Falklands War. Lisa Jardine recognised the tendency to re-read Henry V in the light of contemporary concerns about nationalism as follows:

> It is no accident and may turn out to be tragedy of our time, that readings
> of Henry V at the present historical moment stumble repeatedly at the
> complexity of representation within the play of nationalism and ethnic
> identity.[14]

The scene with the four captains representing Scotland, Ireland, England and Wales has received a great deal of critical attention recently because of the interest in devolution. Various readings of this scene are discussed below.[15]

Henry V is commonly referred to as a 'patriotic King' and the play as Shakespeare's most patriotic. In fact the purpose of *Henry V* was to make a hero of the King, not to glorify England. This does not mean that awareness of English national identity was absent from the play, but fusion between monarch and nation was taken for granted in the ultimate expression of Shakespeare's ideal of unity. Henry was referred to as 'Harry England' (Act III, Sc. v, 48,) in a way that was not used for other Kings. There were expressions of patriotism, for example in the chorus before Act II:

O England! model to they inward greatness,

Like little body with a mighty heart,

What mightst thou do, that hour would thee do,

Were all thy children kind and natural!

Canterbury was confident of victory against the French, and reminisced about England's past glories, such as the successes of the Black Prince:

O noble English that could entertain

With half their forces the full pride of France

And let another half stand laughing by,

All out of work and cold for action!

[Act I, Sc. ii, 113-116]

But Henry, himself, did not use patriotism as an encouragement to loyalty in the way one would expect from a 'patriot King.' His speech before Harfleur contained only two passing references to the fact that they were English:

. . . On, on you noblest English,

Whose blood is fet from fathers of war-proof!

. . . And you, good yeomen,

Whose limbs were made in England, show us here

The mettle of your pasture;

[Act III, Sc. ii, 17-19,25-27]

Before Agincourt he spoke of honour, fellowship and fame, but not of service to the country. (Act IV, Sc. iii) In the previous scene Henry gave his opinion on war without availing himself of the opportunity to discourse on war as a service to England. He argued that the King was not responsible for the deaths and that war could be God's way for punishing sinners. His conquest of France and wooing of Catherine are conducted in terms of dynastic rather than national ambition.

Some writers in the first half of the twentieth century allowed their own notions of patriotism to cloud their interpretation of sixteenth-century attitudes to England. This applies especially to the assumption that the patriot automatically identified with his country's government. This was not the case in politics, and it was certainly not the case in Shakespeare's plays, as can be seen by considering Richard II.

There was no clash of loyalties in Henry V but in Richard II Shakespeare illustrated how patriotism could be used against a monarch. Bolingbroke responded to his exile as follows:

Then England's ground, farewell; sweet soil adieu;

My mother and my nurse, that bears me yet!

Where'er I wander, boast of this I can,

Though banish'd yet a true born Englishman.

[Act I, Sc. iii 304-7]

Probably the best known expression of patriotism in Shakespeare comes from Gaunt, again in opposition to the King:[16]

> This Royal throne of Kings, this scepter'd isle,
> This earth of majesty, this seat of Mars,
> This other Eden, demi-paradise;
> This fortress built by Nature for herself
> Against infection and the hand of war;
> This happy breed of men, this little world,
> This blessed plot, this earth this realm, this England.

Gaunt is describing an idealised England. He is nostalgic for a golden age when King and feudal nobility worked together to form a strong government. He is critical of conditions under Richard's government:

> That England that was wont to conquer others,
> Hath made a shameful conquest of itself.
>
> [Act II, Sc. i, 40-5, 50, 65-6]

Gaunt's speech was built up as a statement of truth from a dying man:

> O, but they say the tongues of dying men
> Enforce attention like deep harmony.
>
> [Act II, Sc. i, 5-6]

Richard's own concern for England's soil, however, was expressed as part of his display of self-pity on facing rebels on his return from Ireland. His speech, which begins:

> Needs must I like it well: I weep with joy
> To stand upon my kingdom once again
>
> [Act III, Sc. ii, 4-5]

is as 'hollow' in its patriotism as the crown he later uses as a vehicle for his eloquence.

Historians and critics alike have puzzled as to why Sir Gilly Merrick should organise a performance of *Richard II* as a prelude to the Essex conspiracy. It is understandable that the government should have been sensitiveabout any play dealing with the deposition of a monarch. John Hayward found that out when he was imprisoned because of his account of Richard II's death in his *The First Part of the Life and Reign of King Henry IV* (1599). But Shakespeare had been careful not to express sympathy with the rebels. The Bishop of Carlisle prophesied chaos in response to Bolingbroke's first hint that he was going to 'ascend the regal throne':

> The blood of English shall manure the ground,
> And future ages groan for this foul act;
> Peace shall go to sleep with Turks and infidels,
> and in this seat of peace tumultuous wars
> Shall kin with kin and kind with kind confound;
>
> [Act IV, Sc. i, 139-143]

and Bolingbroke went through the conventional ritual of hinting that he wanted to be rid of Richard, but pretending remorse when taken at his word. The play ended with Bolingbroke's speech:

I'll make a voyage to the Holy Land,
To wash this blood off from my guilty hand:
March sadly after; grace my mournings here;
In weeping after this untimely bier.

[Act V, Sc.v , 59-62]

This led Strachey to conclude:

Sir Gilly must have been more conversant with history than literature
for how otherwise could he have imagined the spectacle of the pathetic
ruin of Shakespeare's minor poet of a hero could have nerved any
man to lift a hand against so oddly different a ruler.[17]

But is it not possible that Essex's supporters were not intending any
comparison to be made between Richard, and Elizabeth, but were aware of
the patriotic stance taken by Richard's opponents?

Shakespeare was not the only dramatist to deal with the dilemma of the
obligation of loyalty to the crown conflicting with patriotism. Marlowe's
*Edward II* followed the same pattern. Edward was depicted as putting
Gaveston before the interests of the country when he welcomed him home:

I have my wish in that I joy thy sight;
And sooner shall the sea o'er wealm my land
Than hear the ship that shall transport thee hence.

[Act I, Sc. ii, 151-3]

From the beginning, the younger Mortimer advocated the overthrow of
Gaveston for the good of the country:

This much I urge is of a burning zeal
to mend the King and do our country good.

[Act I Sc. iv, 258-9]

Lords, sith that we are, by sufferance of heaven,
Arriv'd and armed in this prices right,
Here for our country's cause swear we to him
All homage, fealty and forwardness;
And for the open wrongs and injuries
Edward has done us, his Queen and land,
We come in arms to wreck it with the sword,
That England's Queen in peace may reposes
Her dignities and honours, and withal
We may remove these flatterers from the King
that havoc England's wealth and treasury.

[Act IV, Sc. iv, 27-27]

After Edward's downfall, both the Queen and Mortimer used the welfare of
the country to justify their actions. Isabella claimed:

I rue my Lord'd ill-fortune; but alas,
Care of my country call'd me to this war:

and was reassured by Mortimer:

Madam, have done with care and sad complaint.
Your King hath wronged your country and himself.

When Spenser replied with the implication that obedience to the monarch
was more important than duty to the country he was dismissed by Mortimer
with 'take him away; he prates.' The justification of duty to the country was
also used by the minor characters. Kent warned Edward against destroying
the realm:

> My Lord, I see your love to Gaveston
> Will be the ruin of the realm and you
>
> [Act II, Sc. ii, 208-9]

and when he changed sides he used the country as an excuse.

> My Lords, Of love of this our native land,
> I come to join with you and leave the King;
> And in your quarrel, and the realm's behoof,
> Will be the first that will adventure life.
>
> [Act II, Sc. iv, 1-4]

Patriotism was not as important on an emotional level in *Edward II* as in
*Richard II* and none of the characters spoke in favour of England. But duty
to the country was used as a justification for action against the King. Elizabeth
was aware of the danger of patriotism being used against the monarchy and
was able to counter the threat by using propaganda to identify crown and
nation. The Stuarts were, of course, unable to maintain this identification.

It is usual to think of the audience for Elizabethan drama from the mid-1580s
onwards, as reflecting a society unified in response to the war. Harbage
wrote of Shakespeare's audience that it was:

> literally popular, ascending from each gradation from potboy to
> Prince. It was the one to which he had been conditioned early and for
> which he never ceased to write. It thrived for a time, it passed quickly
> and its like has never existed since. . . . It reached its peak when the
> audience formed a great amalgam, and it began to decline when the
> amalgam was split in two.[18]

The split was heralded by the so-called 'war of the theatres,' of 1600-
1601 when Ben Jonson retreated to the relative safety of the private theatres
and began to attack the public audiences, which in turn were defended by
John Marston and Thomas Dekker. Rowse argued that this quarrel put an end
to 'Elizabethan integration and national unity.'[19] But did this 'national unity'
really exist? We have seen that dramatists responded in a variety of ways to
the war with Spain and that not all of these responses were based on national
unity.[20] Conversely, not all patriotism involved anti-Spanish chauvinism.

By the mid-1590s a rift between dramatists and government was becoming
obvious. I have mentioned the fact that both Marlowe and Shakespeare,
especially in Edward II and Richard II, were aware that patriotism and loyalty
to the monarch were not necessarily synonymous, and that Elizabeth
disapproved of John Hayward's Henry IV. It was at this time that the
government banned all history plays not specifically sanctioned by the
Council. Unfortunately, Nashe and Jonson's Isle of Dogs is no longer extant

so we do not know what aspect of the play upset the authorities, but we do know that the authors were imprisoned for a time (in 1597) and that there was a threat from the Council to close all theatres. When one considers that the theatres were under fire from the Puritans for encouraging sin[21] and from the city authorities for encouraging the plague,[22] one wonders where this idea of national integration comes from.

## Notes

1. Simon Trussler, ed., *The Fair Maid of the West by Thomas Heywood*, 1986. According to Trussler, *The Fair Maid of the West* was probably first performed in 1599. This edition was the script of the Royal Shakespeare Company's production and includes material from *The Fair Maid of the West*, part two, first performed in 1630. The verses quoted are from the first part of the play.
2. Act V, sc. ii, 322-340.
3. Sally Purcell, ed., *George Peele: Selected with an Introduction*, 1972, p. 47.
4. ibid. pp 48, 54, 33.
5. Bob Hodge, *Literature Language and Society in England 1580-1680*, 1981, p. 102.
6. David Bevington, *Tudor Drama and Politics, A Critical Approach to Topical Meaning*, Cambridge, Mass., 1968, p. 187.
7. ibid p. 187.
8. Trussler, op. cit., pp45, 59.
9. See chapter eight.
10. Shakespeare's concern for order was stressed by E.M.W. Tillyard in his *Shakespeare's History Plays*, 1944. See above chapter one p. 30. The recognition that Tillyard had appropriated Shakespeare for his own ideological purposes should not lead us to dismiss the importance of his contribution to our understanding of the plays.
11. Kathleen M. Burton, ed, *Thomas Starkey's A Dialogue between Reginald Pole and Thomas Lupset*, 1948, p55.
12. Adrian Hastings, *The construction of nationhood: Ethnicity, religion and nationalism*, Cambridge, 1997, p. 57.
13. See chapter one.
14. Lisa Jardine, *Reading Shakespeare Historically*, p. 7.
15. See chapter 8.
16. This is a different reading of Gaunt's speech from that of Graham Holderness who sees it as an example of 'royalist patriotism' and the language as 'uncompromisingly royalist,' 'Shakespeare's History: Richard II' *Literature and History*, 7, 1981, p. 13.
17. Lytton Strachey, *Elizabeth and Essex*, 1950, p. 191.
18. A. Harbage, *Shakespeare's Audience*, Columbia University Press, 1941, p. 159.
19. A.L. Rowse, *The Elizabethan Renaissance: The Cultural Achievement*, 1972, p. 30.
20. In concluding his study of patriotism in Elizabethan drama, 'we should have learned no more however, than that the Elizabethan Englishman loved, England because it was England,' Lindabury seriously underestimates the disparity both of the patriotic experience and of dramatists responses to it. R.U. Lindabury *A Study of Patriotism in Elizabethan Drama*, Oxford 1931, p. 201.
21. Philip Stubbes, writing in 1583 believed 'in the theatre you will learn to condemn God and his laws to care neither for Heaven or Hell', *Anatomie of Abuses* 1583, p. 145. Quoted in Jonathan Dollimore, *Radical Tragedy: Religion Ideology and power in the Drama of Shakespeare and his Contemporaries*, 1989, p. 23.
22. The theatres were closed because of the plague in 1592 and 1593.

# VII

# 'The renouned Isle of Great Britain':
## National Consciousness in Sixteenth-Century Poetry

When Elizabethan dramatists scoured chronicles for plots, they knew that stories of past English victories had patriotic potential which would both appeal to audiences and appease critics of the theatre. In reply to his detractors the playwright Thomas Heywood wrote:

> To turn to our domestic histories: What English blood seeing the person of any bold Englishmen there presented and does not hug his fame and honey at his valour, pursuing him in his enterprise with his best wishes . . . what coward, to see his own countrimen valiant, would not be ashamed of his own cowardice ?[1]

Many of the elite poets, however, did not consider events of national significance, whether historical or contemporary, as suitable subject matter for their poetry. In his elegy, *To my Dearly Loved Friend Henry Reynolds, Esquire,* Michael Drayton praised English poets from Chaucer and Gower through to Jonson. But he delivered a mild rebuke to Samuel Daniel for being 'too much a historian in verse' and suggested his subject matter would be better expressed in prose.[2] Philip Sidney wrote his *Apologie for Poetry* to defend poets against an attack by Stephen Gossom in his *The School of Abuses*: *containing a pleasant invective against Poets, Pipers, Players, Jesters and such like caterpillars of the Commonwealth*, published in 1589. Gosson, an ex-poet and playwright turned Puritan, argued that poems and plays undermined the nation's virtue, making Englishmen effeminate and licentious. Sidney's response was to emphasise that poets should transcend the natural world, dealing with the ideal rather than the actual and it was this approach that encouraged the elite poets to eschew direct description of national events in preference to more esoteric concerns.

Throughout the sixteenth century, such poets expressed their love for their country, not through patriotic subject matter but through their concern for the English language and their belief that the country's reputation was enhanced by the achievements of their fellow writers. The antiquary, John Leyland, whose patriotism has already been noted[3] wrote a series of elegies on Thomas Wyatt. He praised the poet for the kudos brought to the country by the eloquence of Wyatt's poetry :

*Anglus par Italis*
Bella suum merito iactet florentia Dantem.
Regia Petrarchae carmina Roma probet.
His non inferior patrio sermone Viatus
Eloquuij secum qui decus omne tulit.

and he was especially laudatory about the effect of his verse on the development of the English language:

Lima Viati

Anglica lingua fuit rudis & sine nomine rhythmus:

Nunc limam agnoscit docte Viate tuam.[4]

George Puttenham also approved of Wyatt's contribution to improving the vernacular in his *Arte of English Poesie*, published in 1589. Puttenham did not mention national themes when discussing subjects suitable for poetry but referred to:

the laud honour and glory of the immortall gods . . . the worthy gests of noble princes, praise of virtue and reproofe of vice . . . finally the common solace of mankind in all his travails and cares of this tranitorie life.

His patriotism became apparent, however, in his call for poets to be honoured for having:

by their thankful studies so much beautified our English tong, as at this day it will be found our nation is nothing inferior to the French or Italian for copie of language and subtiltie of devise, good method and proportion in any form of poem.[5]

Sidney was full of praise for the language of the poets in his *Apologie for Poetry:*

For the uttering sweetly and properly the conceits of the minde, which is the end of speech, that hath it equally with any other tongue in the world.[6]

Sidney was in turn commended by Drayton for enhancing the reputation of the mother tongue:

The noble Sidney with this last arose,

That hero for numbers and for prose,

That thouroughly paced our language as to show

The plenteous English hand in hand might go

With Greek and Latin, . . .[7]

The acclamation of the English language did not imply a nationalistic perception of the mother tongue. Drayton regretted that he could not reach a wider audience with his poetry:

O, why should Nature niggardly restraine!

That Foraine Nations rellish not our Tongue.

Else should my lines glide on the waves of the *Rhene*

And crowne the *Pirens* with my living song.

The rest of the poem shows that he saw his audience as anyone who could understand his language whether or not they lived within the boundaries of the English state.

But bounded thus, to Scotland get you forth,

Thence take you wing unto the Orcades,

There let my verse get glory in the North,

Make my sighs to thaw the Frozen Seas.

And let the Bards within that *Irish* Ile,

To whom my Muse with fierce wings shall passe,

Call back the stiffe-necked Rebels from Exile

And mollifie the slaughtering Galliglasse.

And why my flowing Numbers they rehearse,

Let Wolves and Beares be charmed with my Verse.[8]

Poets did not confine their approbation to their own language and were especially complimentary about Welsh. Again Drayton can serve as an example. He had no particular connections with Wales but in the section on Queen Katherine and Owen Tudor in *England's Heroical Epistles* he had friendly things to way about the Welsh language. Katherine, addressing Owen, is understandably polite about his country:

And Wales as well as haughty England boasts

Of Camelot and all her Pentecosts,

To have precedence in Pendragon's race,

At Arthur's table challenging the place.

and goes on to talk of past Welsh victories. She then moves on to personal compliments to Owen which include the following reference to his speech:

The British language[Welsh], which our vowels wants,

And jars so much upon harsh consonants,

Comes with such grace from thy mellifluous tongue

As do the sweet notes of a well-set song,

And runs as smoothly from those lips of thine

As the pure Tuscan from the Florentine.[9]

This enabled Drayton to express his appreciation for the Welsh and Tuscan languages.

When the elite poets wanted to deal with England they did so via allegory rather than direct description. Ballad writers did report events of national significance in the form of news. Were these events handled in a patriotic way and how did the elite poets respond to changes in national awareness throughout the century ? The ballad writers were influenced by the demands of their audience and the elite poets by the concerns of their patrons. Did this have any effect on the patriotic content of the different types of verse? These questions can be considered by a more detailed survey of sixteenth century poetry.

It is unusual to find examples of patriotism in any genre of early sixteenth-century poetry, despite the growing use of appeals to national interest in official propaganda. When Henry VIII' s government severed links with Rome in the 1530s it vilified the Popes as greedy foreigners, sucking the country dry.[10] Poets did not follow this lead. Ballads which dealt with the Break with Rome were anti-clerical and strongly anti-Papal but the Pope was attacked for his worldliness rather than for his country of origin.[11] Personal exploits caught the public imagination and provided material for ballads. For example the Scotsman, Andrew Barton, was a popular subject. He was a pirate who was defeated and killed by Lord Thomas Howard in 1512. Sailors were treated as individuals, motivated by avarice or courage rather than concern for their native land. Events of national significance, such as the defeat of the Scots at the Battle of Flodden Field in 1513 were seized upon by the poets as opportunities to emphasise honour and feudal martial obligation. An anonymous poem, *Scottish Field* written in 1515 opens with the Earl of Surrey asking for help and various members of the feudal elite responding by rounding up their private armies. The importance of feudal symbolism is indicated in the following section of the poem which refers to the Stanley crest of an eagle's foot with three crowns:

> Sir John Stanley, that stout knight, that sturn was of deeds,
> With four thousand fierce men that followed him after.
> They were tenants that they took, that tenden on the bishop,
> Of his household, I you hete, hope yee no other.
> Every burn had on his breast, broidered with gold
> A foot of the fairest fowl that ever flew on wing,
> With three crowns full clear all of pure gold.

The 'country' is the region of origin and not England and the battle itself is an account of regional and not national gains and losses:

> Yorkshire like yorn men eagerly hey foughten:
> So did Derbyshire that day deyred many Scots:
> Lancashire like lions laiden them about.[12]

Thomas Wyatt's *Tagus Farewell* is a rare early example of a patriotic poem written by a member of the educated elite:

> Tagus, farewell, that westward with thy streams,
> Turns up the strains of gold already tried:
> With spur and sail for I go seek the Thames,
> Gainward the sun that shew'th her wealthy pride.
> And to the town which Brutus sought by dreams,
> Like bended moon doth lend her lusty side.
> My King, my Country, alone for whome I live,
> Of mighty love the wings for this me give.[13]

Wyatt, however, was a victim of this attack of patriotism, not because of any feelings for his homeland as such, but because of his personal circumstances. He had been recalled from his embassy to the court of Charles V of Spain, partly because he had antagonised Bishop Bonner and partly because of the imminent downfall of his patron, Thomas Cromwell. Alistair Fox has suggested an alternative reading by positing a romantic rather than a political motivation for the poem but the orientation remains personal.[14]

A patriotic response from Elizabethan poets to events of national importance such as the defeat of the Spanish Armada is to be expected. Before looking at poems written in direct response to such events it is worthwhile to consider the effect they had on *The Mirror for Magistrates* which was verse written for and by the ruling elite and which went through a series of editions. The authors, William Baldwin, George Ferris, Thomas Chaloner, Thomas Phear, Thomas Sackville and John Doleman had three things in common: their ability to stay in favour for four reigns, the fact that they were all distinguished men of letters and their familiarity with the affairs of the court and the nation.[15]

Baldwin, chosen as editor by the printer Thomas Marshe, dedicated his *Treatise on Moral Philosophy* to the Earl of Hertford, son of the Duke of Somerset. He was working on plays and pastimes for the court during the Christmas of 1552-3 and his play *Love of Lyve* was produced at court in 1556. Ferrers, the translator of *Magna Carta* had been a protégé of Cromwell. He was also a servant of the Dukes of Somerset and Northumberland during the reign of Edward VI and helped to put down Wyatt's rebellion in Mary's reign. Chaloner, author of the section on Richard II in *The Mirror*, was employed by four rulers, usually as an ambassador. Phear, a Physician and lawyer, dedicated his translation of *The Aeneid* to Mary. Sackville and Doleman were also lawyers who were associated with the Inner Temple at the time of the production of their play *Gorboduc* in 1560.[16]

*The Mirror* was written as a moral example to those in power. Baldwin's original preface described his purpose as the production of 'a Myrrour for al men as well noble as others' but the dedication was to 'the nobility and all others in office'. Throughout the work the explanatory introductions to the tragedies stressed that they were aimed at 'learned magistrates'. Although the implication is always there that, in the words of Baldwin in his dedication '. . . the goodness or badness of any realm lyeth in the goodness or badness of the rulers', the emphasis in the earlier editions was on personal tragedy. The consequences of sin were emphasised and it was to avoid these consequences rather than to benefit their realm that magistrates were exhorted to avoid pride, ambition and vengeance. The connection between sin and retribution in *The Mirror* can be illustrated by a selection of titles from the 1578 edition:

1. Robert Tresilian cheif justice of England hange at Tyburn and his fellow justices banished for miscontruing the lawes.

15. Richard Plantagenet D. of York, slaine through his over rash boldness. . . .

16. The Lord Clifford for his abhominable cruelty came to a sodaine end.

Richard Earl of Warwick was portrayed as meeting his end because of his concern for the 'common weal' without any implication that this was praiseworthy. The death of Richard II, which was to provide Shakespeare with an opportunity to stress the duties of kingship in a patriotic context,[17] was at this stage being treated as an individual tragedy:

I am a Kynge that ruled by lust,
That forced not of virtue, tyght of lawe,
But always put false flatterers most in trust,
Ensuing such as could my vices clawe.

The tragedies added in the 1578 edition were still warning against failings such as pride, as in the case of Eleanor, Duchess of Gloucester, or against the dangers and responsibilities of those close to the crown, as with Humphrey, Duke of Gloucester. There was, however, a distinct change of tone with a strong patriotic element becoming apparent in the 1587 edition of *The Mirror*. The section on Cardinal Wolsey still moralised about the outcome of pride and ambition, but the other three provided opportunities for the expression of patriotic feelings. The description of the battle of Flodden, unlike the contemporary celebration of the victory mentioned above, listed the people taking part so that their descendants could be proud of the way they had served their country. James IV's downfall was brought about solely because he had dared to co-operate with the French against such a country as England. The story of Sir Nicholas Burdet is a cautionary tale of the miseries resulting from civil dissension and contained the following patriotic rhetoric:

> Haue you oft heard the like, of cowards such before?
> Those forty thousand, Bretons, Frenche and Scots,
> Fowre score them foyled, made them flee like sots.
> I meant to make them fishe the poole without the bayte
> Protestin ere they there should get the wal
> Wee would as English die, or gieve our foes the fall.
> Yee worthy wights alive, which love your countryeys weale
> And for your princes porte such warres do undertake,
> Learne so for country yours with foryne foes do deale,
> See that of manhood good, so great accompts yee make.

The editor points out that additions made to the 1587 edition were probably written much earlier, in 1563 and were based on Holinshed. Why then did the 1587 editor and printer choose to include them? It is certainly not because of literary merit – with the possible exception of the section on Sir Nicholas Burdet, the verse is of a lower standard than the rest of *The Mirror*. As there was no change in the personnel making the decisions, one can only assume that their choice was based on the judgement that there had been an increase in audience receptiveness for material of a patriotic nature because of the war with Spain.

The continuation of the war did not exert a permanent influence on the portrayal of the downfall of kings, which still had a dynastic rather than a national orientation. They suffered retribution for their sins rather than punishment for failing the country. An example is provided in Sir Francis Hubert's treatment of the death of Edward II in his long poem which was written in 1597-1598. Edward is reminded that even Kings are subject to the law of God:

> But now I find by proofe that One there is
> (And well it is that there is such an One)
> Who is not hood-winckt unto our amisse,
> And he can pull us from our Kingly Throne
> For all our Guards, our forts, our walles of stone
> Know King, how great-soever that thou be,
> The King of Kings still ruleth over thee

and towards the end of the poem he regrets the sins which have led to his downfall:

> But now my Soule groanes with the weight of sin
> And I lye prostrate at my Makers feet.

I doe confesse how sottish I have bin,
How my distast hath taken sower for sweet.
I finde a God whose judgements now I meet.
  Damn'd atheist, thou that say'st there is  no God-
Thou wilt confesse one when thou feel'st  his rod.[18]

The tone is very different from that of Marlowe's play Edward II where
the King's selfishness is contrasted with the patriotism of his opponents.[19]

There was some correlation between government policy and the line taken
by poets. When Elizabeth had still been anxious to prolong the peace with
Spain, those poets who had an eye on official preferment could risk an anti-
war stand. George Gascoigne is a case in point. He had a promising early
career; after studying law at Cambridge he spent some time abroad then
became M.P. for Bedford in 1558 and the Queen's almoner in 1559. But he
was constantly in debt, not least because of a series of expensive court cases
brought about by the fact that his bride, one Elizabeth Breton, was already
married. His poem, *The Fruits of Warre*, was based on his experiences in the
Netherlands, where he fled as a mercenary soldier to escape his debtors.
Gascoigne followed patriotic conventions: the collection in which the *Fruits
of Warre* appeared – *The Posies of George Gascoigne Esquire* – was
undertaken 'to the end thereby might be encouraged to employ my penne in
some exercises which might tend both to my preferment, and to the profit of my
country.' In the poem itself he refers to 'Our English bloudes' and 'worthy English
men'. But he does not glorify death for one's country. He claims that poets,
painters, astronomers and travellers lie about war and he wants to tell the truth:

[16] If Painter craft have truly warre dysplayde,
Then it as woorsse (and badde it is at best)
Where townes destroyde, and fields with bloud berayde,
Young children slaine, olde widdowes foule opprest,
Maydes ravished, both men and wives distrest:
Short tale to make, where sworde and cindering flame
Consume as much as earth and ayre may frame.

He urges Princes and various groups within society to be satisfied with what
they have and not to risk war for greed or glory. The bulk of the poem is
taken up with a description of his own experiences from which he concludes
that nothing can be gained from war. As England was not yet involved in the
continental conflict he was able to praise Elizabeth as a peace keeper:

(193) O noble Queen, whose high forsight provides,
That wast of warre your realmes doth not destroye,
But pleasaunt peace, and quiet concord glydes,
In every coast, to drive out darke anoye,
O vertuous dame, I say Pardonez moy,
That I presume in worthlesse verse to warne,
Thambitious Prince, his duties to descerne.[20]

It was not always the case, however, that public sentiment and government
policy coincided. In the following pasquin, xenophobia was directed against

France and the writer was critical of the Queen's plans to marry Francis, Duke of Alencon, brother of the King of France:

The King of France shall not advance his ships in Englishe sande.

Nor shall his brother have the ruling of the land.

We subjects true unto our Queen, the foreign yoke defy,

Where to we plight our faithful hearts, our limbs our lives and all,

thereby to have our honour rise or take our fatal fall

Therefore, good Francis, rule at home, resist not our desire

for here is nothing else for thee, but only sword and fire.[21]

Members of the Council were sensitive when patriotism was used against government policy. John Stubbs lost his right hand for a pamphlet entitled *The discoverie of a gaping gulf where unto England is likely to be swallowed by another French marriage if the Lord forbid not the bans* which took a similar line to the pasquin.

The change of tone in *The Mirror for Magistrates* in response to the threat from the Armada was mentioned above. But what of the attitudes of the poets who dealt directly with the event? Ballads which described the naval incidents were understandably chauvinistic but patriotism appeared alongside and was subordinated to praise for Elizabeth and thanks to God for a Protestant victory. One of Thomas Delony's ballads described the horrors which the Spaniards had in store for their English victims:

One sort of whips, they had for men

so smarting, fierce, and fell,

As like as never could be devised

by any devil in hell:

The strings whereof with wiry knots,

like rowel they did frame

that every stroke might tear the flesh,

they laid on with the same.[22]

Deloney had been a silk weaver before turning to ballads and tales and his livelihood depended on catering to popular taste. Popular taste, however, would not be satisfied simply by anti-Spanish rhetoric and the ballad was also news. In one of his offerings, Deloney described the events which took place on the 21st and 29th July, 1588 -shortly after the first sighting of the Armada – and the ballad was printed and for sale on the streets within a few days. The ballad has patriotic elements, as can be seen from the opening lines:

O noble England, fall down upon thy knee:

And praise thy GOD with thankful heart which still maintaineth thee

and England is later referred to as 'our pleasant country, so fruitful and so faire', but the main theme is religious. The ballad is a prayer of thanks for salvation from the Catholics and an exhortation to the people to remain steadfast, not to their country but to their faith. This can be illustrated by the title: *A Joyfull New Ballad Declaring the happie obtaining of the great Galleazzo wherein Don Pedro de Valdes was the chiefe, through the mighty*

*power and providence of God: being a speciall token of His gracious and*
*fatherly goodnes towards us; to the great encouragement of all those that*
*willingly fight in the defence of his gospel and our good Queene of England.*[23]
The theme that God had chosen to defeat the Armada to save England for
Protestantism, permeated contemporary ballads as in the following example:

> From merciless invaders,
>> From wicked men's device,
> O God! arise and help us,
>> to quele our enemies.
>
> Sinke deepe their potent navies,
>> Their strength and courage breake,
> O God! arise and arm us,
>> For Jesus Christ his sake.
>
> Though cruel Spain and Parma
>> With heatherns legions come,
> O God! arise and arm us,
>> We'll dye for our home!
>
> We will not change our credo
>> For Pope nor book nor bell;
> And if the devil come himself,
>> We'll hound him back to hell.[24]

Elizabeth was given her share of credit, alongside God, for saving England
from invasion and patriotism was combined with gushing adulation for the
Queen. *A Proper Ballad, wherein is plain to be seen how God hath blessed*
*England for love of our Queen,* opened with the following lines, which set
the tone for the rest of the verses:

> London, London, singe and praise thy lord!
>> let England's joy be seene;
> Trew subjects, quickly shew with one accorde,
>> youre love unto your Queene Elizabeth so brave.

The ballad was not dated, but must have been written after the defeat of the
Armada as it referred to the way God dealt with the 'Spanish spite by
drowning'.[25] Another Thomas Deloney ballad on the defeat of the Armada
combined patriotism with praise of Elizabeth:

> And yours dear brethern!
>> which beareth arms this day,
> For safeguard of your native soil;
>> mark well what I shall say!
> Regard your duties!
>> think on your country's good!
> And fear not in defence thereof,
>> to spend your dearest blood!
> Our gracious Queen,

doth greet you every one!
And saith she will among you be
in every bitter storm!
Desiring you
true English hearts to bear
To God! to her! and to the land
wherein you nursed were![26]

War with Spain continued until after the end of the reign so ballad writers were provided with further opportunities for patriotic accounts of naval and military incidents. *The Famous Fight at Malango*, relates with relish the destruction, not only of the Spaniards, but also their wives, their children, their houses and their churches.[27] Delony continued to respond to newsworthy events and wrote a ballad to celebrate the taking of Cadiz by the Earl of Essex and Lord Howard on the 21st of June, 1596. The ballad concentrates on praise for the 'most valient and hardye' Essex and on the spoils and profits:

'Now' quoth the noble Earl 'courage my soldiers all,
Fight and be valiant, the spoil you shall have;
and be well rewarded from all great and small'

and later:

Full of rich merchandize, every ship catched our eyes
Damasks and satterns and velvets full fayre,
Which soldiers measured out be the lenth of their swords;
Of all commodities eche had a share.

Despite the emphasis on personal gain, however, the ballad does have a patriotic tone which is set by the opening stanza:

Long the proud Spaniards had vanted to conquer us,
Threatening our country with fyer and sword;
often preparing their navy most sumptuous
With as great plenty as Spain could afford.
Dub a dub, dub a dub, thus strikes their drums.
Tantara, tantara the Englishman comes.[28]

It was noted above[29] that the expedition to Cadiz had been less than successful. The military objectives were not achieved and the voyage was marred by squabbling between the leaders. The government could often rely on ballad writers to skip over the negative aspects of the war against Spain which did not go well after the initial success against the Armada. In Gervase Markham's hands the loss of the Revenge and the death of Grenville became an example of patriotic behaviour rather than an act of lunacy.[30]

Poets writing for a narrower audience also found inspiration in the exploits of Englishmen. Michael Drayton had various noble patrons and there is a tradition that he was employed by Elizabeth on a diplomatic mission to Scotland.[31] With Drayton, one finds a widening of patriotism away from the limits of chauvinism, to encompass love of and pride in his native land. He praised Lord Willoughby for his action against the enemy:

Then courage, noble Englishmen,

> And never be dismayed,
> If that we be but one in ten
> We will not be afraid
> To fight with common enemies
> And set our countries free;
> And thus I end the bloody bout
> Of brave Lord Willoughby.

He also wrote of national as well as personal honour for those involved in colonisation in *To The Virginian Voyage*:

> You brave heroic minds
> Worthy your country's name:
> That honour still pursue;
> Go and Subdue!
> Whilst loitering hinds
> Lurk here at home with shame!

His *To the Cambro-Britons, and Their Harp, His Ballad of Agincourt* was on one level a glorification of a national victory as indicated by the last verse:

> Upon Saint Crispin's day
> Fought was this noble fray,
> Which fame did not delay
> To England carry;
> O, when shall English men
> With such acts fill a pen,
> Or England breed again
> Such a King Harry?

But patriotism appeared in the poem alongside a continuing emphasis on feudal values and the quest for personal honour dominated the description of the fighting:

> Warwick in blood did wade,
> Oxford the foe invade,
> And cruel slaughter made
> Still as they ran up;
> Suffolk his axe did ply,
> Beaumont and Willoughby
> Bare them right doughtily,
> Ferrers and Fanhope.[32]

Although his *Barrons Wars*, the subject of which is the rebellious pride of Edward II's barons, can be read as a warning against the internal conflict which was a threat to England's greatness, it too was basically a story of personal tragedy. Long verse chronicles were fashionable among the upper classes in the 1590s. Samuel Daniel was a tutor to the Herbert and Clifford families and began work on his *The Civile War between the Two Houses of Lancaster and Yorke*. Like Drayton, he warned of the danger to the country brought about by internal disunity. In the following stanza, Richard II appeals to England's interests:

> 'Well; so it seem dear cousin' said the King,
> 'Though you might have procured it otherwise.
> And I am here content, in everything
> To right you, as yourself shall best devise.
> And God vouchsafe the force that here you bring
> Beget not England greater injuries.'[33]

Writing of the symbolism of Elizabethan political propaganda, Frances Yates commented that 'Tudor imperialism is a blend of nascent nationalism and surviving medieval universalism.'[34] No single work of literature reflects this blend more than Edmund Spenser's *Faerie Queen*. Una, representing the one pure religion and the peace of the 'golden age' had ancestors who were:

> Ancient Kings and Queens that had of yore
> Their scepters strecht from East to Western shore
> And all the world in their subjection held.
>
> Book I, canto I, 5.

She was the symbol of universal rather than national unity. Merlin's famous prophecy to Britomart referred to universal peace as a sequel to national defence:

> Renowned kings and sacred Emperors,
> Thy fruitfull Offspring shall from thee descend;
> Brave captaines, and most mighty warriours,
> That shall their conquests through all lands extend
> And their decayed kingdomes shall amend
> The feeble Britons, broken with long warre,
> They shall upreare, and mightily defend
> against their forreign foe, that comes from farre,
> Till universall peace compound all ciull iarre.
>
> Book III, canto III, 23.

But the glory of England was a crucial secondary theme. In canto X of Book I, the Red Cross Knight is shown a vision of the Jerusalem built by God 'For those to dwell in that are chosen his, His chosen people purg'd from sinful guilt'. The Knight replies that the beauty of this new Jerusalem surpassed even the city 'in which the Faerie Queen doth dwell' and this presented an opportunity to praise England as follows:

> Yet is Cleopolis' for earthly frame
> The fairest peece that eye beholden can:
> And well beseemes all knights of noble name,
> That couet in th'immortal booke of fame
> To be eternized, that same to haunt,
> And doen their service to that soueraigne Dame,
> That glorie does to them for guerdon graunt;
> For she is heavenly borne, and heaven may justly vaunt.

And the Red Cross Knight was associated with St George:

> For thou amongst those saints, whom thou doest see,
> Shaly be a saint, and thine own nation's friend
> And Patron: thou Saint George shalt called bee,

Saint George of merry England, the sign of victoree.

Book I, canto X, 57,59,62.

In his letter to Raleigh, which prefaced the *Faerie Queen*, Spenser explained his choice of Arthur as hero as follows:

I chose the historye of King Arthur as most fitte
for the excellency of his person, being made famous
by many mens former works, and also furthest from
the danger of envy and suspition of the present time.

Arthur represents the realm of Britain to which the Faerie Queen as Britomart is inexorably linked. The legend of Britain's Trojan origins is used to glorify her past when Arthur, visiting the House of Temperance, discovers an ancient book which traces the history of Britain from Brutus to Uther Pendragon. In Book III, the triumph of Temperance is used as an opportunity to prophesy the triumph of the British Empire. The prophecy made by Merlin to Britomart tells of the return of the Troy-descended line to power; of the union of the houses of York and Lancaster in the Tudors; and of the eventual advent of a 'royal Virgin' who would establish world peace:

Thenceforth eternall union shall be made
Betweene the nations different afore,
And sacred peace shall lovingly persuade
The warlike minds, to learn her godly lore,
And civile armes to excersie no more:
then shall a royall virgin raine, which shall
Strech her white rod over Belgicke shore,
And the great Castle smite so sore with all
That it shall make him shake, and shortly learne to fall.

Book III, canto III, 49.

The patriotism of the *Faerie Queen* is expansionist at a time when Elizabeth had resisted pressure to accept sovereignty of the Netherlands and was trying to limit the scope of naval involvement overseas. Frances Yates has suggested that this partly accounts for the chilly reception which Spenser received when he was introduced to Court by Raleigh in 1592.[35]

Elizabeth's fear of the expansionist implications of patriotic propaganda was discussed above.[36] It is also possible that the patriotic content of descriptions of England had dangerous implications if not for Elizabeth herself then for the future of the monarchy. Michael Drayton's most famous work, *Poly-Olbion*, shows a deep affection for England. The title is a Greek word meaning 'rich in blessings' and is intended as a pun on 'Albion', and the laudatory tone is illustrated by the alternative title:

A chronographical description of all the Tracts, Rivers, Mountains,
Forrests, and other parts of the renowned Isle of Great Britain, with
intermixture of the most remarkable Stories, Antiquities, Wonders,
Rarities, Pleasures and commodities of the same.

The first eighteen songs of *Poly-Olbion* were published in 1612 but a reference by Francis Mere indicates that Drayton was working on the poem from 1598.[37]

Richard Helgerson cites the poem as an example of the way personification of the land was replacing dynastic imagery. He believes it is significant that Drayton removed all royal insignia when he used eighteen illustrations from Christopher Saxton's collection of county maps. This could be explained, however, by the fact that the insignia reflected Saxton's patronage and were no longer relevant to Drayton or that there had been a change of ruler by the time the work was published. Helgerson does have a point in reading the frontispiece to Poly-Olbion as undermining the cult of monarchy. An allegorical personification of Britannia is dressed in a map which represents the land. The Britannia pose is similar to that of Elizabeth on Saxton's frontispiece which in turn was based on the familiar icon of the Virgin Mary as Queen of Heaven. The figures on the edge represent conquerors of England – 'Aeneas nephew, Brut,', 'Laureate Caesar', the Saxon Hengist and the Norman, William – but the continuity and stability comes from the country.[38] The emphasis on the land in opposition to rather that juxtaposition with the monarchy is not confined to the early Stuart period but can be seen in a long line of descriptions of England including John Leyland's *Itinerary*, based on material gathered between 1535 and 1543, William Harrison's *Description of Britain*, first published in 1577, and William Camden's *Britannia* (1586).

When one considers how matters of national significance were dealt with in sixteenth-century poetry it becomes clear that concern for the country was exhibited alongside or often subordinated to religious, feudal or personal considerations. Any patriotism which did exist could represent a challenge to the Government. The nature of any cultural nationalism can only be fully assessed when attitudes to foreigners have been considered and this will be the subject of the next chapter.

# Notes

1. Thomas Heywood, *An Apologie for Actors*, Shakespeare Society, 1841, p. 21.
2. Vivien Thomas, ed., *Michael Drayton: Selected Poems*, Manchester, 1977, p. 73, lines 126-8.
3. See chapter two.
4. John Leyland, 'Naeniae in mortem Thomae Viati equitis incomprabilis', in Patricia Thomson, ed, *Wyatt: The Critical Heritage*, 1974, p. 25. (*The English the Italian's equal*. Beautiful Florence extols the merits of Dante. Royal Rome approves the songs of Petrarch. No less inferior in his own country, Wyatt bore the praise for eloquence and beauty of language. *The file of Wyatt*. The English language was rough and its verses worthless. Now learned Wyatt, it has benefit of your file.)
5. G.D. Willcock and A Walker, eds, *George Puttenham's The Arte of English Poesie*, Cambridge, 1936, pp 24,59.
6. Sir Philip Sidney 'An Apologie for Poetry' in G.G. Smith, ed., *Elizabethan Critical Essays*, Oxford, 1904, pp 148-207.
7. Thomas, op. cit., p. 72, lines 85-89.
8. Michael Drayton, 'Idea: The Shephard's Garland', 1593, first printed 1599, in H.R. Woudhuysen, ed, *The Penguin Book of Renaissance Verse, 1509-1659*, 1992, pp 727-8. 'Orcades' refers to the Orkneys, 'Pirens' to the Pyrenees and

'Galliglasses' are Irish retainers.

9. Emrys Jones, ed, *The New Oxford Book of Sixteenth Century Verse*, Oxford, 1992, p. 544 l.83-86, p. 545 l.125-130.

10. See chapter two, p. 9.

11. F.J. Furnivall and W.R. Morfill, eds, *Ballads from Manuscripts*, Ballad Society, 1868-1873, vol. 1, pp 56-59, 104-107.

12. *Sixteenth-Century Verse*, pp 67-73 ll.36-42,191-193.

13. ibid. p86.

14. Alistair Fox, *Politics and Literature in the Reigns of Henry VII and Henry VIII*, London, 1989, p. 275.

15. Lily B. Campbell, ed., *The Mirror for Magistrates*, Cambridge, 1938, p. 21.

16. Chapter six, pp 1-2.

17. ibid pp 17-19.

18. Bernard Mellor, ed, *The Poems of Sir Francis Hubert*, Oxford, 1961, pp 9, 132.

19. See chapter six pp 20-22.

20. J.W. Cunliffe, ed, *The Complete Works of George Gascoigne*, 2 vols. Cambridge, 1907-1910, I, pp 5, 160, 144, 145, 179.

21. Furnivall and Morfill, op. cit., p. 114.

22. A.F. Pollard, *Tudor Tracts, 1532-1588*, 1903, p. 499.

23. ibid, p. 485.

24. Christopher Stone, *Sea Songs and Ballads*, Oxford, 1906, pp 80-81.

25. Furnivall and Morfill, op. cit., ii, pp 92-96.

26. Pollard, op. cit., p. 490.

27. Stone, op. cit., pp 87-90.

28. Guy N. Pocock, ed, *Ballads and Poems*, Glasgow, 1921.

29. Chapter six.

30. Gervase Markham, *The Most honourable Tragedie of Sir Richard Grenville, Knight*, 1595.

31. *Dictionary of National Biography*.

32. Thomas op. cit., pp 58-62, lines 116-120, 105-112.

33. Jones, op. cit., p. 515.

34. Frances Yates, *Astraea: The Imperial Theme in the Sixteenth Century*, 1975, p. 87.

35. Frances Yates, *The Occult Philosophy in the Elizabethan Age*, 1979, p. 85.

36. See chapter one.

37. Thomas, op. cit., p. 12.

38. Richard Helgerson, 'The Land Speaks: Cartography, Chorography and Subversion in Renaissance England', *Representations*, 16, 1986, pp 59-64,

# VIII
# 'Hans van Belch' and 'bursten bellied sots':
# Foreigners in Sixteenth-Century Literature

Hostility to foreigners in non-literary sources is well documented. Despite the growing *detente* with the French government after 1570, there is evidence of a continued dislike for the traditional enemy. This surfaced especially when Elizabeth conducted marriage negotiations with the French King's brother, the Duke of Alencon, in 1579.[1] William Maltby has discussed the growing resentment against Spain[2] which can be explained partly by Protestant propaganda which was especially virulent from the Dutch rebels. As in the case of Spain, attitudes to foreigners were not necessarily determined by national prejudices as international ties of faith remained strong. Many English Catholics still looked to Rome for deliverance and large numbers of exiles lived in Spain during Elizabeth's reign.[3] The Protestants also had international aspirations and hoped that Elizabeth would lead a crusade of Protestants in Europe against the Spanish Antichrist.[4] I will suggest that, in literature, if one considers either stereotypical or more realistic portrayals, the role of foreigners remained traditional and the attitudes of writers was far removed from cultural nationalism.

It was fashionable for English gentlemen to complete their education with a period of foreign travel after university, with Italy the favourite destination. However, the influence of Renaissance culture was not universally welcomed. Many felt that, although travel had a great deal to offer, the Englishman would be tainted with sin if not on his guard. Roger Ascham in *The Schoolmaster* warned:

> I was only once in Italie myselfe; but I thanke God my abode there was only ix days – And yet I saw in that little tyme in one citie more libertie to sinne than ever I heard tell of in our noble citie of London in IX yeare.[5]

Robert Greene seems to have enjoyed his time abroad, but claimed that he was never the same again:

> Being at the University of Cambridge I light among wags as lewd as myselfe, with whom I consumed the flower of my youth, who drew me into travell in Italy and Spaine, in which places I saw and practizde such villainnie as is abhominable to declare.

He went on to tell how difficult he found it to settle to a steady job when he returned home.[6]

This idea that foreign travel might contaminate the Englishman was used in literature to highlight morality themes. For example, in Thomas Dekker's play *Old Fortunatus*, which was first printed in 1600, travel is associated with vice. Old Fortunatus is given a choice by Fortune of wisdom, strength, health, beauty, long life or riches. He chooses the last and decides to travel.[7] While he is away the dramatist establishes the character of two sons and a servant. Ampedo represents virtue, Andelocia vice and the servant, Shadow, is portrayed as sensible and down to earth. This meant that when Dekker presented both sides in the travel debate, the audience was left in no doubt that travel was immoral. Andelocia (Vice) sets the scene by anticipating changes in his father:

> Come come, when the old traveller my father comes home, like a young Ape, full of fantasticke trickes, or a painted parrat stucke full of outlandish feathers, heele leade the world in a string.
>
> [Act II, sc ii, 24-27]

And Ampedo (Virtue's) response to his father's return is to suggest that all travellers are liars. Old Fortunatus claims that he has returned from Babylon in one minute (actually he has – it's that kind of play!) Ampedo replies: 'How? in a minute father? I see travellers must lie.' Shadow emphasises the point – 'Tis their destine: the fates do so conspire.' (Act II, sc ii, 126-7) The clearest condemnation of travel comes in exchange between Andelocia and Shadow.

> Andelocia: Thou dolt, weele visit the kings courts in the world.
>
> Shadow: So we may, and return dolts home, but what shall we learne by trauaile?
>
> Andelocia: Fashions.
>
> Shadow: Thats a beastly disease: me thinks it better staying in your own countrie.
>
> Andelocia: How? In mine owne countrie? like a Cage-birde and see nothing?
>
> Shadow: Nothing? yes you may see things enough, for what can you see abroad that is not at home? The same sun calls you up in the morning, and the same man in the Moone lights you to bed at night, our fields are as greene as theirs in summer, and their frosts will nip us more in winter: Our birds sing as sweetly, and our women are as fair: In other countries you shall have one drinke to you, whilst you kisse your hand, and ducke, heele poison you: I confesse you shall meete more ffoles, and asses, and knaves abroad then at home (yet God be thanked we have prettie store of all) but for Punckes we put them downe.
>
> [Act II, sc ii 393-410]

Not all writers came down so decisively in favour of the merits of staying at home and being content with one's lot. Thomas Nashe's *The Unfortunate Traveller, or the Life of Jack Wilton* (1594) is usually interpreted as a caveat against foreign travel. The novel describes the adventures abroad of Jack Wilton, a page in the service of the Earl of Surrey. He encounters scenes of sex, violence, rape, romance and intrigue in Florence, Venice and Rome. Nashe is full of commendation for the cities his hero visits. There is, for example, a long passage praising Rome for the beauty of its gardens, orchards, baths, vineyards, and merchants' houses, which is designed to contrast with a later description of a city hit by the plague. The most specific criticism of travel comes from an earl who has just rescued Wilton from the gallows:

> Countriman, tell me what is the occasion of thy straying so farre out of England, to visit this strange Nation? If it be languages thou maist learn them at home, nought but lasciviousnesse is to be learned here. Perhaps to be better accounted of, than other of thy condition, thou ambitiously undertaken this voyage; these insolent fancies are but Icarus feathers, whose wanton wax melted against the sunne, will betray thee into a sea of confusion.

He goes on to point out that God cursed the Israelites by leading them out of their own land and to criticise Englishmen who left their native country through choice. He ridicules those failings which would contaminate the English traveller in France Italy or Spain. But were these the views of the author? The Earl is characterised as a pedantic old bore from whom Jack is anxious to escape, although, as things go from bad to worse towards the end of the novel, Jack regrets 'deriding such a grave and fatherly advertiser.' Rather than producing a polemic against travel, Nashe presented the dilemma contrasting the benefits and pleasures against the moral danger involved.[8]

Shakespeare seemed to take travel for granted as part of education. There is an exchange in *Two Gentlemen of Verona*, for example, where Antonio and Panthino are discussing the former's son. Panthino suggests various reasons why the son should spend some time abroad to complete his education:

> Some to the wars, to try their fortunes there;
> Some to discover islands far away;
> Some to the studious universities;
>                                      [Act I sc iii, 9-11]

and stresses that it would be to his detriment in his adult life if he'd never travelled in his youth. Antonio agrees:

> I have considered well his loss of time,
> And how he cannot be a perfect man
> not being tried and tutor'd in the world:

He did, however recognise the pitfalls. In *As You Like It*, Rosalind attributes Jaques' melancholy to the fact that he has travelled:

> A traveller! By my faith you have great reason to be sad: I fear you have sold your own lands to see other men's; then you have seen too much, and to have nothing, is to have rich eyes and poor hands.
>                                      [Act IV sc i 18-21]

> Farewell, Monsieur traveller; look you lisp and wear strange suits; disable all the benefits of your own country; be out of love with your nativity and almost chide God for making you the countenance that you are.
>                                      [28-31]

Shakespeare, in common with many Elizabethan writers, ridiculed the 'Italianate Englishman' who had been influenced by foreign fashions.

In *Richard II*, the Duke of York complained that Richard listened only to flatterers and was interested in:

> Report of fashions in proud Italy,
> Whose manners still our tardy apish nation
> Limps after in base imitation.

[Act II sc i 21-23]

The moralists' invective was directed not so much against foreigners as against Englishmen who allowed themselves to be corrupted by alien influences. These influences were taken seriously by some commentators as a symptom of a deep malaise in the English commonwealth. Greene's pamphlet, *A Quip for an Upstart Courtier*, (1592), an allegorical critique of English society, took the form of a debate between Clothbreeches and Velvetbreeches, as to which was more fitted to reside in the commonwealth. The former, wearing clothes 'such as our grandfathers wore', was associated with the 'good old days' of stability and prosperity, when everybody knew their place. The latter dressed in Italian style and epitomised evil:

> Thou camest not alone but accompanied with multitude of abominable
> vices, hanging on thy bombast nothing but infectious abuses, and
> vainglory, selfelove, sodomie and strange poisonings wherewith thou
> had infected this glorious island.[9]

This idea that 'aping' foreign, and especially Italian, dress represented a rejection of traditional ideals was a commonplace in late sixteenth-century works. In his pamphlet *The English Ape*, (1588) the Puritan, William Rankins saw the influence of foreign fashions as a reflection of the corruption within society.[10] For Nashe, foreign styles were a rejection of the national past: 'Other countries fashions they see, but never look back to the attire of their forefathers, or consider what shape their own country should give them'.[11] John Decon painted a wider but equally hostile picture of the way the innocent Englishmen were corrupted by evils from abroad. In his dialogue, *Tobacco Tortured*, (1616) he wrote:

> We leave our ancient simplicitie eftsoones in a forreine ayre: and
> (instead thereof) do greedily sucke up from foreigners, not their
> virtues, but vices, and monstrous corruptions, as well as religion and
> manners, as also in framing the whole course of our life . . . from
> whence cometh it now to pass, that so many of our Englishmens minds
> are terribly Turkished with Mahometan trumperies; thus ruefully
> Romanized with superstitious relikes; thus treacherously Italianized
> with sundry antichristian toyes.[12]

Decon accepted that foreigners had virtues and blamed the English for copying only the vices. Similarly, George Gascoigne criticised his fellow countrymen for surpassing as well as adopting foreign defects:

> Ah las, we Englishemen can mocke and scoffe at all Countreyes for
> their defects, but before they have many times musteres before us, we

can learn by little and little to exceed and pass them all, in all that which, at first sight, we accounted both vile and villanous: The Spanish codpeece on the bellye: the Itallyan waste under the hanch bones: the Frenche Ruffes: the Polonian Hose: the Dutch Jerkin: and the Turkie Bonnet: all these at first we despised, and had in derision. But immediately (Mutat(a) opinione) we do not only retain them, but we do so far exceed them. That of a Spanish codpeece, we make an English footeball: of an Itallyan wast, an English Petycoate: of a French Ruffe, an English Chytterling: of a Polonian Hose, and English bowgette: of a Dutch Jerkin, an old English Habergeone, and of a Turkish bonnet, a Copentank for Caiphas.[13]

When considering comments on travel one should, however, guard against too literal an interpretation of place. For example, in John Lyly's *Euphues*, (1579) Athens, which produced Euphues, was Oxford, which produced Lyly; and Naples was London. So that when Lyly criticised travel: 'Let not your mindes be caryed away with vaine delights, as with travailing into farre and straunge countries, wher you shall see more wickednesse then learn virtue and wit,'[14] he was warning against the influence of London.

Direct knowledge of foreigners was limited to the educated elite and those living near the large numbers of Flemish immigrants working in England.[15] People living in counties bordering Wales and Scotland may have come across the occasional Welshman and Scotsman. Within the circles of those meeting visiting diplomats or scholars or travelling abroad themselves, direct contact with other nationalities was common. The educated would have access to books by travel writers such as Andrew Borde. He studied medicine abroad in the late 1520s and in 1535 he was sent to Europe by Cromwell to report on reactions to Henry VIII. Later his lengthy and widespread travels included a stay at Montpelier university where he wrote his *First Booke of the Introduction of Knowledge*, a survey of the customs and characteristics of some thirty-three countries and regions, which was published in 1542. Borde's patriotism and his attitude to the English language were discussed above.[16] His love of his native land did not engender any hostility to foreigners. His accounts of foreign countries include portrayals of national characteristics which are occasionally unflattering but never malicious.[17] Fynes Moryson's *Itinerary*[18] (1617) also includes a survey of national traits and Thomas Wilson uses a list of national characteristics as a rhetorical device in his *Art of Rhetoric*[19] (1553). Chroniclers often included detailed descriptions of other parts of the British Isles as well as England; for example William Harrison's *An historical description of the iland of Britaine*, and Richard Stanihurst's *De rebus Hibernia gestis, libri iv*, which contained a view of the ancient and present state of Ireland and the manners and customs of the Irish inhabitants.[20]

When writers of pamphlets and travel books included accounts of national characteristics they were influenced by long-standing traditions of the portrayal of foreign stereotypes in literature. These images continued to be used by dramatists and poets for either comic or moral effect. For example, in Dekker's play *Sir Thomas Wyatt*, which was first printed in 1607, Spaniards were used both for comic effect and to personify pride. The play is not a patriotic one.[21] At the beginning of the play, Wyatt is one of Mary's most ardent supporters and he is shown to turn against her because she is to marry a Spaniard. But the dramatist cannot afford to sympathise with this, as Wyatt is to be hanged as a traitor. The sympathy instead is directed (not very successfully) towards Lady Jane Grey and her husband, Guilford Dudley, whose fathers, the Earl of Suffolk and the Duke of Northumberland, had tried to divert the succession away from Mary. The couple come over as innocent (if rather pathetic) lovers whose death at the end of the play has been caused by their fathers' pride. The play closes with a speech from the Duke of Norfolk:

> Thus we have seen her Highnesse will perform'd
> And now their heads and bodies shall be joined
> And buried in one grave as fits their loves.
> Thus much ile say on their behalfes now dead,
> Their Fathers pride their lives have severed.
>
> [Act V sc ii, 182-6]

The theme of condemnation of pride echoes earlier references to Spain:

> Philip is a Spaniard, a proud nation,
> Whome naturally our Countrimen abhoue.
>
> [Act III sc i, 161-2]

While he has Spaniards, if not on stage, at least in the wings of his play, Dekker is able to use popular conceptions of their physical defects to provide light relief, as in the exchange between Alexander Brett, a captain, and a clown:

> Brett: A Spaniard is cald so, because hee's a Spaniard: his yard is but a span.
>
> Clown: That's the reason our Englishwomen love them not.
>
> Brett: Right, for he carries not the Englishmans yard about him, if you deal with him look for hard measure: if you give him an inch hee'le take an ell: if he giue an ell, youle take an inch.
>
> [Act IV, sc ii, 62-68]

There is a similar reference in Spanish Tragedy, as Balthazar and Hieronimo trade insults:

> Balthazar:   Thou inch of Spain
>                Thou man, from thy hose down, scarce so much;
>                Thou very little longer than they beard;
>                Speak not such big words;
>
> [Sc x, 33-36]

Spanish pride was also ridiculed in a lighthearted way in Chapman's play The Blind Beggar of Alexandria (1596).[22] The Spaniard, Braggadino is introduced into one scene as a rival to the Count for the affections of Elimine. His nationality is emphasised in the opening comment from the Count: 'How now shall I be troubled with this rude Spaniard now.' (Sc II, 20) They agree to compete and that the loser will follow the happy couple, walking backwards and biting his thumbs. The audience knows what to expect – firstly Braggadino's showing off is ridiculed:

> Brag: Sweete Nimph, a Spaniard is compared to a great elixar or golden medicine.
>
> Count: What dost thou come upon her with medicines, dost thou think she is a sore.
>
> [54-6]
>
> Brag: I say a Spaniard is like a Philosophers stone.
>
> Count: An I say an other mans stone may be as good as a philosopher at all tymes.
>
> [60-62]

Elimine, of course, chooses the Count and Braggadino is bullied into making a fool of himself by complying with the terms of the agreement.

Spanish pride is used with more serious moral intent – to warn against vice – in the cautionary ballad: *A Warning Piece to England against Pride and Wickedness: Being the fall of Queen Eleanor, Wife to Edward I King of England; who for her pride by God's Judgements sunk into the ground at Charingcross and rose at Queen-Hithe*. At the beginning of the ballad, Eleanor is shown to be a bad influence on the homely English:

> 2. She was the first that did invent
>    In coaches brave to rise;
>    She was the first that brought this land
>    To deadly sin or pride.
>    No English Taylor here could serve
>    To make her rich attire
>    But sent for taylors into Spain
>    To feed her vain desire.

As in the examples above, foreign fashions are used to represent vice:

> 3. They brought in fashions strange and new
>    With golden garments bright;
>    The farthingale and mighty ruff
>    With gowns of rich delight;
>    The London dames in Spanish pride
>    Did flourish everywhere;
>    Our Englishmen, like women then
>    Did wear long locks of hair.

Eleanor becomes resentful that the English look as good as the Spaniards so asks her husband to cut their hair off. He agrees after first cutting his own. The Queen then asks that the women should have their breasts cut off – giving an opportunity for a bit of bloodthirstiness which always went down well in ballads:

> 7. That ev'ry woman kind should have
>    Their right breast cut away,

> And then with burning irons sear'd
> The blood to staunch and stay.

Edward agrees to the request, but only if the Queen agrees to be the first. As the ballad progresses the Queen becomes more sinful and finally comes to a nasty end herself. The moral comes in the final verse:

> Thus have you heard the fall of pride,
> A just reward of sin;
> For those who will forswear themselves
> God's vengeance daily win.
> Beware of pride ye courtly dames,
> Both wives and maidens all;
> Bear this imprinted on your minds,
> That pride must have a fall.[23]

One of the best known uses of the national stereotype comes in the 'casket scene' of *The Merchant of Venice*. The story is a traditional one. Following instructions left by her father, Portia has to present all her suitors with a choice of three caskets, gold, silver and lead. Those choosing wrongly have to promise never to marry – a symbol of the castration which was the forfeit in some versions of the tale. A list of suitors is dismissed before the scene proper begins and Shakespeare is able to create an image of these people in the minds of the audience by making them national stereotypes – the horse-mad Neapolitan, the adaptable Frenchman, the inarticulate Englishman and the drunken German. The ethnic differentiation continues as we meet the other suitors. With the Prince of Aragon we get the usual image of the proud Spaniard. He rejects the gold because of its slogan 'Who chooseth me shall gain what many men desire':

> I will not choose what many men desire,
> Because I will not jump with common spirits,
> And rank me with the barbarous multitudes.

> [Act II, sc ix, 31-33]

He chooses silver – 'Who chooses me shall get as much as he deserves' because of his high opinion of his own worth. But the Prince has a further role to play; he is in the scene to represent the white Christian as opposed to the black Moor who is the other suitor we meet in person. Portia draws attention to the Moor's colour before meeting him: 'if he have the condition of a saint and the complexion of the devil, I had rather he should shrive me than wive me' (Act I sc ii). The Prince of Morocco is a dignified and honourable character, who makes a plea that his colour should not be held against him:

> Mislike me not for my complexion,
> The shadow'd livery of the burnish'd sun,
> To whom I am a neighbour near and bred.

> [Act II, sc i, 1-3]

He loses, but makes his choice of gold as a compliment to Portia and not through arrogance. He is dismissed with a further reference to his colour by Portia:

> A gentle riddance. Draw the curtains go.
> Let all of his complexion use me so.
>                                [Act II, sc viii, 80-81]

The Elizabethan audience would not expect the Prince of Morocco to succeed, whatever his personal qualities, as they were familiar with the image of black as evil. This was not a racial judgement – the ethnic connections of 'Moors' in sixteenth century literature were varied and often vague[24] – but colour was used as antithetical to the European ideal of a stable Christian society. The religious nature of the contrast is shown by a comment made by Lazarotto in Kyd's The *First Part of Hieronimo* which was written between 1585 and 1587. He and Lorenzo are plotting to murder Andrea. When the latter asks whether he is afraid of damnation, Lazarotto replies:

> Dare I? Ha! Ha!
> I have no hope of everlasting height;
> My soul's a Moor, you know, salvation's white.
> What dare not I enact then?
>                                [Sc iii, 59-63]

In Peele's *Battle of Alcazar*, (1589) the negro, Muly Hamet, is a figure of absolute evil, in contrast to the hero, King Sebastian of Portugal. He is introduced by the presenter as follows:

> Blacke in his looke and bloudie in his deeds,
> And in his shirt stained with a cloud of gore,
> Presents himselfe with naked sword in hand,
> Accompanied as now you may behold,
> With devils coted in the shapes of men.
>                                [14-18]

Later references stress his sinfulness – 'damned wits' line 22, 'unbelieving Moore', line 31, 'Vengeance on this accursed Moore for sinne', line 39. Aaron is in Titus Andronicus to represent barbaric disorder and Eleazer in Lusts Dominion is pure villainy. It is these preconceptions of the Moor that make Othello work so effectively. By the end of the play Othello has been deprived of everything his mythical 'Moorishness' implied. He has taken on Christian virtues and become the leader of Christendom against the Turks. Conversely Iago has become the personification of evil usually reserved for the Moor.

This utilization of foreigners because of their role in God's providence applies especially to the Jews. Sixteenth-century anti-semitism was religious rather than racial. In June 1594 Dr Roderigo Lopez, a Jewish physician, was hanged, drawn and quartered for attempting to poison the Queen. This increased the public interest in Marlowe's *Jew of Malta*, which was first performed in 1592, but was put on 15 times in 1594. Shakespeare probably wrote The Merchant of Venice to capitalise on the excitement caused by the Lopez trial. A great deal has been written about the crude anti-semitism behind Marlowe's Barabas and the more subtle characterization of Shakespeare's dignified tyrant, Shylock. Frances Yates wondered why there was such strong feeling against Jews when there was so little direct connection with them and speculated that the government might have been planning to re-admit them into England.[25] This explanation is plausible, but not necessary. The Jews were well enough known by their role in Christian mythology as the murderers of Christ. The key to the religious interpretation of the Jews is in the daughters, who are not automatically condemned because of their race. Shylock's daughter deserts both her father and her faith, so is allowed a happy ending with a Christian husband. Abigail also deserts her father, Barabas, albeit with greater reluctance and ends up in a Christian convent.

The Jewish stereotype could be put to a variety of uses. The ballad, *Gernutus, Merchant of Venice*, used the same 'pound of flesh' story as Shakespeare as a way of warning against the outcome of greed. The central character was a 'cruel Jew' who could not sleep for fear of being robbed and who schemed to deceive the poor. The moral in the final verse was a religious one:

> Frome whome the Lord deliver me,
> And every Christian too,
> And send them like sentence eke
> That meaneth so to do.[26]

In the play Three Ladies of London, (1581) Wilson used the image of the Jew to dramatise the saying 'worse than a Jew'. Mercatore, the Christian merchant tries to cheat Gernutus, the Jew. When they meet in Turkey Mercatore tries to get out of his debt by becoming a Turk. Gernutus is so horrified by this betrayal of religious birthright that he cancels the debt rather than let the conversion happen.

One of the commonest national stereotypes in both fact and fiction was the Flemish drunkard. The view was a traditional one. *The Libel of English Policy* of 1436 had a lot to say about the habits of foreigners and included the following:

> Ye have herde that two fflemynges togedere
> Wol undertake, or they goo any whethere,
> Or they rise onys, to drinke a barrelle fulle
> Of goode berkyne. So sore they hale and pulle,
> Undre the borde they pisses, as they sitte:[27]

Andrew Borde seems to have had a similar impression. He opened the section on Flanders in his Introduction with:

> I am a Flemyng, what for all that,
> Although I wyll be drunken other whyles as a rat?

He makes a distinction between the habits of the Dutch and the Germans.

> I am a base Doche man, borne in the Netherlands;
> Diverse times I am so cupshoten, on my feet I cannot stand;
> My reason is suche, I can not speke a word;
> Than am I tonge tayed, my feete doth me fayle,
> And then I am harnesyed in a cote of mayle;
> Then wyl I pysse in my fellowes shoes and hose.

The people of Bonn, on the other hand, did not use the floor: 'they will have in diverse places a tub or a great vessell standyng under the bord to pusse in,'[28]

In fiction, Dutch characters were usually drunk, with names like Hans van Belch in Dekker and Webster's Northwood Ho! (1605). Why was this image so popular? Hunter suggests it was derived from familiarity with the Dutch: 'It seems as if the Dutch were too close to the eyes of the English beholders for anything more than detailed idiosyncrasies to be observable.'[29] A further explanation could be that the English writers saw a lot of their fellow countrymen in the Dutch reputation of drunkenness and wanted to distance themselves from it. In Pierce Peniless (1592), Nashe refers to the Danes as 'bursten-bellied sots, that are to be confuted with tankards and quart pots . . . they have no ears but their own mouths, no sense but of that which they swallow down their mouths'. But he later admits that the English have a similar fault: 'It is not for nothing that other countries, whom we upbraid with drunkenness call us bursten bellied gluttons; for we make our greedy paunches powdering tubs of beef, and eat more meat in one meal than the Spaniards or Italians in a month.[30] The stereotype of the drunken Englishman is presented by Shakespeare in Othello. There is an exchange between Iago and Cassio where the former sings a drinking song then explains: 'I learned it in England where they are indeed most potent in potting: your Dane, your German and your swagbellied Hollander, – Drink, ho! are nothing to your English'. When Cassio asks if the English are expert drinkers he gets the following reply: 'Why he drinks with facility your Dane dead drunk; he sweats not to overthrow your Almain; he gives your Hollander a vomit ere the next pottle can be filled.'[31] To the Englishmen in the audience this would be praise indeed!

The English writers were prepared to identify their own countrymen with the reputation for gluttony of the Dutch and Germans, but they related strange stories concerning the nationalities with which they were less familiar – such as the Icelandic partiality for candles. Borde wrote in his Introduction ' They (natives of Iceland) wyll eate talowe candells, and candells endes, and olde greece, and restye tallowe and other fylthy things'.[32] Harrison tells of how, when a great man from Iceland 'came of late into one of our ships which went thither for fish, to see the form and fashion of the same, his wife apparelled in fine sables, abiding in the decks whilst her husband was under the hatches with the mariners, espied a pound or two of candeles hanging at the mast, and being loth to stand their idle alone, she fell to and eat them up every one, supposing herself to have been at a jolly banket'.[33]

An unlikely source of moral edification came from the Welsh proclivity for toasted cheese. Borde refers to this addiction and the image was a popular one in literature. There is a story in A Hundred Merry Talys which was first printed by John Rastell in 1526 that one day God had been in a tolerant mood and had let too many Welshmen into heaven. As they were driving the other inhabitants to distraction with their constant chatter, God made St Peter responsible for getting rid of them. Peter reckoned it would be an easy problem to solve – all he had to do was to go to the gates of heaven, shout 'toasted cheese', all the Welshmen would run out and he would be able to shut the door behind them.[34] The story had a cautionary intent, the moral being that if people were overfond of earthly pleasures they would lose eternal salvation, and was not meant to be a hostile caricature.

'Welshness' was put to comic effect in The Merry Wives of Windsor, through the character of Sir Hugh Evans. Much of the entertainment comes from his portrayal as a typical pedagogic parson and he was made Welsh so that his long-windedness could be exaggerated. Again, the cheese makes an appearance. In the final scene when Falstaff realises that Evans is dressed as a fairy his response is 'Heavens defend me, lest he transform me into a piece of cheese,' and later:

> Have I laid my brain in the sun and dried it, that it wants matter to prevent such gross over-reaching as this? Am I ridden with a Welsh goat too? shall I have a coxcomb of frize? 'Tis time I were choked with toasted cheese.

This leads to an exchange which uses language as a source of amusement:

> Evans: Seese is not good putter; your pelly is all putter.
> Falstaff: 'seese' and 'putter'? Have I lived to stand of one must make fritters of English? This is enough to be the decay of lust and of late walking through the realm.

[Act V, sc v, 137-149]

Shakespeare was fond of amusing his audience with the pomposity of language, as with Don Armado in Love's Labour's Lost. He is the person we all recognise – the foolish pedant who is over-fond of his own voice and oblivious to the ridicule to which he is constantly subjected. This figure of fun is a Spaniard, but there is not implication that he is typically Spanish. He shares his scenes with the schoolmaster, Holofernes, who is ridiculed for repeating everything he says in Latin.[35] Shakespeare was scathing towards anyone who misused language, as did Polonius in Hamlet, whatever their nationality.

Shakespeare is able to derive humour from the English perception of the French language in a variety of ways. In Henry V there is a comic scene based on misunderstanding. Pistol takes a French soldier, when asked his name, replies 'O Seigner Dieu!', whereupon Pistol assumes he is talking to a Signieur Dew. The soldier begs for mercy – 'avez pitie moi' and Pistol replies:

> Moy shall not serve: I shall have forty moys
> Or I will fetch thy rim out at they throat.
> In crimson drops of blood.

[Act IV, sc iv, 12-14]

In The Merry Wives of Windsor, the Frenchman Dr Caius, raises a laugh by his broken English and foreign mannerisms. In the following exchange the humour comes from the host deliberately using words a foreigner would not understand; it is the idiomatic nature of language which makes the joke possible:

> Host: A word, Monseur Mock-water.
> Caius: Mock-vater! vat is dat?
> Host: Mock-water, in our English tongue, is valour, bully.
> Caius: By gar, den, I have as much mock-water as de Englishman.

> Scurvy Jack-dog priest! by gar, me vill cut his ears.
> Host: He will clapper-claw thee tightly bully.
> Caius: Clapper – de – claw! vat is that?
> Host: That is he will make thee amends.
> Caius: By gar, me do look he shall clapper – de-claw me;
>    By gar, me will have it.
>
> [Act II, sc iii, 65-74]

The opportunity for puns in two languages was too good to miss as Princess Katherine of France learns English from her maid, Alice, in Henry V.[36] Katherine discusses the name for various parts of her body. The first laugh comes from her mispronunciation of elbow. The humour takes a more sinister turn as neck becomes Nick (the devil) and chin becomes sin; and becomes more risky as Katherine ask what is the English for 'le robe'. The reply 'de foot' and 'de coun' – Alice's version of 'gown', sound to Katherine like the French 'foutre' and 'con'; she goes on to say that English was not fit to be repeated by polite French ladies in front of French gentlemen, in case any of the audience had missed the point of the double-entendres. One would imagine the audience would enjoy the dirty joke rather than ponder the significance of Shakespeare's subconscious 'queasiness before female sexuality' as some modern critics are prone to do.[37]

Language has a more romantic purpose in the final scene between Henry and Katherine. Henry is glad she does not understand him or she would be aware of the simplicity of his language. He modestly contrasts his own plain soldier's speech, which represents constancy, with that of 'these fellows of infinite tongue, that can rhyme themselves into ladies favour, they do always reason themselves out again'. As the scene progresses language differences, rather than being a barrier between them, become the focal point of the courtship.[38]

Language is a barrier to communication between lovers in I Henry IV. Glendower's daughter is married to Mortimer. In a farewell scene he regrets that they have no common language as she speaks only Welsh, but adds that tears and kisses make talking unnecessary:

> I understand they looks: that pretty Welsh
> Which though pourest down from these swelling heavens
> I am too perfect in; and but for shame,
> In such a parley should I answer thee.

There followed a compliment to the beauty of the Welsh language: Mortimer says he would like to be able to speak Welsh as her tongue:

> Makes Welsh as sweet as ditties highly penn'd,
>    Sung by a fair Queen in a summer's bower,
>    With revishing division to her lute.
>
> [Act III, sc i, 198-202]

Kyd uses language to symbolise confusion in The Spanish Tragedy (1588). The climax comes when Hieronimo is to avenge his son's death during a play to be performed by the leading characters. Hieronimo explains that the play is to be acted in different languages and as the scene ends he links this with the

chaos he hopes to create (Act IV, sc i). At the end of the play he asks for a
return to their vulgar tongue which represents the return to reality. The device
of a play within a play, during which Hieronimo kills his enemies, is used to
emphasise the formalities of the tragic convention, and language is a device
to differentiate the two tiers of unreality.

Occasionally language was associated with patriotism. In Richard II
Mobray's reaction to his exile shows that he linked banishment from his
native land with loss of his native language:

> The language I have learn'd these forty years,
> My native English, now I must forego:
> And now my tongue's use is to me no more
> Than an unstringed viol or a harp;
> Or like a cunning instrument cased up,
> Or being open, put into his hands
> That knows no touch to tune the harmony.
>
> Act I, sc iii

But on the whole Elizabethan dramatists were fascinated with language as
a source of humour and a facet of communication rather than as a badge of
nationality.[39]

Literary representations of foreigners had little connection with official
diplomatic relations with their countries. In the 1520s there had been isolated
examples of entertainments produced for specific occasions which portrayed
individual foreigners in a bad or good light depending on the circumstances.
A play put on for Charles V's visit to England in 1522 has been described by
Hall.[40] A group of allegorical figures – Friendship, Prudence and Might –
tamed a wild horse, Francis I of France. A few years later Henry VIII had
been let down by the Emperor, so was looking for friendship with France. In
1527, John Ritwise and the children of St Paul's performed a Latin play for
Henry and the French ambassador, which was hostile to Charles and the
Spaniards. Wolsey, the hero of the play, united England and France against
the enemies of the Church, humiliating Charles and freeing Francis' sons.[41]
Later in the sixteenth century, however, when dramatists were writing for a
wider audience, they could not be relied upon to tow the government line.
There were complaints from the Spaniards in the early part of Elizabeth's
reign at a time when the government was trying to preserve the alliance with
Spain as protection against France and Scotland. The Count of Feria protested
that Burghley was behind efforts of playwrights which offended him.[42] In
1559 the Venetian ambassador seems to have been annoyed at the way Philip
II was being represented on stage,[43] and in 1562, Bishop Quandra sent home
a section of Bale's satire on Philip II as his complaints to the Queen about
'books farces and songs prejudicial to other Princes' were falling on deaf
ears.[44] The patriotic reactions to the defeat of the Armada from dramatists
and ballad writers, tended not to make any difference to the stereotype of the
Spaniard. Shakespeare's history plays were popular in the 1590s because

England was at war with Spain and the audience wanted to be reminded of past glories or warned against repeating past mistakes. The French, the opponents at the time the plays were set, could represent the national enemy as easily as the Spaniards.

Writers did seem to be more aware of political realities in their fictional representations of the Scots. In *Henry V*, Shakespeare included a scene built round the tradition of the Scots taking advantage of the English kings' absences in France. During a discussion of his plans to invade France, Henry brings up the subject of what to do about the Scots. In response to Canterbury's suggestion that the people of the Marches can cope with a few 'pilfering borderers', Henry points out that the problem could be more serious:

> We do not mean the coursing snatches only,
> But fear the main intendment of the Scot,
> Who hath been still a giddy neighbour to us;
> For you shall read that my great-grandfather
> Never went with his forces into France,
> But that the Scot on his unfurnished kingdom
> Came pouring like the tide into the breach.
>
> Act I, sc ii 136-42

Westmorland agrees and gives a graphic description of the relationship with the Scots:

> For once the eagle England being in prey,
> To her unguarded nest the weasel Scot
> Comes sneaking and so sucks her princely eggs,
> Playing the mouse in the absence of the cat,
> To tear and havoc more than she can eat.
>
> Act I, sc ii 162-6

Henry was referring to August 1346 when David, King of Scotland had launched a diversion in the North of England to help his French ally while Edward III was fighting the Battle of Crecy. Shakespeare's audience would be aware of a more recent example of the Scottish 'mouse' taking advantage of the absence of the English 'cat'. James IV had invaded England in 1513, when Henry VIII had been attracted to the idea of spending August in France. Shakespeare's portrayal of individual Scotsmen, however, is not hostile. In *I Henry IV*, it suited Shakespeare's purpose for the Earl of Douglas to be valiant and honourable. After all, there was no prestige to be had from defeating a weak and cowardly enemy. He is referred to as 'the brave Douglas' and his forces as 'Ten thousand bold Scots' in order to increase the impact of Hotspur's victory over them. When Hotspur is driven to rebel, he turns to his former enemy who had to have been a worthy adversary for this to be plausible. Later, Prince Henry can show the merciful side of his character by the way he treats Douglas after defeating him:

> Go to Douglas and deliver him
> Up to his pleasure, ransomless and free:
> His valour shown upon her crests today

Hath taught us how to cherish such high deeds
Even in the bosom of our adversaries.
                              [I Henry IV, Act V, sc v 28-32]

In the 1580s, some writers responded to the fact that Scotland was no longer the national enemy in a way that did not happen in attitudes towards the French. James VI was a Protestant and a possible heir to the English throne and these factors were more important than his nationality. William Elderton invented a typical Englishman, Brown, to protect the young Scottish King against a variety of plots; such as in the 1581 ballad entitled *Declaring the great treason conspired against the young King of Scots, and how one Andrew Browne, an Englishman who was the king's Chamberlaine, prevented the same*. Three ballads showed a sympathetic interest in James' marriage and one in the birth of his eldest son.[45]

Shakespeare also responded to changes in relations with Scotland. The scene in Henry V which introduced the Scotsman, Captain Jamy, together with the Irish Captain Macmorris and the Welshman, Fluellen was introduced for comic relief rather than to further the plot; it was common practice for dramatists to bring on the foreigners when they wanted to lighten the tone. But the scene may have had an additional purpose. It is possible that it was added for a performance at court in 1605 and that the sympathetic treatment of Jamy was designed to offset any offence James might have taken by earlier references to his fellow countrymen. Philip Edwards assumed that the scene was in the original play but was dropped in the 1600 folio as 'Captain Jamy' was seen as an insult to James VI of Scotland.[46] This is unlikely. Jamy is a more sympathetic character than the other captains and in 1600 James' succession, although probable, was neither inevitable nor imminent.

The scene has received much attention recently and it is taken more seriously than, perhaps it deserves.[47] Lisa Jardine reads the exchange between the captains as symbolic of disunity between England, Ireland, Scotland and Wales:

United English troops deconstruct themselves into an Englishman, an Irishman, a Welshman and a Scot, distinct in their speech, attitude and interests, and at loggerheads, uncovering the fiction of a 'pure' English nation, and provoking the passionate cry from the Irish Macmorris 'What ish my nation?'[48]

Curtis Breight's account of abuse and repression in the English army was referred to above.[49] He too takes the characters seriously. His reference to 'four useless captains' reflects his own agenda, which is to search out and expose corruption wherever it occurs! He is correct to point out that:

Shakespeare's audience would have viewed these men not as an example of 'British solidarity' – an anachronism – but as the kind of cowardly captains so prevalent in contemporary culture and discourse.[50]

Philip Edwards appears not to have noticed the flaws in the captains' characters, referring to Fluellen and MacMorris as 'fine hard working devoted soldiers.'[51] Edward's theme was the 'interactions between drama and nationality in Shakespeare's England and Yeats's Ireland.'[52] He therefore deals in some detail with an exchange between Fluellen and MacMorris. The latter is portrayed as a man of action while the former, true to his stereotype as a 'Welsh windbag' wants to talk tactics, proposing 'a few disputations...as partly touching or concerning the discipline of war.'

> Fluellen: Captain Macmorris, I think look you, under our correction, there is not many of your nation. . . .
> Macmorris: Of my nation? What ish my nation? Ish a villain and a bastard and a knave, and a rascal.. What ish my nation? Who talks of my nation?

According to Edwards, Macmorris is flying off the handle at the discrimination shown by Fluellen in using the phrase 'your nation'. He paraphrases what Macmorris meant as follows:

> What is this separate race you're implying by using the phrase 'your nation'? Who are you, a Welshman to talk of the Irish as though they were a separate nation from you? I belong to this family as much as you do.[53]

Because his theme is the inauguration of Great Britain and the conquest of Ireland, Philips reads Shakespeare teleologically giving Macmorris a sensitivity to his country of origin that Shakespeare may not have intended.[54] The word 'nation' was conceivably used here in the way Ascham used it to refer to a 'nation of scholars'.[55] He could have been asking 'what community are you suggesting I belong to – a confederacy of villains, perhaps or an association of rascals?' Many editions of Henry V, also based on the 1623 Folio, have the phrases in a different order so the response reads: 'What ish my nation? Who talks of my nation is a villain, and a bastard and a knave and a rascal.' In this case Macmorris is being aggressive and insulting towards Fluellen, rather than over-sensitive about his 'nation'. Edwards resents the comedy in the scene as a sign of English superiority and condescension towards the Welsh and Irish.[56] It is likely, however, that for Shakespeare and his audience the comedy was the main purpose of the scene.

Foreigners from outside the British Isles were differentiated by class and status, or by religion, rather than on the basis of ethnic origin. For example, George Gascoigne was a witness to the sack of Antwerp by Spanish soldiers in 1576 and wrote of his experiences. He was critical of the common soldiers, but not of all Spaniards. In fact he was at pains to point out in his preface that he did not blame Philip II:

> These outrages and disordered cruelties done to our nation proceeded but from the common soldiers: neither was there any of the twelve which entered the English house, a man of any charge or reputation.

He hoped that Philip would offer compensation for any damage done and that he and Elizabeth would remain friends.[57]

Protestants emphasised their Anglo-Saxon origins, claiming to be returning to the pure early church before it was contaminated by the Normans. This approach affected their attitude to contemporary Frenchmen. John Aylmer was a Marian exile who became Bishop of London under Elizabeth. Writing in Switzerland in

1556 he was hostile to the 'effeminate Frenchmen: Stoute in bragge, but noting in deede', and would not admit that the French had made any positive contribution to English culture: 'We have a few hunting terms and peddlars French in the louyse lawe, brought in by the Normans, yet remaining: But the language and customs be Englishe and Saxonyshe'.[58] The attitude towards Spaniards in Mary's reign depended on religious sympathies, not nationalist prejudices. The Protestant, John Bradford, printed a letter addressed to 'various noble lords declaring the nature of the Spaniards and discovering the most detestable treasons, which they have pretended most falsely againste our moste noble Kyngdome of England.' He printed a ballad with the letter entitled *a tragicall blast on the Papisticall trompet for maintenaunce of the Pope's kingdome in England*, which had the Pope exhorting Catholics against England. Each verse ended:

> Now al shaven crownes to the standerd
> Make roome, pul down for the Spaniard.

But the prospect of a Spanish King and a half-Spanish heir (or, more accurately, three-quarters Spanish) was welcomed by the Catholics. When Mary was thought to be pregnant in 1555, *A ballad of Joy upon the publication of Queen Mary, Wife of King Philip, her being with child*, welcomed the news:

> How manie good people were long in dispaire,
> That this letel England shold lack a right heire:
> But now the swet marigold sprineth so fayre,
> That England triumpheth without anie care.[59]

In literature, the representation of Spaniards could be affected if the antagonists were Christians and the Infidel. The bravery of the Spaniards was praised if they were enemies of the Turks. In this polarization the dramatists were responding to the popular rather than the official perception. In 1571, a combined Christian fleet, let by Don John of Austria, Philip II's half brother, defeated the Turkish fleet at Lepanto. By this time England's relations with Spain were already deteriorating. The Spanish ambassador had been expelled for his part in the Ridolfi plot earlier in the same year. The plot in turn had been encouraged by the Pope's excommunication of Elizabeth in the previous year. Lepanto was, therefore, a victory for England's enemies. Yet it was welcomed in England as a triumph for Christendom. Holinshed tells of a sermon preached in London by William Foulks of Cambridge 'to give thanks to almighty God for the victorie, which of his mercifull clemencie it had pleased him to grant to the Christians in the Levant seas against the common enemies of our faith, the Turks,' and describes the celebrations held because the defeat of the Turks was so important for the Christian Commonwealth'.[60] In general the Turks were portrayed as being outside the laws of Christendom and the expression 'to turn Turk' was used to mean to betray one's baptism.[61] In Richard III, when Buckingham is trying to persuade the audience of his and Richard's good intentions he says:

> What think you we are Turks or Infidels?
> Or that we would, against the form of law
> proceed thus rashly. . . ?

>                    [Act III, sc v, 41-3]

Richard's downfall is, in fact, brought about because of his disregard for the law, so the association with the Turks was an additional condemnation.

Even when England was at war with Spain after 1585, dramatists did not feel obliged to present a hostile view of the Spaniards. This can be illustrated by an examination of Thomas Kyd's plays, *The First Part of Hieronimo* written between 1585 and 1587, and *The Spanish Tragedy*,[62] first performed in 1588. The Senecan model on which the plays were based required two countries recently at war, with the one owing tribute to the other. Spain and Portugal fitted the bill. It is possible to take the odd line out of context to indicate anti-Spanish feeling[63] such as when Balthazar, son of the King of Portugal, makes a rousing speech before the fight:

> Let all the tribute that proud Spain receiv'd
> Of all those captive Portugales deceased
> Turn into chafe, and choke thri insolence.
>
> [Sc x, 6-8]
>
> Your country's reputation, your lives' freedom,
> Indeed your all that may be termed revenge,
> Now let your bloods be liberal as the sea;
> And all those wounds that you receive of Spain,
> Let theirs be equal to quit yours again.
>
> [12-17]

But this is admiration for patriotism in general and the audience is not encouraged to associate it with one country in particular. The play's main theme is the honour of war and equal praise is given to the valiant on both sides. There is an exchange between Balthazar and Andrea, the Spaniard who is the play's hero, as they prepare to fight, which is designed to show that they are both equal and worthy combatants, after which Alexandro butts in with the comment 'My liege, two nobler spirits never met' (Sc iv). In scene ten nobles on both sides are challenging their opponents, in preparation for the battle. Andrea comments:

> Can we be foes, and all so well agreed?

to which Balthazar replies:

> Why, man, in war there's bleeding amity;
> And he this day gives me the deepest wound,
> I'll call him brother.
>
> [Sc x, 99-102]

There were also dishonourable characters of both nationalities. While Andrea was away the Spaniard, Lorenzo plotted to kill him and seduce his lover, Bel-imperia. Andrea was eventually killed by Portuguese soldiers. The avenging of Andrea's death is the theme of *The Spanish Tragedy*. Again there is no hostility in the portrayal of either the Spaniards or the Portuguese. The action takes place after the conflict between the two countries and both sides show excessive honour in the treatment of, and friendship towards their former enemies; much to the disgust of Andrea's ghost, who urges them to get on with the revenge (Act I, sc vi). The play was first performed in 1588,

so some patriotism was called for, but this took the form of praise for past
English successes and was not xenophobic. Hieronimo, Andrea's father, put
on a masque where three English knights were represented:

The first knight:

> Was English Robert, Earl of Gloucester,
> Who, when King Stephen bore sway in Albion,
> Arrived with five and twenty thousand men
> In Portugal, and by success of war
> Enfor'd the king, then but a Saracen,
> To bear the yoke of English monarchy
>
> Act I, sc. v, 26-31

The second:

> Was Edmond, Earl of Kent in Albion,
> When English Richard wore a diadem.
> He came likewise, and razed Lisbon walls,
> And took the King of Portingal in fight.
>
> 37-40

The third:

> Was, as the rest, a valiant Englishman,
> Brave John of Gaunt, the Duke of Lancaster,
> As by his scutcheon plainly may appear.
> He with a puissant army came to Spain,
> And took our King of Castile prisoner.
>
> 48-52

The scene was superfluous to the plot and must have been contrived in
response to the public interest in English exploits.

If one is looking for hostility to foreigners based on real experiences one
must turn to resentment on economic grounds rather than diplomacy. In times
of economic difficulty it is always the outsider who becomes the scapegoat.
In the May Day riots of 1517, 2,000 apprentices had sacked the houses of
French and Flemish artificers and insulted Florentine and Genoese merchants.
The riots were sparked off by a preacher who alleged that 'strangers not only
deprived the English of their industry and profits arising therefrom but
dishonoured their dwellings by taking their wives and daughters.[64] These
events fired the imagination of later writers as in the ballad *The Story of Ill
May Day*[65] and the play *Sir Thomas More*.[66]

The collapse of the over-expanded wool industry in 1551 led to economic
distress, the impact of which was still apparent in the beginning of Elizabeth's
reign. In the mid to late 1560s, Spanish oppression in the Netherlands meant
that further trade disruption coincided with increased immigration of Flemish
craftsmen who were fleeing from religious persecution. Criticisms of foreigners
living and working in England were many and varied in early Elizabethan
drama. William Wager in *Enough is as good as a feast*, George Wapull in *The
Tide Tarrieth for no man* and Thomas Lupton in *All for Money* blamed aliens
for inflated rents and resulting eviction of Englishmen. They tended to blame

the greed of the landlords rather than the aliens themselves. For example, in *Enough* a character complains (in a Somerset accent):

> And they are no zo covetoue to ask nother, ich beleeve,
> But a zort of volles are ready to give;
> And espetially straungers, ye, a shameful zort,
> Are placed now in England, and in every port,
> That we, our wives and children, no houses can get
> Wherein we may live, such price on them is zet.[67]

Similarly in *Tide Tarrieth:*

> For among us now, such is our contry zeal,
> That we live best with strangers to deal.
> To sell a lease dear, whosoever that will,
> At the French or Dutch church let him set up his bill
> And he shall have chapmen, I warrent you good store,
> Look what an Englishman bids, they will give as much more.[68]

The anonymous play *The Pedlar's Prophecy* was a general critique of the ills of English society, which defended the church and the Queen, but attacked the upper classes for allowing problems to arise. The problems outlined included rising prices, rents and evictions caused by foreigners. The play also warned against the dangers of a mixed population:

> Tree parts of London are alreadie Alians,
> Other mongrels. Alians children, michieuously mixed,
> And that with the most detestable Barbarians,
> Which there forever hatht their dwellings fixed:
> Still you mariners bring them in daily. . . .
> Ye shall see them one day play their parts gaily,
> When ye think least, they shall cut their throats.[69]

Resentment of alien workers was also prevalent during the economic crisis of the 1590s. Thomas Deloney had been a silk weaver before turning ballad and pamphlet writer. His pamphlet of 1595, *Complaint of the Yeoman Weavers against the Immigrant Weavers*, discussed the problems faced by the weavers of Norwich as they tried to compete with foreign craftsmen who would not respect price and practice agreements. The pamphlet was distributed to the aliens and copies sent to the aldermen and the Lord Mayor, as a result of which Deloney and eleven others spent some time in Newgate prison.

At the point where patriotism degenerates into nationalism, perception of foreigners becomes hostile and racist. This did not happen in sixteenth-century literature. Writers showed an ambivalent attitude to foreign travel, as poets and dramatists contrasted the educational benefits with the danger of contamination by 'unEnglish' ideas, modes of speech or dress. There was also uncertainty as to the influence that foreign visitors or residents would have on the English people. But the debates were conducted in moral rather than nationalistic tones. 'Abroad' was used allegorically to represent the strange or the unknown and the desire for travel to represent dissatisfaction with one's allotted role in society.

National stereotypes had a significant place in sixteenth-century literature. Generalizations made by travel writers fed upon and fuelled traditional images – the proud Spaniard, the drunken Dutchman, the 'cheese-mad' Welshman. As these images were immediately recognisable by the audiences, they could be used as allegorical morality figures or for comic effect. One could argue that it is a short step from poking fun at a foreigner because of his speech to indulging in hate-inspiring ridicule, but this step had not been taken in the sixteenth century.

In some instances characterisation moved away from the stereotypical to a more realistic representation of foreigners. With the possible exception of the Scots, diplomatic circumstances had little direct influence and religion was more important than race in determining attitudes. The traditional polarization of Christian against Infidel survived alongside the newer antagonism of Protestant against Catholic. It is in the economic sphere that the beginnings of the hostility to foreigners, which is a component of nationalism, can be discerned. Immigrants were disliked for taking jobs and accommodation and for working for low wages. Nascent racism was apparent as some dramatists complained about 'mongrelization'.

## Notes

1. John Stubbe, *The Discovery of a Gaping Gulf where unto England is likely to be swallowed by another French Marriage if the Lord Forbid not the bans*, 1579.
2. William Maltby, *The Black Legend: The Development of Anti-Spanish Sentiment, 1588-1610*, Durham, North Carolina, 1971.
3. Albert J. Loomie, *The Spanish Elizabethans: The English Exiles at the Court of Philip II*, New York, 1963.
4. See chapter two.
5. Roger Ascham, *The Schoolmaster*, 1570, p. 88.
6. 'The Repentance of Robert Greene', in A.B. Grosart, *The Life and Complete Works of Robert Greene*, 15 vols, 1881, vol XII, p. 172.
7. Fredson Bowers, ed, *The Dramatic Works of Thomas Dekker*, 4 vols., Cambridge, 1953. vol I, p. 122, Act I, sc i, 224.
8. Thomas Nashe, 'The Unfortunate Traveller or the Life of Jack Wilton' 1594, in *Shorter Elizabethan Novels*, Everyman, 1928, pp 321-3 333, 337.
9. Robert Greene, *A Quip for an upstart Courtier: or a Quaint dispute between Velvet Breeches and cloth-breeches*, 1592, sig.B2.
10. William Rankins, *The English Ape, The Italian imitation, the footsteps of France*, 1588.
11. R.B. McKerrow, ed., *The Works of Thomas Nash*, 5 vols, Oxford, 1958, II, p. 141.
12. John Deacon, *Tobacco Tortured, Or, Filthie Fume of Tobacco Refined*, 1616, pp 6-10.
13. 'A Delicate Dyet for Droonkards', 1576, J.W. Cunliffe, ed, *George Gascoigne's Complete Works*, 2 vols, Cambridge, 1907-1910, vol I, p. 466.
14. J.J. Jusserand, *The English Novel in the Time of Shakespeare*, 1966, p. 733, where Lyly's comment is cited as an example of a denunciation of foreign travel.

15. For information on the numbers of immigrants see C.K. Hunter, 'Elizabethans and Foreigners', *Shakespeare Survey,* 1964, vol 17 p. 45. cf. W. Cunningham, *Alien Immigrants to England,* 1897.

16. See chapter three.

17. F.J. Furnivall, ed *The First Booke of the Introduction of Knowledge made by Andrew Borde,* Early English Text Society, 1870, pp 119, 118, 120.

18. Fynes Moryson, *Itinerary, containing his ten years travel,* 1617.

19. G.H. Hair, ed *Thomas Wilson's Art of Rhetoric,* Oxford, 1909, pp 178 ff.

20. Both published in Henry Ellis, ed *Raphael Holinshed's Chronicles,* 6 vols, 1807-8.

21. Bowers, ed *The Dramatic Works of Thomas Dekker* vol I. 'Sir Thomas Wyatt' was written in collaboration with John Webster.

22. Allan Holaday, ed, *The Plays of George Chapman, The Comedies,* University of Illinois Press 1971.

23. J. Roberts, ed, *A Collection of Old Ballads,* 3 vols, 1723, vol I, pp 103-7.

24. C.K. Hunter, 'Othello and Colour Prejudice' *Dramatic Identities and Cultural Tradition,* Liverpool, 1978, pp 31-59.

25. Frances A. Yates, *The Occult Philosophy in the Elizabethan Age,* 1979, p. 119.

26. *The Pepys Ballads,* vol VIII, p. 45.

27. T. Wright, *Political Songs,* vol II, p. 169.

28. Borde, op. cit., pp 147, 155-156.

29. Hunter, op. cit., p. 45.

30. J.B. Steane, ed *Thomas Nashe's The Unfortunate Traveller and Other Woks,* 1971, pp 77, 99.

31. Act II, sc iii.

32. Borde, op. cit., p. 142.

33. William Harrison, 'Description of Britain', published with the second edition of *Holinshed's Chronicles,* book iii, chpt 7, p. 321.

34. Borde, op. cit., p. 126, Oesterley, ed, *A Hundred Merry Talys,* 1866, p. 131. First printed by Rastell, 1526.

35. Act IV, sc ii and Act V, sci.

36. Act III, sc 1

37. Leslie A. Fiedler, *The Stranger in Shakespeare,* 1972, p. 45.

38. Act V sc ii.

39. See chapter three.

40. Edward Hall, *The Union of Two Noble and Illustrie Families of Lancaster and York,* 1550, lxxxxviii-lxxxxix. cf a letter from Martin se Salinas, ambassador of Archduke Ferdinand, who accompanied Charles, in G.A. Bergenroth et al, eds, *Calender of Letters, Dispatches and State Papers, Relating to the negotiations between England and Spain,* 1862, vol II, 1509-1525, pp444-445.

41. Referred to in David Bevington, *Tudor Drama and Politics: A Critical Approach to Topical Meaning,* Cambridge, Mass, 1968, p. 127.

42. *Cal. S.P., Sp. ,* NSI, 1558-67, p. 62.

43. *Ven. Cal,* vol VIII, pp 80-1.

44. *Cal. S. P., Sp,* NSI, (1558-67) p. 247.

45. C.H. Firth, 'The Ballad History of the Later Tudors' *Transactions of the Royal Historical Society,* Third Series, vol III, 1909, pp 100, 111.

46. Philip Edwards, *Threshold of a Nation: A Study in English and Irish Drama,* Cambridge, 1979.

47. Of the many discussions of the lines surrounding Macmorris's question 'What

ish my nation?', David Baker's is the only one to point out that the lines do not actually make sense, David J. Baker, *Between Nations: Shakespeare, Spenser and Marvell and the Question of Britain*, Stanford, 1997 p39.

48. Lisa Jardine, *Reading Shakespeare Historically*, 1996, p. 14. cf Andrew Murphy, *But the Irish Sea Betwixt Us: Ireland, Colonialism and Renaissance Literature*, Lexington, 1999, pp 118,120.

49. See chapter one.

50. Curtis Breight, *Militarism, Surveillance and Drama*, 1996, p. 222.

51. Edward, op. cit., p74.

52. ibid p. 1.

53. ibid p. 75.

54. Edwards' approach has been admired and followed by a number of writers e.g. Alan Sinfield, *Faultlines: Cultural Materialism and the Politics of Dissident Reading*, Oxford, 1992, p. 125. (the chapter was co-written with Jonathan Dolimore).

55. See chapter one.

56. Edwards op. cit. p. 75.

57. Gascoigne, op. cit., vol II p. 589.

58. A. MacDougall, *Racial Myth in English History*, New England, 1982, p37.

59. Firth, op. cit., p. 66.

60. *Holinshed's Chronicle*, vol IV, p. 262.

61. *Hamlet*, Act III, sc ii, 287; *Much Ado About Nothing*, Act III, sc iv, 57.

62. Andrew S. Cairncross, ed *Thomas Kyd's The First Part of Hieronimo and the Spanish Tragedy*, 1967.

63. R.U. Lindabury, *A Study of Patriotism in Elizabethan Drama*, Oxford, 1931, p. 201.

64. *Ven. Cal.*, vol II, p. 382.

65. 'The Story of Ill May Day' in W. Chappell, ed, *Johnson's Crown Garland of Golden Roses*, part ii, Percy Society, 1845, p. 39.

66. The original play, *Sir Thomas More*, written by Anthony Munday, was refused a licence. The play was then rewritten by a group of five dramatists.

67. Seymour de Ricci, ed, *William Wager's Enough is as Good as a Feast*, Huntington Facsimile Reprints, New York, 1920, E.

68. Ernst Ruhl, ed, *George Wapull's The Tide Tarrieth for no Man*, 1907, pp 496-501.

69. *The Pedler's Prophecy*, anon, 1561, Malone Society Reprints, 1907. The Play was published anonymously but has been attributed to Robert Wilson on internal evidence. Pettegree has pointed out that the dramatists of the day expressed the same grievances as were more commonly put forward in the formal petitions against the activities of foreigners in London such as over-crowding and rent increases; Andrew Pettegree, *Foreign Protestant Communities in Sixteenth Century London*, Oxford, 1986, pp 282 ff.

# BIBLIOGRAPHY

## Contemporary Sources

*Acts of the Privy Council of England*, ed. J.R. Dasent, 32 vols. 1890-1907

Allen, William, *A True Sincere and Modest Defence of English Catholics*, ed Robert M. Kingdom, New York, 1965

*An admonition to the people of England and Ireland concerning the Present Warres*

Ascham, Roger, *Toxophilus*, 1545

*The Schoolmaster*, 1570 Cassell's National Library, 1888

Bale, John *Select Works of John Bale*, ed H. Christmas, Parker Soc., 1849

*New Years Gift*, ed W.A. Copinger (privately printed in Manchester), 1895

Baker, George, trans., *Conrad Gesner's The Newe Jewell of Healthe*, 1576

Becon, Thomas, *An Humble Supplication to God*, Strasburg, 1554

*A Comfortable Epistle to God's faithful People in England*, Strasburg, 1554

'The Policy of War' in *Early Works*, ed, J. Ayre, Parker Soc., 1843

Best, George, *A True Discourse of the Late Voyages of Discovery*, 1578

Betham, Peter, trans, *The Precepts of Warre*, 1544

Billingsly, Henry, trans, *Euclids Elements of Geometrie*, 1570

Bilson, Thomas, *The True Difference between Christian Subjection and Unchristian Rebellion*, 1585

Borde, Andrew, *The First Boke of the Introduction of Knowledge made by Andrew Borde* and *The Brevery of Health*, 1547. ed F.J. Furnivall, E.E.T.S., 1870

Breight, Curtis C., *Surveillance, Militarism and Drama in the Elizabethan Era*, 1996

Brende, John, trans, *Quintius Curtius, Historie of the Acts of the Great Alexander*, 1553

*Calendar of State Papers, Spanish,* 13 vols 1862-1954 and 4 vols, 1892-9

*Calendar of State Papers, Venetian*, 1862-1954 and 4 vols, 1892-9

*Calendar of State Papers, Venetian*, 1864-98

Camden, William, *The History of the most Renowned and Virtuous Princess Elizabeth, late Queen of England. . . . Composed by way of Annals*, 1610, ed. Thomas Hearne, 3 vols., 1717.

*Britannia*, 1586, ed Richard Gough, 3 vols 1789

Campbell, Lily B., ed, *The Mirror for Magistrates*, Cambridge, 1938

Campden, Hugo of, *Kynge Boccus and Syndrake*, 1530

Caraman, Philip, trans and ed, *William Weston's Autobiography of an Elizabethan*, 1611, 1951

Castiglione, Baldassare, *The Book of the Courtier*, trans, Sir Thomas Hoby, Everyman, 1928

Cecil, William, *The Execution of Justice in England*, ed Robert Kingdon, New York, 1965

Cheke, John, *The Hurt of Sedition*, 1549. In *Holinshed's Chronicles*, iii

*The Gospel according to St Matthew and part of the first chapter of the gospel according to St Mark, translated into English from the Greek original notes by Sir John Cheke*, ed James Goodwin

Cox, Leonard, *Arte or Crafte of Rhetoryke*, 1524

Cranmer, Thomas, *Miscellaneous Writings and Letters of Thomas Cranmer*, ed J.E. Cox, Parker Society, 1846.

Crowley, Robert, *The Select Works of Robert Crowley*, ed J.M. Cowper, E.E.T.S. extra series, XV 1872.

Daniel, Samuel, 'Musophilus: Containing a General Defence of learning' in *The Poetical Essays of Sam. Danyel, Newly Corrected and Augmented*, 1599

Dee, John, *General and rare Memorials pertaining to the Perfect Art of Navigation*, 1577

Dekker, Thomas, 'Wonderful Year', 1603, *The Dramatic Works of Thomas Dekker*, ed. Fredson Bowers, 4 vols Cambridge, 1953

*The Determination of the Most Famous Universities of Italy and France, that it is unlawful for a man to marry his brothers wife and that the Pope has no power to dispence therewith*. Nov. 1531

Doleman, R. (pseudonym for Robert Parsons) *A Conference about the next Succession to the Crowne of England*

Drayton, Michael, *Complete Works*, ed J.W. Hebel, Oxford, 1961

Dudley, Edmund, *The Tree of Commonwealth*, 1509, ed D.M. Brodie, Cambridge, 1948

Eden, R., *A Very Necessarie and Profitable Book Concerning Navigation* 1579

Elyot, Thomas, *Castel of Health*, 1539 trans. Plutarch. *The Governor*, ed S.E. Lehmberg, Everyman, 1962

*Of the Knowledge Which Maketh a Man Wise*, ed E.J. Howard, Oxford, Ohio, 1946.

D'Ewes, Sir Simonds, *A Complete Journal of the Votes, Speeches and debates both of the House of Lords and the House of Commons throughout the whole reign of Queen Elizabeth*, 1693

Fenner, Dudley, *The Artes of Logike and Rhetorike, plainly set forth in the English tongue . . . and for the whole in the resolution or opening of certain parts of Scripture*, 1584

Fox, Edward, *De Vera Differentia*, 1534

Foxe, John, *Acts and Monuments of John Foxe*, 8 vols. ed. Josiah Pratt, 1870

Fraunce, Abraham, *The Archadian Rhetoric: or the Praecepts of Rhetorike made plain by examples, Greeke, Latin, English, Italian, French and Spanish*, 1588

Gardiner, Stephen, ' The Oration of True Obedience' in *Obedience in Church and State, trans and ed P. Janelle*, Cambridge, 1933 *The Letters of Stephen Gardiner*, ed J.A. Muller, Cambridge, 1933

*A Machiavellian Treatise by Stephen Gardiner*, ed P.S. Donaldson, Cambridge 1975

Gascoigne, George, *Compete Works*, ed J.W. Cunliffe, 2 vols, Cambridge 1907-1910

Gee, Henry and Hardy W.J. eds, *Documents Illustrative of Church History*, 1897

Goodman, Christopher, *How Superior Powers Ought to be Obeyed*, 1558, ed Charles H. McIlwain, Facsimile Text Society, New York, 1932

Griffiths, J. ed, *The Two Books of Homilies, Appointed to be read in Churches*, Oxford, 1859

Grosart, A.B., ed, *The Life and Complete Works of Robert Greene*, 15 vols 1881

Hakluyt, Richard, *The Principle Navigations, Voyages and Discoveries of the English Nation, made by sea or land*, 1589, 8 vols Everyman, 1962

Hall, Edward, *Henry VIII*, 1548, ed, C. Whibley, 2 vols 1904

*The Union of the Two Illustrie Families York and Lancaster*, ed Henry Ellis, 1809

Harrison, William, *Description of Britain*, Published with the second edition of *Holinshed's Chronicles*

Hart, John, *An Orthographie*, 1568

Hartwell, Abraham, *A Collection of Voyages and Travells*, 1745

Harvey, Gabriel, 'Pierces Supererogation' in *Archaica*, ed Sir E. Brydges, 1815 II

Hastings, Adrian, *The Construction of Nationhood: Ethnicity, Religion and*

*Nationalism*, Cambridge, 1997

Henry VIII, *The Letters of King Henry VIII,* ed M.St.C. Byrne, 1936

Heywood, Thomas, *An Apology of Actors,* Shakespeare Soc 1841

Holderness, Graham, '"What ish my nation?": Shakespeare and national identities', *Textual Practice*, vol 5, pp 73-93

Holinshed, Raphael, *The First Volume of the Chronicles of England, Scotland and Ireland*, 1577, ed Hay, Camden Soc., 1950

Hooker, Richard, *Works*, ed J. Keble, revised R.W. Church and F. Paget, Oxford, 1988

Howard, Jean and Phyllis Rackin, *Engendering a Nation: A Feminist account of Shakespeare's English Histories*, 1997

Hughes, P.L. & Larkin, J.F., *Tudor Royal Proclamations*, 3 vols, New Haven,1964-9

Jackson, W.A. & Ferguson, F.S., completed by Katherine F. Pantyer, *A Short Title Catalogue of Books Printed in England, Scotland and Ireland and English Books Printed abroad,* 1475-1642, vol I, 1986, vol II, 1976

Jewel, John, *A Defence of the Apologie of the Church of England*, 1567

Ker, W.P., ed, *Tudor Translations*, Oxford, 1926-7

Kyd, Thomas, Thomas Kyd's *The First Part of Hieronimo and the Spanish Tragedy*, Andrew S. Cairncross, ed, 1967.

*Leicester's Commonwealth*, Paris, 1584

Leland, John, *The Itinerary of the Famous John Leland*, ed Lucy Toumlin Smith, 1906

*Letters and Papers of the Reign of Henry VIII, 1509-1547*, ed J.S. Brewer and James Gairdner, 21 vols, 1862-1910 and R.H. Brodie, 1920

Lever, Ralph, *The Art of Reason rightly termed witcraft, teaching the perfect way to argue and dispute*, 1573

Lloyd, Humphrey, trans, *John XXI's Treasury of Health*, 1550

Major, John, *History of Great Britain, 1521*, 8 vols, ed A. Constable, Edinburgh, 1892

Maley, Willy, ' "This Sceptered Isle": Shakespeare and the British Problem' in J. Joughin, ed, *Shakespeare and National Culture*, Manchester, 1996

Markham, Gervase, *The Tragedy of Sir Richard Grenville*, 1595

Marlow, Christopher, *Complete Plays*, ed J.B. Steane, 1969

Middleton, Christopher, *The Famous Historie of the Union of England and Wales*, ed W.E. Mead, E.E.T.S., old series, 165, 1925

Monmouth, Geoffrey of, *History of the Kings of Britain*, trans L. Thorpe, 1966

More, Thomas, *The Works of Sir Thomas More, written in the English tongue*, 1557, ed W.E. Campbell and A.W. Reed, 2 vols, 1927-31

    *Utopia,* trans Ralph Robinson, 1551

Morison, Richard, *Apomaxis,* 1537 or 1538

    *An Exhortation to stir all Englishmen to the Defence of their country*, 1539

    *A Lamentation in which it is shown that ruin and destruction cometh of seditious rebellion,* 1536

*A Remedy for Sedition*, 1536

Mulcaster, Richard, *The First Part of the Elementarie which Entreateth Cheflie the Right Writing of our English Tong*, 1582, ed R.C. Alston Menston, 1970

Nashe, Thomas, *The Works of Thomas Nashe*, R.B. McKerrow, ed, 5 vols, Oxford, 1958

Nicholas, J.G., ed *The Chronicles of Queen Jane*, Camden Soc., 1850

Peacham, Henry, *The Garden of Eloquence conteyning the Figures of Grammer and Rhetorick . . . and also helpeth much for the understanding of the Holy Scriptures,*

1577

Pettie, George, *The Civile Conversation of M Stephan Guazzo*, 1586

Pocock, Nicholas, *Records of the Reformation – The Divorce, 1527-33*, II Oxford, 1870

Pollard, A.F., ed, *Tudor Tracts, 1532-1588*, 1903

Ponet, J., *A Short treatise of Politike Power*, ed. Winthrop S. Hudson, in John Ponet: *Advocate of Limited Monarchy*, Chicago, 1942

Poyntz, Sir F., *The Table of Cebes the Philosopher*, 1530

Proctor, John, 'The History of Wyatt's Rebellion', 1554 in *Tudor Tracts*, ed Pollard

Puttenham, George, *The Arte of English Poesie*, ed G.D. Willcock and A. Walker, Cambridge, 1936

Rastell, W., trans, *Julius Cesars Commentaryes*, 1530

Ricci, Seymour de, ed, *William Wager's Enough is as Good as a Feast*, New York, 1920

Robinson, Hastings, ed *Original Letters Relative to the English Reformation, 1531-58*, 2 vols, Parker Society, 1846-7

Roper, William, *The Life of Sir Thomas More*, Knight, ed A.L. Rowse, 1980

Sherry, Richard, *A Treatise of Schemes and Tropes*, 1550

Sidney, Philip, *The Prose Works of Sir Philip Sidney*, ed. Albert Feuillerat, Cambridge, 1962

Skelton, John, *Complete Poems*, ed, Philip Henderson, 1949
trans., *Biblioteca Historia of Diodorus Siculus*, ed F.M. Salter and H.L.R. Edwards, E.E.T.S. 1957

Southwell, Robert, *An Humble Supplication to Her Majestie*, by Robert Southwell, ed R.C. Bald, Cambridge, 1953

Spenser, Edmund, *The Faerie Queen*, Everyman, 1910

Standish, John, *A Discourse where it is debated whether it be expedient that the Scripture should be in English for all men to read at will*, 1554

Starkey, Thomas, *An Exhortaion to the People instructing them to unite and obedience*, 1536

*A Diologue Between Reginald Pole and Thomas Lupset*, ed Kathleen M. Burton, 1948

*State Papers Published under the Authority of his Majesty's Comm – King Henry VIII*, 11 vols, 1830-52

State Trials, *Cobbett's Complete Collection of State Trials*, I, 1809

*Statutes of the Realm*, ed A. Luders et al., 11 vols 1810-28

Stow, John, *The Survey of London*, Everyman, 1965

Stubbe, John, *The Discovery of a Gaping Gulf Whereunto England is likely to be swallowed by Another French Marriage if the Lord Forbid not the bans*, 1579

Tawney, R.H. & E. Power, ed *Tudor Economic Documents*, University of London History Series, 14, 1924

*A Treatise of Treasons against Queen Elizabeth and the Crowne of England*, Louvain, 1572

Taverner, R., *Proverbs and Adages of Erasmus*, 1539

Thorndike, A. ed *The Minor Elizabethan Drama*, 1910, 'Gorboduc' Thomas Norton and Thomas Sackville

Turner, W., *A New Booke of Spirituall Physik*, 1555

Udall, Nicholas, 'Answer to the Commons of Devonshire and Cornwall' 1549 in *Troubles Connected with the Prayer Book*, ed N. Pocock, Camden Soc, 1884

Vergil, Polydore, *History of England*, ed Henry Ellis, 1846

Watson, William, *Important Considerations which ought to move all sound Catholics*

*who are not wholly jesuited to acknowledge that the proceedings of her majesty . . .*
*have been most mild and merciful*

Wilson, Thomas, *The Arte of Rhetorique*, Facsimile reproduction, New York, 1977
Wyatt, Thomas, *The Governauce of Good Health, Beynge Erasmus Interpretoure*, 1530
Williams, C.H. ed English Historical Documents, V & VI, 1967

## Secondary Sources

Anderson, Benedict, *Imagined Communities: Reflections on the Origins and Spread of Nationalism*, 1983

Baker, David J., *Between Nations: Shakespeare, Spencer, Marvell and the Question of Britain*, Stanford , 1997

Barber, Charles, *Early Modern English*, 1976

Bauckman, Richard, *Tudor Apocalypse*, Appleford, Berks, 1978

Bauman, Richard, *Explorations in the Ethnography of Speaking*, Cambridge, 1974

Baumer, F. Le Van, *The Early Tudor Theory of Kingship*, New Haven, 1940

Bennett, H.S. *English Books and Readers, 1475-1603*, 2 vols., Cambridge, 1952

Bevington, David, *Tudor Drama and Politics: A Critical Approach to Topical Meaning*, Cambridge, Mass., 1968

Bolton, W.F., *The English Language, Essays by English and American Men of Letters*, Cambridge, 1966

Bradshaw, Brendan, *The Irish Constitutional Revolution of the Sixteenth Century*, Cambridge, 1979

Breuilly, John, *Nationalism and the State*, Manchester, 1982

Bush, M.L. *The Government Policy of Protector Somerset*, 1975

Butterworth, C.C., *The English Primers, 1529-1545*, Philadelphia, 1953

Capp, B.S., *The Fifth Monarchy Men*, 1972

Carlisle, Nicholas, *A Concise Description of the Endowed Grammer Schools*, 1878, reprinted 1974

Chaytor, H.J., *From Script to Print, An Introduction to Medieval Vernacular Literature*, 1945.

Clancy, Thomas H., *Papist Pamphleteers: The Allen-Parsons Party in the Political Thought of the Counter Reformation in England, 1572-1615*, Chicago, 1964

Clark, Cumberland, *Shakespeare and National Character*, 1934

Coleman, C. & D.R. Starkey, eds., *Revolution Reassessed: Revisions in the History of Tudor Government and Administration*, Oxford, 1986

Cohen, Walter, *Drama of a Nation, Public Theatre in Renaissance England and Spain*, New York, 1985, pp 29, 137

Coleman, Janet, *English Literature in History*, 1981
   *Medieval Vernacular Literature*, 1945

Collinson, Patrick, *The Birthpangs of Protestant England: Religious and Cultural Change in the Sixteenth and Seventeenth Centuries*, 1988

Cressy, David, *Literature and the Social Order: Reading and Writing in Tudor and Stuart England*, Cambridge, 1980
   *Bonfires and Bells: National Memory and the Protestant Calendar in Elizabethan and Stuart England*, 1989

Cross, Claire, *Church and People, 1450-1660*, 1976

Davies, Norman, *The Isles: a History*, 1999

Deutsh, Karl, *Nationalism and Social Communication: An Enquiry into the Foundation of Nationality*, Cambridge, Mass., 1953

Dickens, A.G., *The German Nation and Martin Luther*, 1974

*Dictionary of National Biography*

Dollimore, Jonathan, *Radical Tragedy, Religion Ideology and Power in the Drama of Shakespeare and his Contemporaries,* 1989

Doob, Leonard W., *Patriotism and Nationalism – Their Psychological Foundations,* Yale, 1964

Durkacz, Victor Edward, *The Decline of the Celtic Languages,* Edinburgh, 1983

Edwards, John, *Language, Society and Identity,* 1985

Eisenstein, Elizabeth, L., *The Printing Press as an Agent of Change,* Cambridge, 1979

Einstein, Lewis, *Tudor Ideals,* New York, 1921

Ellis, Steven, G, *Tudor Ireland: Crown, Community and the Conflict of Cultures, 1470-1603,* 1985

   *Ireland in the Age of the Tudors, 1447-1603,* 1998

Elton, G.R., *The Tudor Revolution in Government,* Cambridge, 1954

   Policy and Police, The Enforcement of the Reformation in the Age of Thomas Cromwell, Cambridge, 1972

Ferguson, Arthur B. *The Indian Summer of English Chivalry,* Durham, N. Carolina, 1960

Fiedler, A Leslie, *The Stranger in Shakespeare,* 1972

Firth, K.R., *The Apocalyptic Tradition in Reformation Britain, 1530-1645,* Oxford, 1979

Foster, R.F. ed., *The Oxford Illustrated History of Ireland,* Oxford, 1991

Fox, A.G. & J.A. Guy, *Reassessing the Henrician Age: Humanism, Politics and Reform, 1500-1550,* Oxford, 1986

Fox, Alistair, *Politics and Literature in the Reigns of Henry VII and Henry VIII,* 1989

Fox, Levi, ed., *English Historical Scholarship in the Sixteenth and Seventeenth Centuries,* 1956

Furnivall, F.J. & W.R. Morfill, *Ballads from Manuscripts,* Ballad Society, 1868-1873

Fussner, F.S. *The Historical Revolution: English Historical Writing and Thought, 1580-1640,* 1962

Garrett, Christina Hallowel, *The Marian Exiles: A Study of the Origins of Elizabethan Puritanism,* Cambridge, 1938

Gaunt, William, *Court Painting in England from Tudor to Victorian Times,* 1980

Gellner, Ernest, *Nations and Nationalism,* Oxford, 1983

   *Encounters with Nationalism,* Oxford, 1994

Gibson, Edgar C.S., *The Thirty-Nine Articles, Explained with an Introduction,* 1896

Goldberg, Jonathan, *James I and the Politics of Literature,* Baltimore, 1983

Greenblatt, Stephen, *Renaissance Self-Fashioning: From More to Shakespeare,* Chicago, 1980

Greenfeld, Liah, *Nationalism: Five Roads to Modernity,* Cambridge Mass, 1922

Guibernan, Montserrat and John Hutchinson, eds, *Understanding Nationalism,* 2001

Guth, DeLloyd J.& John W. McKenna, eds. *Tudor Rule and Revolution: Essays for G.R. Elton by his American Friends,* Cambridge, 1982

Guy, John, *Tudor England,* Oxford, 1990

Haller, William, *Foxe's Book of Martyrs and the Elect Nation,* 1963

Harbage, Alfred, *Annals of English Drama, 975-1700,* Philadelphia, 1940

   *Shakespeare's Audience,* 1941

Heal, Felicity and Rosemary O'Day, eds., *Church and Society in England: Henry VIII to James I,* 1977

Helgerson, Richard, *Forms of Nationhood: The Elizabethan Writing of England,* Chicago, 1992

Hobsbawm, *Nations and Nationalism since 1780,* Cambridge, 1990

Hodge, Bob, *Literature, Language and Society in England, 1580-1680,* 1981

Huizinga, J., *The Waning of the Middle Ages,* 1955

Hunter, C.K., *Dramatic Identities and Cultural Tradition*, Liverpool, 1978

Hurstfield, Joel, *Elizabeth I and the Unity of England*, 1971
    *Freedom Corruption and Government in Elizabethan* England, 1973

Jardine, Lisa, *Reading Shakespeare Historically*, 1986

Jenner, H., *A Handbook of the Cornish Language*, 1904

Jones, Edwin, *The English Nation: the Great Myth*, 1998

Jones, Emrys, ed., *The New Oxford Book of Sixteenth-Century Verse*, Oxford, 1992.

Jones, N.L., *Faith by Statute: Parliament and the Settlement of Religion, 1559*, Royal
    Historical Society Studies in History

Jones, R.F., *The Triumph of the English Language*, Oxford, 1953

Jones, W.R.D., *The Tudor Commonwealth, 1529-1559*, 1970

Kearney, Hugh, *The British Isles, A History of Four Nations,* Cambridge, 1989

Kedourie, Elie, *Nationalism,* 1960

Kohn, Hans, *Nationalism: Its Meaning and History*, New York, 1955

Lehmberg, S.F., *Thomas Elyot, Tudor Humanist*, Austin, Texas, 1960

Leith, Dick, *A Social History of English*, 1983

Levy, F.J., *Tudor Historical Thought*, San Marino, 1967

Lindabury, R.U., *A Study of Patriotism in Elizabethan Drama*, Oxford, 1931

Loades, D.M., *Two Tudor Conspiracies*, Cambridge, 1965

Loomie, Albert, *The Spanish Elizabethans: The English Exiles at the Court of Philip II,*
    New York, 1963

Macdougal, A., *Racial Myth in English History,* New England, 1982

Major, J.M., *Sir Thomas Elyot and Renaissance Humanism*, Lincoln, 1964

Maltby, William s. *The Development of Anti-Spanish Sentiment, 1558-1660,* Durham,
    North Carolina, 1971

Marcu, E.D., *Sixteenth-Century Nationalism*, New York, 1976

Mattieson, F.O., *Translation – an Elizabethan Art*, Cambridge, Mass., 1931

McConica, J.K., *English Humanists and Reformation Politics under Henry VIII and
    Edward VI,* Oxford, 1965

McGrath, Patrick, *Papists and Puritans under Elizabeth I,* 1967

McLuhan, M., *The Gutenberg Galaxy, The Making of Typographical Man*, 1962

Mattingley, Garrett, *The Defeat of the Spanish Armada,* 1959

Mellor, Bernard, ed., *The Poems of Sir Francis Hubert*, Oxford, 1961

Merriman, R.B., *The Life and Letters of Thomas Cromwell*, Oxford, 1962

Mews, Stuart, ed*., Religion and National Identity: Studies in Church History*, XVIII,
    Oxford, 1982

Moore, Quintin and Geoffrey Nowell Smith, eds., and trans., *Selections from the Prison
    Notebooks of Antonio Gramsc*i, 1971

Mouffe, Chantel, ed., *Gramsci and Marxist Theory*, 1979

Murphy, Andrew, *But the Irish Sea Betwixt us: Ireland, Colonialism and Renaissance
    Literature*, Lexington, 1999

Neale, J.E., *Elizabeth and her Parliaments*, 2 vols., 1953 & 1959
    *Essays in Elizabethan History*, 1958

Newey, Vincent and Ann Thompson, eds., *Literature and Nationalism*, Liverpool, 1991

Newman, Gerald, *The Rise of English Nationalism: A Cultural History, 1740-1830*, 1987

Norbrook, D., *Poetry and Politics in the English Renaissance*, 1984

Olson, V. Norslov, *John Foxe and the Elizabethan Church*, 1973

Orgel, Stephen*, Illusion of Power: Political Theatre in the English Renaissance*, Berkeley,
    1975

Palmer, Roy, *A Ballad History of England from 1588 to the Present Day*, 1979

Parry, G.J.R., *A Protestant Vision: William Harrison and the Reformation of Elizabethan*

*England,* Cambridge, 1987

Patrides, C.A., *The Apocalypse in English Renaissance Thought and Literature,* Manchester, 1984

Perry, Maria, *The Word of a Prince: A Life of Elizabeth Through Contemporary Documents,* 1990

Purcell, Sally, ed, *George Peele: Selected with an Introduction,* Oxford, 1972

Ranum, O., ed, *National Consciousness, History and Culture in Early Modern Europe,* Baltimore, 1975

Redworth, Glyn, *In Defence of the Church Catholic: The Life of Stephen Gardiner,* 1990

Renolds, P., *The Wisbech Stirs, 1595-98,* Catholic Record Society, 1955

Rowse, A.L., *The English Spirit,* 1946.
  *The Elizabethan Renaissance: The Cultural Achievement,* 1972

Scarisbrick, J.J., *Henry VIII,* 1966

Seton-Watson, Hugh, *Nation States: An Enquiry into the Origins of Nations and the Politics of Nationalism,* 1977

Shafer, Boyd C., *Nationalism: Myth and Reality,* 1955

Simon, Roger, *Gramsci's Political Thought,* 1982

Slavin, Arthur, J. ed., *Thomas Cromwell on Church and Commonwealth: Selected Letters,* New York, 1969

Southern, A.C., *Elizabethan Recusant Prose, 1559-1582,* 1950

Smith, Alan, G.R., *The Emergence of a Nation State, 1529-1660,* 1984

Smith, Anthony, *Theories of Nationalism,* 1971

Smith, G.G.S., *Elizabethan Critical Essays,* Oxford, 1904

Spufford, Margaret, *Small Books and Pleasant Histories: Popular Fiction and its Readership in Seventeenth-Century England,* Cambridge, 1981

Steinberg, S.H., *Five Hundred Years of Printing,* 1961

Stone, Christopher, *Sea Songs and Ballads,* Oxford, 1906

Strachey, Lytton, *Elizabeth and Essex,* Oxford, 1963

Strong, Roy, *Portraits of Elizabeth,* Oxford, 1963

Strype, J. *The Life of the Learned Sir John Cheke,* Oxford, 1821
  *Annals of the Reformation and Establishment of Religion and other Various Occurrences in the Church of England, During Queen Elizabeth's Happy Reign,* 4 vols., Oxford, 1824

Tillyard, E.M.W. *Shakespeare's History Plays,* 1944

Thompson, Patricia, ed., *Wyatt: The Critical Heritage,* 1974

Tonkin, Elizabeth, Maryon McDonald and Malcolm Chapman, eds, *History and Ethnicity,* 1989

Traversi, Derek, *Renaissance Drama,* 1980

Wakelin, Martyn F., *Language and History in Cornwall,* Leicester, 1975

Williams, Gwyn A, *The Welsh in their History,* 1982

Wingfield-Straford, Esme, *The History of English Patriotism,* 2 vols., 1913
  *The Foundations of British Patriotism,* 1940

Wright, T., *Political Songs,* Rolls Series II, 1859-1861

Yates, Frances, *Astraea: The Imperial Theme in the Sixteenth Century,* 1975
  *The Occult Philosophy in the Elizabethan Age,* 1979

Zeeveld, W. Gordon, *Foundations of Tudor Policy,* Cambridge, Mass. 1948

# Articles

Adair, E.R., William Thomas: A Forgotten Clerk of the Privy Council, in R.W. Seton-Watson, ed., *Tudor Studies*, 1924, pp 142-160

Anglo, Sydney, The British History in Early Tudor Propaganda, *Bulletin of the John Rylands Library*, 44, 1961, pp 17-48

Ashton, Margaret, Lollardy and Sedition, 1381-1431, *Past and Present*, 17, 1960, pp 1-44

Barker, Felix, If Parma had Landed, *History Today*, 38, 1988, pp 34-41

Bayley, C.C., Petrarch, Charles V and the Renovatio Imperii, *Speculum*, XVIII, 1942, pp 226-242

Bradshaw, Brendan, George Browne, first Reformation Archbishop of Dublin, 1536-1554, *Journal of Ecclesiastical History*, xxi, 1970, pp 312-313

Sword, Word and Strategy in the Reformation in Ireland, *The Historical Journal*, 1978, pp 475-502

Brennan, Gillian E., Papists and Patriotism in Elizabethan England, *Recusant History*, 19, 1988, pp 1-15

Patriotism Language and Power, *History Workshop*, 27, 1989, pp 18-35

The cheese and the Welsh: foreigners in Elizabethan literature, *Renaissance Studies*, 1994, Vol 8, no 1, pp 40-64.

Language and nationality: the role of policy towards Celtic Languages in the consolidation of Tudor Power, *Nations and Nationalism*, vol 7, part 3 2001, pp 317-338

Burke, Peter, Languages and Anti-Languages in Early Modern Italy, *History Workshop*, 11, 1981, pp 24-32

Butterworth, C.C., Robert Redman's Prayers of the Bible, *The Library*, III, 5th series, 1948, pp 279-286

Canny, Nicholas, Religion, Politics and Gaelic Literature, 1580-1750, *Past and Present*, 95, 1982, pp 91-116

Cross, Claire, Great Reasoners in Scripture, Women Lollards, 1380-1530 in D. Baker, ed., *Medieval Women, Studies in Church History*, Oxford Subsidia I, 378, 1978

Cunningham, Hugh, The Language of Patriotism, 1750-1914, *History Workshop*, 12, 1981, pp 8-33

Ebel, Julia, G. A Numerical Survey of Elizabethan Translations, *The Library*, 30, 1967, pp 104-127

Eisenstein, Elizabeth, L., Some Conjectures about the Impact of Printing on Western Society and Thought, *Journal of Modern History*, 40, 1968, pp 1-56

Ellis, Steven G. Ellis, Tudor Policy and the Kildare Ascendancy in the Lordship of Ireland, 1496-1534, *Irish Historical Studies*, xx, pp 245-250

Elton, G.R., The Tudor Revolution – a Reply, *Past and Present*, 29, 1964, pp 26-49

Ferguson, Arthur B., Renaissance Realism in the Commonwealth Literature of Early Tudor England, *Journal of the History of Ideas*, pp 287-305

Firth, C.H., The Ballad History of the Later Tudors, *Transactions of the Royal Historical Society*, Third series, III, 1909, pp 51-124

The Ballad History of the Reigns of Henry VII and Henry VIII, *Transactions of the Royal Historical Society*, Third series, II, 1907-8, pp 21-50

Galbraith, V.H., Nationalism and Language in Medieval England, Transactions of the Royal Historical Society, Fourth series, XXIII, 1941, pp 113-128

Gawthrop, Richard and Gerald Strauss, Protestantism and Literacy in Early Modern Germany, *Past and Present*, 104, 1984, pp 31-55

Graham, Howard Jay, Our Tong Maternall Marvellously Amendyd: The First Englishing and Printing of the Medieval Statutes at Large, 1530-1553, *U.C.L.A. Law Review*, 13, 1965, pp 58-97

Helgerson, Richard, The Land Speaks: Cartography, Chorography, and Subversion in Renaissance England, *Representations*, 16, 1986, pp 59-64

Hicks, L., Father Parsons and the Book of Succession, *Recusant History*, IV, 1957, pp 104-137

Hill, Christopher, God and the English Revolution, *History Workshop*, 17, 1984, pp 19-37

Holderness, Graham, Shakespeare's History: Richard II, *Literature and History*, 7, 1981, p. 2-24

   Agincourt 1944: Readings in the Shakespeare Myth, in Peter Humm, Paul Stignant and Peter Widdowson, eds., *Popular Fictions: Essays in Literature and History*, 1986, pp 178, 192

Jenkins, Gladys, The Archpriest Controversy and the Printers, *The Library*, fifth series, II, 1948, pp 180-186

Keeney, Barnaby C, Military Service and the Development of Nationalism in England, 1271-1327, *Speculum*, XIII, 1947, pp 534-549

Kingdon, Robert, M., William Allen's use of Protestant Political Argument, in Charles H. Carter, ed., *From the Renaissance to the Counter Reformation, Essays in Honour of Garrett Mattingly*, 1966, pp 164-178

Koebner, Richard, The Imperial Crown of this Realm: Henry VIII, Constantine the Great and Polydore Vergil, *Bulletin of the Institute of Historical Research*, XXVI, 1953, pp 29-52

Kohn, Hans, The Genesis and Character of English Nationalism, *Journal of the History of Ideas*, I, 1940, pp 69-94

Loach, Pamphlets and Politics, 1553-1588, *Bulletin of the Institute of Historical Research*, 48, 1975, pp 31-2

Loades, D.M., The Press under the Early Tudors – A Study in Censorship and Sedition, *Transactions of the Cambridge Bibliographical Society*, IV, 1964, pp 29-50

Loomis, L.R., Nationality and the Council of Constance, *American History Review*, 44, 1938-9

McCann, Timothy J., The Parliamentary Speech of Viscount Montague Against the Act of Supremacy 1559, *Sussex Archaeological Collections*, 108, 1970, pp 50-57

Meritt, Herbert, The Vocabulary of Sir John Cheke's Partial Version of the Gospels, *Journal of English and Germanic Philology*, XXXIX, 1940, pp 450-455

Neild, Keith and John Seed, Waiting for Gramsci, *Social History*, 6, 1981, pp 209-227

Parker, Geoffrey, If the Armada had Landed, *History*, 61, 1976, pp 358-368

Potter, D.C., The Treaty of Boulogne and European Diplomacy, *Bulletin of the Institute of Historical Research*, 55. 1982

Roberts, P.R., The Union with England and the Identity of Anglican Wales, *Transactions of the Royal Historical Society*, 1972, pp 66 ff

Thorpe, Malcolm, Religion and the Wyatt Rebellion of 1554, *Church History*, 47, 1978, pp 363-380

Wyatt, Thomas, Aliens in England before the Huguenots, *Huguenot Soc. Proc.*, 19, 1953, pp 79-94

Zeeveld, W.G., Thomas Starkey and the Cromwellian Polity, *Journal of Modern History*, 15, 1943, pp 117-191

# Index